Contents

Question index

The headings in this checklist/index indicate the main topics of questions.

Questions set under the old syllabus *Preparing Financial Statements* Paper are included because their style and content are similar to those which appear in the F3 exam.

We also include some longer **preparation questions** so that you can practise fully the techniques involved.

ACCA

PAPER F3

FINANCIAL ACCOUNTING
(UK STREAM)

PRACTICE & REVISION KIT

In this January 2009 new edition

- We discuss the **best strategies** for revising and taking your ACCA exams

- We show you how to be well prepared for the **2009 exams**

- We give you **lots of great guidance** on tackling questions

- We provide you with **three** mock exams including the **Pilot paper**

- We provide the **ACCA examiner's answers** as well as our own to the Pilot Paper as an additional revision aid

Our **i-Pass** product also supports this paper.

FOR EXAMS IN 2009

BPP LEARNING MEDIA

First edition 2007
Third edition January 2009

ISBN 9780 7517 6654 7
(previous ISBN 9780 7517 4678 5)

British Library Cataloguing-in-Publication Data
A catalogue record for this book
is available from the British Library

Published by

BPP Learning Media Ltd
BPP House, Aldine Place
London W12 8AA

www.bpp.com/learningmedia

Printed in the United Kingdom

We are grateful to the Association of Chartered Certified Accountants for permission to reproduce past examination questions. The answers to past examination questions have been prepared by BPP Learning Media Ltd.

Your learning materials, published by BPP Learning Media Ltd, are printed on paper sourced from sustainable, managed forests.

Part B: Objective test questions

Mock exam 1

Paper-based exam

Mock exam 2

Computer-based exam

Mock exam 3 (Pilot paper)

Using your BPP Learning Media Practice and Revision Kit

Tackling revision and the exam

You can significantly improve your chances of passing by tackling revision and the exam in the right ways. Our advice is based on feedback from ACCA examiners.

- We focus on Paper F3; we discuss revising the syllabus, how to approach different types of question and ways of obtaining easy marks

Selecting questions

We provide a full **question index** to help you plan your revision

Making the most of question practice

At BPP Learning Media we realise that you need more than just questions and simple answers to get the most from your question practice. We include workings and explanations to show you how we arrived at the right answer and why the wrong answers were incorrect.

Attempting mock exams

There are three mock exams that provide practice at coping with the pressures of the exam day. We strongly recommend that you attempt them under exam conditions. **Mock exam 1** reflects the question styles and syllabus coverage of the paper-based exam. **Mock exam 2** reflects what you will see in a computer-based exam. **Mock exam 3** is the Pilot paper. To help you get the most out of doing these exams, we provide help with each answer. The examiner's answers to the Pilot paper are included at the back of the kit.

Using your BPP Learning Media products

This Kit gives you the question practice and guidance you need in the exam. Our other products can also help you pass:

- **Learning to Learn Accountancy** gives further valuable advice on revision
- **Passcards** provide you with clear topic summaries and exam tips
- **Success CDs** help you revise on the move
- **i-Pass CDs** offer tests of knowledge against the clock
- **Learn Online** is an e-learning resource delivered via the Internet, offering comprehensive tutor support and featuring areas such as study, practice, email service, revision and useful resources

You can purchase these products by visiting www.bpp.com/mybpp.

You can view demonstrations of i-Learn and i-Pass products by visiting www.bpp.com/acca/study-materials/#ilearn. Scroll down the page until you find the sections for i-Learn and i-Pass and click on the appropriate 'View demo' button.

Revising F3

General exam support from BPP Learning Media

BPP Learning Media is committed to giving you the best possible support in your quest for exam success. With this in mind, we have produced **guidance** on how to revise and techniques you can apply to **improve your chances of passing** the exam. This guidance can be found on the BPP Learning Media web site at the following link:

www.bpp.com/acca/examtips/Revising-for-ACCA-exams.doc

A paper copy of this guidance is available by e-mailing learningmedia@bpp.com.

As well as written guidance, an excellent presentation entitled **'Exam technique – advice from the experts at BPP Learning Media'** is available at the following link:

www.bpp.com/learningmedia/acca/accaexamskills/player.html

Whilst a substantial amount of the presentation focuses on written exams (papers F4 – P7), you will still find the sections on your **attitude and preparation** before the exam very useful.

Topics to revise

The examiner will test **every area of the syllabus** so you must revise **all topics**. Selective revision will limit the number of questions that you can answer and reduce your chance of passing.

Although the Paper F3 exam does not require you to submit written workings, it is still essential that you **practise the steps** involved in different techniques. If you are familiar with these steps, you will be more confident about tackling any question on the topic.

But do not spend too long on any one topic – it will probably only feature in a few questions.

Question practice - paper based or computer based?

You may take Paper F3 as a **paper based** exam or a **computer based** exam. It is very much a personal choice which one you choose – however your final revision should be tailored towards your choice of exam. You can find general details about computer based exams on page x.

The **computer based** exam contains a **mixture of multiple choice and objective test questions**, whilst the **paper based** exam contains **only multiple choice questions**. Before you decide on the mode of exam you might prefer, it is a good idea to have a look at multiple choice and objective test question banks in this kit to get a feel for the different styles of questions you might be faced with.

Mock Exam 1 and **Mock Exam 3** (pilot paper) are paper based (multiple choice questions only), **Mock Exam 2** contains the style of questions you might face in a computer based exam (even though it is on paper!) The computer based version of the pilot paper is available on the ACCA web site (see below for link).

(i) **Paper based exams**

If you choose the paper based route, your revision must include the following:

- Read 'Tackling multiple choice questions' on page viii

- Attempt all the multiple choice and objective test questions in this kit (you can never get enough question practice!)

- Do Mock Exam 1 and Mock Exam 3 (the pilot paper) under exam conditions

- If time allows, do Mock Exam 2 for additional question practice.

(ii)   **Computer based exams**

If you decide to take the exam on computer, you must include the following in your revision plan:

- Read 'Tackling multiple choice questions' on page viii and 'Tackling objective test questions' on page ix

- Attempt all the multiple choice and objective test questions in this kit

- Do **Mock Exam 2** in this kit and the **computer based version of the pilot paper** which can be accessed on the ACCA web site using the link http://62.254.188.145/main.html. Both should be attempted **under exam conditions** (note that the computer based pilot paper does not subject you to time constraints the way the real exam would, but impose your own two hour time limit to make it realistic).

- **If time allows**, do Mock Exam 1 for additional question practice.

Tackling multiple choice questions

The MCQs in your exam will contain two, three or four possible answers. You have to **choose the option that best answers the question**. The incorrect options are called distracters. There is a skill in answering MCQs quickly and correctly. By practising MCQs you can develop this skill, giving yourself a better chance of passing the exam.

You may wish to follow the approach outlined below, or you may prefer to adapt it.

Step 1   Skim read all the MCQs and identify which appear to be the easier questions.

Step 2   Work out **how long** you should allocate to each MCQ bearing in mind the number of marks available. Remember that the examiner will not expect you to spend an equal amount of time on each MCQ; some can be answered instantly but others will take time to work out.

Step 3   Attempt each question – **starting with the easier questions** identified in Step 1. Read the question thoroughly. You may prefer to work out the answer before looking at the options, or you may prefer to look at the options at the beginning. Adopt the method that works best for you.

You may find that you recognise a question when you sit the exam. Be aware that the detail and/or requirement may be different. If the question seems familiar, read the requirement and options carefully – do not assume that it is identical.

Step 4   Read the five options and see if one matches your own answer. Be careful with numerical questions, as the distracters are designed to match answers that incorporate **common errors**. Check that your calculation is correct. Have you followed the requirement exactly? Have you included every stage of the calculation?

Step 5   You may find that none of the options matches your answer.

- **Re-read the question** to ensure that you understand it and are answering the requirement

- **Eliminate any obviously wrong answers**

- **Consider which of the remaining answers** is the most likely to be correct and select that option

Step 6   If you are still unsure, **continue to the next question**. Likewise if you are nowhere near working out which option is correct after a couple of minutes, leave the question and come back to it later. Make a note of any questions for which you have submitted answers, but you need to return to later. The computer will list any questions for which you have not submitted answers.

Step 7   Revisit unanswered questions and other questions you're uncertain about. When you come back to a question after a break, you often find you can answer it correctly straightaway. If you are still unsure, have a guess. You are not penalised for incorrect answers, so **never leave a question unanswered!**

Tackling objective test questions

What is an objective test question?

An objective test (**OT**) question is made up of some form of **stimulus**, usually a question, and a **requirement** to do something.

- **MCQs**. Read through the information on page viii about MCQs and how to tackle them.

- **True or false**. You will be asked if a statement is true or false.

- **Data entry**. This type of OT requires you to provide figures such as the answer to a calculation, words to fill in a blank, single word answers to questions, or to identify numbers and words to complete a format.

- **Multiple response**. These questions provide you with a number of options and you have to identify those that fulfil certain criteria.

- **Multiple response matching**. This OT question format could ask you whether certain figures will increase or decrease if a particular event happens, or which combination of information is consistent with the data in the question.

OT questions in your exam

If you are sitting your exam on computer your exam will contain different types of OT questions. It is not certain how many questions in your exam will be MCQs and how many will be other types of OT, nor what types of OT you will encounter in your exam. For maximum preparation, attempt all the different types of OT questions in this kit.

Dealing with OT questions

Again you may wish to follow the approach we suggest, or you may be prepared to adapt it.

Step 1   Work out **how long** you should allocate to each OT, taking into account the marks allocated to it. Remember that you will not be expected to spend an equal amount of time on each one; some can be answered instantly but others will take time to work out.

Step 2   **Attempt each question**. Read the question thoroughly, and note in particular what the question says about the **format** of your answer and whether there are any **restrictions** placed on it.

Step 3   Read any options you are given and select which ones are appropriate. Check that your calculations are correct. Have you followed the requirement exactly? Have you included every stage of the calculation?

Step 4   You may find that you are unsure of the answer.

- Re-read the question to ensure that you understand it and are answering the requirement

- Eliminate any obviously wrong options if you are given a number of options from which to choose

Step 5   If you are still unsure, **continue to the next question**. The computer will list any questions for which you have not submitted answers.

Step 6   Revisit unanswered questions and other questions you are uncertain about. When you come back to a question after a break you often find you are able to answer it correctly straight away. If you are still unsure have a guess. You are not penalised for incorrect answers, so **never leave a question unanswered!**

Exam information

Format of the exam

	Number of marks
Paper-based exam (2 hours)	
40 2-mark MCQs	80
10 1-mark MCQs	10
	90
Computer based exam (2 hours)	
50 OTQs (40 2-mark questions and 10 1-mark questions)	90

The pass mark for both papers is 50%.

The computer based examination

In 2002, the ACCA introduced computer based examinations (CBE) (in addition to the conventional paper based examinations).

Computer based examinations must be taken at ACCA Approved Computer Examination Centres. A full list of approved centres can be found on the ACCA web site using the following link:

http://www.accaglobal.com/students/study_exams/exams/cbe/where

How does CBE work?

- Questions are displayed on a monitor and candidates enter their answers directly onto the computer

- When the candidate has completed their examination (two hours are allowed), the computer automatically marks the file containing the candidate's answers

- Candidates are provided with a certificate showing their results before leaving the examination room

- The CBE Licensed Centre uploads the results to ACCA (as proof of the candidate's performance)

Benefits

- **Flexibility** as a CBE and resits can be sat at any time, with no restrictions on number of sittings.

- **Instant feedback** as the computer displays the results at the end of the CBE

- Results are notified to ACCA **within 48 hours**

- **Extended closing date periods** (see ACCA website for further information)

Multiple choice questions

1 Preparation question: Accounting concepts (PFS 12/05)

State four accounting concepts, and explain how each one contributes to fair presentation in the financial statements.

2 Accounting concepts I   24 mins

1   The historical cost convention

    A   fails to take account of changing price levels over time
    B   records only past transactions
    C   values all assets at their cost to the business, without any adjustment for depreciation
    D   has been replaced in accounting records by a system of current cost accounting   **(2 marks)**

2   The *main* aim of accounting is to

    A   maintain ledger accounts for every asset and liability
    B   provide financial information to users of such information
    C   produce a trial balance
    D   record every financial transaction individually   **(2 marks)**

3   The accounting concept or convention which, in times of rising prices, tends to understate asset values and overstate profits, is the

    A   going concern concept
    B   prudence concept
    C   realisation concept
    D   historical cost convention   **(2 marks)**

4   The accounting concept which requires assets to be valued at their net book value, rather than their 'break-up' value is the

    A   materiality concept
    B   going concern concept
    C   historical cost convention
    D   business entity convention   **(2 marks)**

5   The accounting equation can be rewritten as

    A   assets plus profit less drawings less liabilities equals closing capital
    B   assets less liabilities less drawings equals opening capital plus profit
    C   assets less liabilities less opening capital plus drawings equals profit   **(1 mark)**

6   If the owner of a business takes goods from stock for his own personal use, the accounting concept to be considered is the

    A   prudence concept
    B   capitalisation concept
    C   money measurement concept
    D   separate entity concept   **(2 marks)**

7   Assets are usually valued under which basis?

    A   Replacement cost
    B   Historical cost
    C   Net realisable value   **(1 mark)**

8 Sales turnover should be recognised when goods and services have been supplied; costs are incurred when goods and services have been received.

The accounting concept which governs the above is the

A   prudence concept
B   materiality concept
C   accruals concept
D   dual aspect concept

(2 marks)

9 The accounting concept which requires that foreseen losses should be anticipated and taken into account immediately is the

A   consistency concept
B   accruals concept
C   prudence concept
D   going concern concept

(2 marks)

10 A sale should be recognised when the goods or services have been provided and the invoice sent out, rather than when the sale is agreed. Which accounting concept does this illustrate?

A   realisation concept
B   consistency concept
C   going concern concept
D   materiality concept

(2 marks)

(Total = 18 marks)

3 Accounting concepts II

20 mins

1 Listed below are some characteristics of financial information.

1   Neutrality
2   Prudence
3   Completeness
4   Timeliness

Which of these characteristics contribute to reliability, according to the ASB's Statement of Principles?

A   1, 2 and 3 only
B   1, 2 and 4 only
C   1, 3 and 4 only
D   2, 3 and 4 only

(2 marks)

2 Which of the following statements about accounting concepts are correct?

1   The money measurement concept is that only items capable of being measured in monetary terms can be recognised in financial statements.

2   The prudence concept means that understating of assets and overstating of liabilities is desirable in preparing financial statements.

3   The historical cost concept is that assets are initially recognised at their transaction cost.

4   The substance over form convention is that, whenever legally possible, the economic substance of a transaction should be reflected in financial statements rather than simply its legal form.

A   1, 2 and 3
B   1, 2 and 4
C   1, 3 and 4
D   2, 3 and 4

(2 marks)

3   Listed below are some comments on accounting concepts.

1   In achieving a balance between relevance and reliability, the most important consideration is satisfying as far as possible the economic decision-making needs of users.

2   Materiality means that only items having a physical existence may be recognised as assets.

3   The substance over form convention means that the legal form of a transaction must always be shown in financial statements, even if this differs from the commercial effect.

Which, if any, of these comments is correct, according to the ASB's Statements of Principles?

A   1 only
B   2 only
C   3 only
D   None of them   **(2 marks)**

---

4   Which of the following explanations of the prudence concept most closely follows that in the ASB's Statements of Principles?

A   The application of a degree of caution in exercising judgement under conditions of uncertainty
B   Revenue and profits are not recognised until realised, and provision is made for all known liabilities
C   All legislation and accounting standards have been complied with   **(1 mark)**

---

5   In times of rising prices, what effect does the use of the historical cost concept have on a company's asset values and profit?

A   Asset values and profit both understated
B   Asset values and profit both overstated
C   Asset values understated and profit overstated
D   Asset values overstated and profit understated   **(2 marks)**

---

6   Which of the following statements about accounting concepts and policies is/are correct?

1   The effect of a change to an accounting policy should be disclosed as an extraordinary item if material.

2   Information in financial statements should be presented so as to be understood by users with a reasonable knowledge of business and accounting.

3   Companies should create hidden reserves to strengthen their financial position.

4   Consistency of treatment of items from one period to the next is essential to enhance comparability between companies, and must therefore take precedence over other accounting concepts such as prudence.

A   1 and 4
B   2 and 3
C   3 and 4
D   2 only   **(2 marks)**

---

7   Which of the following most closely describes the meaning of prudence, as the term is defined in the ASB's Statements of Principles?

A   Ensuring that accounting records and financial statements are free from material error.
B   The use of a degree of caution in making estimates required under conditions of uncertainty.
C   Understating assets and gains and overstating liabilities and losses.
D   Ensuring that financial statements comply with all accounting standards and legal requirements
                                                                                     (2 marks)

8   Which, if any, of the following statements about accounting concepts and the characteristics of financial information are correct?

   1   The concept of substance over form means that the legal form of a transaction must be reflected in financial statements, regardless of the economic substance.

   2   The historical cost concept means that only items capable of being measured in monetary terms can be recognised in financial statements.

   3   It may sometimes be necessary to exclude information that is relevant and reliable from financial statements because it is too difficult for some users to understand.

   A   1 and 2 only
   B   2 and 3 only
   C   1 and 3 only
   D   None of these statements is correct   (2 marks)

                                                                                    (Total = 15 marks)

4 Preparation question: Sampi

Sampi is a manufacturer of garden furniture. The company has consistently used FIFO (first in, first out) in valuing stock, but it is interested to know the effect on its stock valuation of using weighted average cost instead of FIFO.

At 28 February 20X8 the company had a stock of 4,000 standard plastic tables, and has computed its value on each basis as:

	Unit cost £	Total value £
Basis		
FIFO	16	64,000
Weighted average	13	52,000

During March 20X8 the movements on the stock of tables were as follows.

Received from factory:

	Number of units	Production cost per unit £
Date		
8 March	3,800	15
22 March	6,000	18

Sales:

	Number of units
Date	
12 March	5,000
18 March	2,000
24 March	3,000
28 March	2,000

On a FIFO basis the stock at 31 March 20X8 was £32,400.

Required

Compute what the value of the stock at 31 March 20X8 would be using weighted average cost.

(In arriving at the total stock values you should make calculations to two decimal places (where necessary) and deal with each stock movement in date order.)

5 Stocks

1   A fire on 30 September 20X2 destroyed some of a company's stock and its stock records.

The following information is available:

	£
Stock 1 September 20X2	318,000
Sales for September 20X2	612,000
Purchases for September 20X2	412,000
Stock in good condition at 30 September 20X2	214,000

Standard gross profit percentage on sales is 25%

Based on this information, what is the value of the stock lost?

A   £96,000
B   £271,000
C   £26,400
D   £57,000   **(2 marks)**

2   Which of the following costs may be included when arriving at the cost of finished goods stock for inclusion in the financial statements of a manufacturing company?

1   Carriage inwards
2   Carriage outwards
3   Depreciation of factory plant
4   Finished goods storage costs
5   Factory supervisors' wages

A   1 and 5 only
B   2, 4 and 5 only
C   1, 3 and 5 only
D   1, 2, 3 and 4 only   **(2 marks)**

3   The closing stock at cost of a company at 31 January 20X3 amounted to £284,700.

The following items were included at cost in the total:

1   400 coats, which had cost £80 each and normally sold for £150 each. Owing to a defect in manufacture, they were all sold after the balance sheet date at 50% of their normal price. Selling expenses amounted to 5% of the proceeds.

2   800 skirts, which had cost £20 each. These too were found to be defective. Remedial work in February 20X3 cost £5 per skirt, and selling expenses for the batch totalled £800. They were sold for £28 each.

What should the stock value be according to SSAP 9 *Stocks* after considering the above items?

A   £281,200
B   £282,800
C   £329,200
D   None of these   **(2 marks)**

4   A company values its stock using the first in, first out (FIFO) method. At 1 May 20X2 the company had 700 engines in stock, valued at £190 each.

During the year ended 30 April 20X3 the following transactions took place:

20X2
1 July   Purchased 500 engines at £220 each
1 November   Sold 400 engines for £160,000

20X3

| 1 February | Purchased 300 engines at £230 each |
| 15 April | Sold 250 engines for £125,000 |

What is the value of the company's closing stock of engines at 30 April 20X3?

A   £188,500
B   £195,500
C   £166,000
D   None of these figures   **(2 marks)**

5   Which of the following statements about the valuation of stock are correct, according to SSAP 9 *Stocks*?

    1   Stock items are normally to be valued at the higher of cost and net realisable value.

    2   The cost of goods manufactured by an entity will include materials and labour only. Overhead costs cannot be included.

    3   LIFO (last in, first out) cannot be used to value stock.

    4   Selling price less estimated profit margin may be used to arrive at cost if this gives a reasonable approximation to actual cost.

    A   1, 3 and 4 only
    B   1 and 2 only
    C   3 and 4 only   **(1 mark)**

6   A company with an accounting date of 31 October carried out a physical check of stock on 4 November 20X3, leading to a stock value at cost at this date of £483,700.

    Between 1 November 20X3 and 4 November 20X3 the following transactions took place:

    1   Goods costing £38,400 were received from suppliers.

    2   Goods that had cost £14,800 were sold for £20,000.

    3   A customer returned, in good condition, some goods which had been sold to him in October for £600 and which had cost £400.

    4   The company returned goods that had cost £1,800 in October to the supplier, and received a credit note for them.

    What figure should appear in the company's financial statements at 31 October 20X3 for closing stock, based on this information?

    A   £458,700
    B   £505,900
    C   £508,700
    D   £461,500   **(2 marks)**

7   In preparing its financial statements for the current year, a company's closing stock was understated by £300,000.

    What will be the effect of this error if it remains uncorrected?

    A   The current year's profit will be overstated and next year's profit will be understated
    B   The current year's profit will be understated but there will be no effect on next year's profit
    C   The current year's profit will be understated and next year's profit will be overstated
    D   The current year's profit will be overstated but there will be no effect on next year's profit   **(2 marks)**

8   At 30 September 20X3 the closing stock of a company amounted to £386,400.

    The following items were included in this total at cost:

    1   1,000 items which had cost £18 each. These items were all sold in October 20X3 for £15 each, with selling expenses of £800.

    2   Five items which had been in stock since 1973, when they were purchased for £100 each, sold in October 20X3 for £1,000 each, net of selling expenses.

What figure should appear in the company's balance sheet at 30 September 20X3 for stock?

A   £382,600
B   £384,200
C   £387,100
D   £400,600   (2 marks)

9   According to SSAP 9 *Stocks,* which of the following costs should be included in valuing the stocks of a manufacturing company?

1   Carriage inwards
2   Carriage outwards
3   Depreciation of factory plant
4   General administrative overheads

A   1, 2 and 4 only
B   2 and 3 only
C   1 and 3 only   (1 mark)

                                                                                      (Total = 16 marks)

6 Preparation question: Riffon (PFS 12/03)

The accounting records of Riffon, a limited company included the following balances at 30 June 20X2:

		£'000
Office buildings	– cost	1,600
	– accumulated depreciation (10 years at 2% per year)	320
Plant and machinery	– cost (all purchased in 20X0 or later)	840
	– accumulated depreciation	
	– (straight line basis at 25% per year)	306

During the year ended 30 June 20X3 the following events occurred:

20X2

1 July   It was decided to revalue the office building to £2,000,000, with no change to the estimate of its remaining useful life.

1 October   New plant costing £200,000 was purchased.

20X3

1 April   Plant which had cost £240,000 and with accumulated depreciation at 30 June 20X2 of £180,000 was sold for £70,000.

It is the company's policy to charge a full year's depreciation on plant in the year of acquisition and none in the year of sale.

Required

Prepare the following ledger accounts to record the above balances and events:

(a)   Office building: cost/valuation
                             accumulated depreciation
                             revaluation reserve

(b)   Plant and machinery: cost
                             accumulated depreciation
                             disposal

7 Tangible fixed assets

1   What is the purpose of charging depreciation in accounts?

    A   To allocate the cost less residual value of a fixed asset over the accounting periods expected to benefit from its use

    B   To ensure that funds are available for the eventual replacement of the asset

    C   To reduce the cost of the asset in the balance sheet to its estimated market value   **(1 mark)**

2   Your firm bought a machine for £5,000 on 1 January 20X1, which had an expected useful life of four years and an expected residual value of £1,000; the asset was to be depreciated on the straight-line basis. The firm's policy is to charge depreciation in the year of disposal. On 31 December 20X3, the machine was sold for £1,600.

The amount to be entered in the 20X3 profit and loss account for profit or loss on disposal, is

    A   profit of £600
    B   loss of £600
    C   profit of £350
    D   loss of £400   **(2 marks)**

3   An asset register showed a net book value of £67,460. A fixed asset costing £15,000 had been sold for £4,000, making a loss on disposal of £1,250. No entries had been made in the asset register for this disposal.

The correct balance on the asset register is

    A   £42,710
    B   £51,210
    C   £53,710
    D   £62,210   **(2 marks)**

4   An organisation's asset register shows a net book value of £145,600. The fixed asset account in the nominal ledger shows a net book value of £135,600. The difference could be due to a disposed asset not having been deducted from the asset register.

    A   With disposal proceeds of £15,000 and a profit on disposal of £5,000
    B   With disposal proceeds of £15,000 and a net book value of £5,000
    C   With disposal proceeds of £15,000 and a loss on disposal of £5,000
    D   With disposal proceeds of £5,000 and a net book value of £5,000   **(2 marks)**

5   Recording the purchase of computer stationery by debiting the computer equipment at cost account would result in

    A   an overstatement of profit and an overstatement of fixed assets
    B   an understatement of profit and an overstatement of fixed assets
    C   an overstatement of profit and an understatement of fixed assets   **(1 mark)**

6   A company's plant and machinery ledger account for the year ended 30 September 20X2 was as follows:

PLANT AND MACHINERY – COST

		£			£
20X1			*20X2*		
1 Oct	Balance	381,200	1 Jun	Disposal account – cost of asset sold	36,000
1 Dec	Cash – addition	18,000	30 Sep	Balance	363,200
		399,200			399,200

The company's policy is to charge depreciation at 20% per year on the straight line basis, with proportionate depreciation in years of purchase and sale.

What is the depreciation charge for the year ended 30 September 20X2?

A   £74,440

B   £84,040

C   £72,640

D   £76,840   **(2 marks)**

---

7   A company bought a property in Chelsea four years ago on 1 January for £170,000. Since then property prices have risen substantially and the property has been revalued at £210,000.

The property was estimated as having a useful life of 20 years when it was purchased. What is the amount transferred to the revaluation reserve?

A   £210,000

B   £136,000

C   £74,000

D   £34,000   **(2 marks)**

---

8   A business purchased a motor car on 1 July 20X3 for £20,000. It is to be depreciated at 20 per cent per year on the straight line basis, assuming a residual value at the end of five years of £4,000, with a proportionate depreciation charge in the year of purchase.

The £20,000 cost was correctly entered in the cash book but posted to the debit of the motor vehicles repairs account.

How will the business profit for the year ended 31 December 20X3 be affected by the error?

A   Understated by £18,400

B   Understated by £16,800

C   Overstated by £18,400   **(1 mark)**

---

9   A company's policy as regards depreciation of its plant and machinery is to charge depreciation at 20 per cent per year on cost, with proportional depreciation for items purchased or sold during a year.

The company's plant and machinery at cost account for the year ended 30 September 20X3 is shown below:

PLANT AND MACHINERY – COST

		£			£
20X2			*20X3*		
1 Oct	Balance (all plant purchased after 20W9)	200,000	30 Jun	Transfer disposal account	40,000
			30 Sep	Balance	210,000
20X3					
1 Apr	Cash-purchase of plant	50,000			
		250,000			250,000

What should be the depreciation charge for plant and machinery (excluding any profit or loss on the disposal) for the year ended 30 September 20X3?

A   £43,000

B   £51,000

C   £42,000

D   £45,000   **(2 marks)**

10　The plant and machinery at cost account of a business for the year ended 30 June 20X4 was as follows:

PLANT AND MACHINERY – COST

		£			£
20X3			*20X3*		
1 Jul	Balance	240,000	30 Sep Transfer disposal account		60,000
20X4			*20X4*		
1 Jan	Cash – purchase of plant	160,000	30 Jun Balance		340,000
		400,000			400,000

The company's policy is to charge depreciation at 20% per year on the straight line basis, with proportionate depreciation in the years of purchase and disposal.

What should be the depreciation charge for the year ended 30 June 20X4?

A　£68,000
B　£64,000
C　£61,000
D　£55,000　　　　　　　　　　　　　　　　　　　　　　　　　　　　　　　**(2 marks)**

(Total = 17 marks)

8 Intangible fixed assets　　　　　　　　　　　　　　　13 mins

1　Which of the following statements about research and development expenditure are correct?

　　1　Research expenditure, other than capital expenditure on research facilities, should be recognised as an expense as incurred.

　　2　In deciding whether development expenditure qualifies to be recognised as an asset, it is necessary to consider whether there will be adequate finance available to complete the project.

　　3　Development expenditure recognised as an asset must be amortised over a period not exceeding five years.

　　A　1, 2 and 3
　　B　1 and 2 only
　　C　1 and 3 only
　　D　2 and 3 only　　　　　　　　　　　　　　　　　　　　　　　　　　　**(2 marks)**

2　Which of the following statements about research and development expenditure are correct according to SSAP 13 *Accounting for Research and Development*?

　　1　If certain conditions are met, an entity may decide to capitalise development expenditure.

　　2　Research expenditure, other than capital expenditure on research facilities, must be written off as incurred.

　　3　Capitalised development expenditure must be amortised over a period not exceeding 5 years.

　　4　Capitalised development expenditure must be disclosed in the balance sheet under intangible fixed assets.

　　A　1, 2 and 4 only
　　B　1 and 3 only
　　C　2 and 4 only
　　D　3 and 4 only　　　　　　　　　　　　　　　　　　　　　　　　　　　**(2 marks)**

3　Which of the following statements concerning the accounting treatment of research and development expenditure are true, according to SSAP 13 *Accounting for Research and Development*?

　　1　Development costs recognised as an asset must be amortised over a period not exceeding five years.

　　2　Research expenditure, other than capital expenditure on research facilities, should be recognised as an expense as incurred.

3   In deciding whether development expenditure qualifies to be recognised as an asset, it is necessary to consider whether there will be adequate finance available to complete the project.

4   Development projects must be reviewed at each balance sheet date, and expenditure on any project no longer qualifying for capitalisation must be amortised through the profit and loss account over a period not exceeding five years.

A   1 and 4
B   2 and 4
C   2 and 3
D   1 and 3   (2 marks)

---

4   SSAP 13 *Accounting for Research and Development* governs the accounting treatment of expenditure on research and development. The following statements about the provisions of SSAP 13 may or may not be correct.

1   Capitalised development expenditure must be amortised over a period not exceeding five years.

2   If all the conditions specified in SSAP 13 are met, development expenditure may be capitalised if the directors decide to do so.

3   Capitalised development costs are shown in the balance sheet under the heading of fixed assets.

4   Amortisation of capitalised development expenditure will appear as an item in a company's statement of total recognised gains and losses.

Which of these four statements are in fact correct?

A   3 only
B   2 and 3
C   1 and 4
D   1 and 3   (2 marks)

---

5   Which of the following statements about goodwill are correct?

1   Goodwill is included in tangible non-current assets on the balance sheet.

2   Internally generated goodwill may not be capitalised.

3   Goodwill is always shown on the face of a company's profit and loss account.

4   Purchased goodwill is the difference between the cost of acquiring a company and the fair value of its identifiable net assets.

A   1 and 3 only
B   2 and 3 only
C   1 and 4 only
D   2 and 4 only   (2 marks)

(Total = 10 marks)

9 Preparation question: XY ledger accounts

At 1 October 20X5, the following balances were brought forward in the ledger accounts of XY:

	Debit £	Credit £
Rent payable account	1,000	
Electricity account		800
Interest receivable account	300	
Allowance for debtors account		4,800

You are told the following.

(a) Rent is payable quarterly in advance on the last day of November, February, May and August, at the rate of £6,000 per annum.

(b) Electricity is paid as follows.

5 November 20X5	£1,000 (for the period to 31 October 20X5)
10 February 20X6	£1,300 (for the period to 31 January 20X6)
8 May 20X6	£1,500 (for the period to 30 April 20X6)
7 August 20X6	£1,100 (for the period to 31 July 20X6)

At 30 September 20X6, the electricity meter shows that £900 has been consumed since the last bill was received.

(c) Interest was received during the year as follows.

| 2 October 20X5 | £250 (for the six months to 30 September 20X5) |
| 3 April 20X6 | £600 (for the six months to 31 March 20X6) |

You estimate that interest of £300 is accrued at 30 September 20X6.

(d) At 30 September 20X6, the balance of debtors amounts to £125,000. The allowance for debtors is to be amended to 5% of debtors.

Required

Write up the following ledger accounts.

(a) Rent payable
(b) Electricity
(c) Interest receivable
(d) Allowance for debtors

and bring down the balances at 30 September 20X6.

---

10 Preparation question: Kate's Coffee House

Included in the balance sheet of Kate's Coffee House at 30 June 20X0 were the following:

	£
Prepayment account (insurance)	450
Accrual account (electricity)	80

The following invoices were received and paid during the year to 30 June 20X1

Date paid		£
5.9.X0	Electricity (quarter to 31 August 20X0)	309
8.12.X0	Electricity (quarter to 30 November 20X0)	320
2.1.X1	Insurance (year to 31 December 20X1)	1,000
7.3.X1	Electricity (quarter to 28 February 20X1)	340
6.6.X1	Electricity (quarter to 31 May 20X1)	321

Required

Calculate the electricity and insurance expenses for the year ended 30 June 20X1.

---

11 Preparation question: Irrecoverable debts

Trade debtors at 31.12.X0 were £76,000. You are told that:

(a) An irrecoverable debt of £3,000 is to be written off;
(b) Specific allowances of £700 and £2,300 are to be made against two doubtful debts;
(c) A general allowance of 6% is to be maintained. The opening balance on the allowance account is £4,000.

Required

Show how the above would be recorded in the ledger accounts.

12 Adjustments to accounts

27 mins

1   A company receives rent from a large number of properties. The total received in the year ended 31 October 20X2 was £481,200.

The following were the amounts of rent in advance and in arrears at 31 October 20X1 and 20X2:

	31 October 20X1	31 October 20X2
	£	£
Rent received in advance	28,700	31,200
Rent in arrears (all subsequently received)	21,200	18,400

What amount of rental income should appear in the company's profit and loss account for the year ended 31 October 20X2?

A   £486,500
B   £460,900
C   £501,500
D   £475,900

(2 marks)

2   A company receives rent for subletting part of its office block.

Rent, receivable quarterly in advance, is received as follows:

Date of receipt	Period covered	£
1 October 20X1	3 months to 31 December 20X1	7,500
30 December 20X1	3 months to 31 March 20X2	7,500
4 April 20X2	3 months to 30 June 20X2	9,000
1 July 20X2	3 months to 30 September 20X2	9,000
1 October 20X2	3 months to 31 December 20X2	9,000

What figures, based on these receipts, should appear in the company's financial statements for the year ended 30 November 20X2?

	P & L account	Balance sheet
A	£34,000 Debit	Prepayment (Dr) £3,000
B	£34,500 Credit	Accrual (Cr) £6,000
C	£34,000 Credit	Accrual (Cr) £3,000
D	£34,000 Credit	Prepayment (Dr) £3,000

(2 marks)

3   A company pays rent quarterly in arrears on 1 January, 1 April, 1 July and 1 October each year. The rent was increased from £90,000 per year to £120,000 per year as from 1 October 20X2.

What rent expense and accrual should be included in the company's financial statements for the year ended 31 January 20X3?

	Rent expense	Accrual
	£	£
A	100,000	20,000
B	100,000	10,000
C	97,500	10,000
D	97,500	20,000

(2 marks)

4   At 31 March 20X2 a company had oil in hand to be used for heating costing £8,200 and an unpaid heating oil bill for £3,600.

At 31 March 20X3 the heating oil in hand was £9,300 and there was an outstanding heating oil bill of £3,200.

Payments made for heating oil during the year ended 31 March 20X3 totalled £34,600.

Based on these figures, what amount should appear in the company's profit and loss account for heating oil for the year?

A   £23,900
B   £36,100
C   £45,300
D   £33,100

(2 marks)

5   At 31 December 20X2 a company's debtors totalled £400,000 and an allowance for debtors of £50,000 had been brought forward from the year ended 31 December 20X1.

It was decided to write off debts totalling £38,000 and to adjust the allowance for debtors to 10% of the debtors.

What charge for irrecoverable debts and debtors allowance should appear in the company's profit and loss account for the year ended 31 December 20X2?

A   £74,200
B   £51,800
C   £28,000
D   £24,200

(2 marks)

6   At 1 July 20X2 the debtors allowance of Q was £18,000.

During the year ended 30 June 20X3 debts totaling £14,600 were written off. It was decided that the debtors allowance should be £16,000 as at 30 June 20X3.

What amount should appear in Q's profit and loss account for irrecoverable debts and debtors allowance for the year ended 30 June 20X3?

A   £12,600
B   £16,600
C   £48,600
D   £30,600

(2 marks)

7   A company has sublet part of its offices and in the year ended 30 November 20X3 the rent receivable was:

Until 30 June 20X3   £8,400 per year
From 1 July 20X3   £12,000 per year

Rent was paid quarterly in advance on 1 January, April, July, and October each year.

What amounts should appear in the company's financial statements for the year ended 30 November 20X3?

	P & L account Rent receivable	Balance sheet
A	£9,900	£2,000 in sundry creditors
B	£9,900	£1,000 in sundry creditors
C	£10,200	£1,000 in sundry creditors
D	£9,900	£2,000 in sundry debtors

(2 marks)

8   At 30 September 20X2 a company's allowance for debtors amounted to £38,000, which was five per cent of the debtors at that date.

At 30 September 20X3 debtors totalled £868,500. It was decided to write off £28,500 of debts as irrecoverable and to keep the allowance for debtors at five per cent of debtors.

What should be the charge in the profit and loss account for the year ended 30 September 20X3 for irrecoverable debts and allowance for debtors?

A	£42,000	
B	£33,925	
C	£70,500	
D	£32,500	(2 marks)

9   At 1 July 20X3 a limited company had an allowance for debtors of £83,000.

During the year ended 30 June 20X4 debts totalling £146,000 were written off. At 30 June 20X4 it was decided that a debtors allowance of £218,000 was required.

What figure should appear in the company's profit and loss account for the year ended 30 June 20X4 for irrecoverable debts and debtors allowance?

A	£155,000	
B	£364,000	
C	£281,000	
D	£11,000	(2 marks)

10   A business compiling its financial statements for the year to 31 July each year pays rent quarterly in advance on 1 January, 1 April, 1 July and 1 October each year. The annual rent was increased from £60,000 per year to £72,000 per year as from 1 October 20X3.

What figure should appear for rent expense in the business profit and loss account for the year ended 31 July 20X4?

A	£69,000	
B	£62,000	
C	£70,000	
D	£63,000	(2 marks)

(Total = 20 marks)

13 Preparation question: Scimitar

Scimitar Ltd proves the accuracy of its sales and purchase ledgers by preparing monthly control accounts. At 1 September 20X7 the following balances existed in the company's accounting records, and the control accounts agreed:

	Debit £	Credit £
Sales ledger control account	188,360	2,140
Purchase ledger control account	120	89,410

The following are the totals of transactions which took place during September 20X7, as extracted from the company's records.

	£
Credit sales	101,260
Credit purchases	68,420
Sales returns	9,160
Purchases returns	4,280
Cash received from customers	91,270
Cash paid to suppliers	71,840
Cash discounts allowed	1,430
Cash discounts received	880
Irrecoverable debts written off	460
Refunds to customers	300
Contra settlements	480

At 30 September 20X7 the balances in the sales and purchase ledgers, as extracted, totalled:

	Debit	Credit
	£	£
Sales ledger balances	To be ascertained	2,680
Purchase ledger balances	90	To be ascertained

An initial attempt to balance the two ledgers showed that neither of them agreed with their control accounts. The differences were found to be due to the following.

(a) A credit balance of £680 had been omitted when listing the sales ledger balances.

(b) A contra settlement of £500 had not been included in the totals of transactions prepared for the control accounts.

(c) A new employee had mistakenly entered five copy sales invoices into the purchases day book as if they had been purchase invoices and entered the amount to new purchase ledger accounts. The total of these invoices was £1,360.

(d) A £20 cash refund to a customer was made out of petty cash, and has not been included in the summary of transactions given above. The £20 was entered to the sales ledger as if it had been a cash receipt from the customer, and this resulted in a £40 credit balance on the account, which was still outstanding at 30 September 20X7.

When these errors had been corrected both control accounts agreed with the ledgers.

Required

Prepare the sales ledger and purchase ledger control (total) accounts for the month of September 20X7 *after* these errors had been corrected, and hence ascertain the missing totals of the ledger balances as indicated above (debit balances in sales ledger and credit balances in purchase ledger).

---

14 Control accounts

27 mins

1 You are given the following information:

Debtors at 1 January 20X3	£10,000
Debtors at 31 December 20X3	£9,000
Total receipts during 20X3 (including cash sales of £5,000)	£85,000

Sales on credit during 20X3 amount to

A £81,000
B £86,000
C £79,000
D £84,000 (2 marks)

---

2 A supplier sends you a statement showing a balance outstanding of £14,350. Your own records show a balance outstanding of £14,500.

The reason for this difference could be that

A the supplier sent an invoice for £150 which you have not yet received
B the supplier has allowed you £150 cash discount which you had omitted to enter in your ledgers
C you have paid the supplier £150 which he has not yet accounted for
D you have returned goods worth £150 which the supplier has not yet accounted for (2 marks)

---

3 The sales ledger control account at 1 May had balances of £32,750 debit and £1,275 credit. During May, sales of £125,000 were made on credit. Receipts from debtors amounted to £122,500 and cash discounts of £550 were allowed. Refunds of £1,300 were made to customers. The closing balances at 31 May could be

A   £35,175 debit and £3,000 credit
B   £35,675 debit and £2,500 credit
C   £36,725 debit and £2,000 credit
D   £36,725 debit and £1,000 credit   **(2 marks)**

4   The debit side of a trial balance totals £50 more than the credit side. This could be due to

A   a purchase of goods for £50 being omitted from the supplier's account
B   a sale of goods for £50 being omitted from the customer's account
C   an invoice of £25 for electricity being credited to the electricity account
D   a receipt for £50 from a customer being omitted from the cash book   **(2 marks)**

5   A sales ledger control account had a closing balance of £8,500. It contained a contra to the purchase ledger of £400, but this had been entered on the wrong side of the control account.

The correct balance on the control account should be

A   £7,700 debit
B   £8,100 debit
C   £8,400 debit
D   £8,900 debit   **(2 marks)**

6   Which of the following items could appear on the credit side of a sales ledger control account?

1   Cash received from customers
2   Irrecoverable debts written off
3   Increase in allowance for debtors
4   Discounts allowed
5   Sales
6   Credits for goods returned by customers
7   Cash refunds to customers

A   1, 2, 4 and 6
B   1, 2, 4 and 7
C   3, 4, 5 and 6
D   5 and 7   **(2 marks)**

7   An inexperienced bookkeeper has drawn up the following sales ledger control account:

SALES LEDGER CONTROL ACCOUNT

	£		£
Opening balance	180,000	Credit sales	190,000
Cash from credit customers	228,000	Irrecoverable debts written off	1,500
Sales returns	8,000	Contras against creditors	2,400
Cash refunds to credit customers	3,300	Closing balance (balancing figure)	229,600
Discount allowed	4,200		
	423,500		423,500

What should the closing balance be after correcting the errors made in preparing the account?

A   £130,600
B   £129,200
C   £142,400
D   £214,600   **(2 marks)**

8   The following sales ledger control account has been prepared by a trainee accountant

		£			£
20X3			**20X3**		
1 Jan	Balance	284,680	31 Dec	Cash received from credit	
31 Dec	Credit sales	189,120		customers	179,790
	Discounts allowed	3,660		Contras against amounts	
	Irrecoverable debts			owing by company in	
	written off	1,800		purchase ledger	800
	Sales returns	4,920		Balance	303,590
		484,180			484,180

What should the closing balance on the account be when the errors in it are corrected?

A   £290,150
B   £286,430
C   £282,830
D   £284,430   **(2 marks)**

---

9   The following control account has been prepared by a trainee accountant:

SALES LEDGER CONTROL ACCOUNT

	£		£
Opening balance	308,600	Cash received from credit customers	147,200
Credit sales	154,200	Discounts allowed to credit	
Cash sales	88,100	customers	1,400
Contras against credit balances in		Interest charged on overdue	
purchase ledger	4,600	accounts	2,400
		Irrecoverable debts written off	4,900
		Allowance for debtors	2,800
		Closing balance	396,800
	555,500		555,500

What should the closing balance be when all the errors made in preparing the sales ledger control account have been corrected?

A   £395,200
B   £304,300
C   £307,100
D   £309,500   **(2 marks)**

---

10   The following sales ledger control account prepared by a trainee accountant contains a number of errors:

SALES LEDGER CONTROL ACCOUNT

		£			£
20X4			**20X4**		
1 Jan	Balance	614,000	31 Dec	Credit sales	301,000
31 Jan	Cash from credit customers	311,000		Discounts allowed	3,400
	Contras against amounts			Irrecoverable debts	
	due to suppliers in			written off	32,000
	purchase ledger	8,650		Interest charged on overdue	
				accounts	1,600
				Balance	595,650
		933,650			933,650

What should the closing balance on the control account be after the errors in it have been corrected?

	A	£561,550
	B	£578,850
	C	£581,550
	D	£568,350

(2 marks)

(Total = 20 marks)

15 Preparation question: Cain

A young and inexperienced bookkeeper is having great difficulty in producing a bank reconciliation statement at 31 December. He gives you his attempt to produce a summarised cash book, and also the bank statement received for the month of December. These are shown below. You may assume that the bank statement is correct and that the first cheque issued in December was number 7654. You may also assume that the trial balance at 1 January did indeed show a bank overdraft of £7,000.12.

CASH BOOK SUMMARY - DRAFT

	£	Dr £	Cr £		
Jan 1					
Opening overdraft		7,000.12	35,000.34	Jan-Nov payments	
Jan-Nov receipts	39,500.54				
Add: discounts	500.02				
		40,000.56			
			12,000.34	Balance Nov 30	
		47,000.68	47,000.68		
Dec 1 brought down		12,000.34		Dec payments	Cheque no
Dec receipts	178.19		37.14		7654
	121.27		192.79		7655
	14.92		5,000.00		7656
	16.88		123.45		7657
		329.26	678.90		7658
Dec receipts	3,100.00		1.47		7659
	171.23		19.84		7660
	1,198.17		10.66		7661
		4,469.40	10,734.75	Balance c/d Dec 31	
		16,799.00	16,799.00		
Jan 1 balance brought down		10,734.75			

BANK STATEMENT – DECEMBER 31

	Withdrawals £	Deposits £	Balance £
1 December			800.00 O/D
7650	300.00	178.19	
7653	191.91	121.27	
7654	37.14	14.92	
7651	1,111.11	16.88	
7656	5,000.00	3,100.00	
7655	129.79	171.23	
7658	678.90	1,198.17	
Standing order	50.00	117.98	
7659	1.47		
7661	10.66		
Bank charges	80.00		
31 December			3,472.34 O/D

Prepare a corrected cash book summary and a reconciliation of the balance on this revised summary with the bank statement balance as at 31 December to establish the remaining difference.

16 Preparation question: George

George has completed his financial statements for the year ended 31 March 20X9, which showed a profit of £81,208, when he realised that no bank reconciliation statement had been prepared for that date.

When checking the cash book against the bank statement and carrying out other checks, he found the following.

(a)   A cheque for £1,000 had been entered in the cash book but had not yet been presented.

(b)   Cheques from customers totalling £2,890 entered in the cash book on 31 March 20X9 were credited by the bank on 1 April 20X9.

(c)   Bank charges of £320 appear in the bank statement on 30 March 20X9 but have not been recorded by George.

(d)   A cheque for £12,900 drawn by George to pay for a new item of plant had been mistakenly entered in the cash book and plant account as £2,900. Depreciation of £290 had been charged in the profit and loss account for this plant.

(e)   A cheque for £980 from a credit customer paid in on 26 March was dishonoured after 31 March 20X9 and George decided that the debit would have to be written off as the customer was now untraceable.

(f)   A cheque for £2,400 in payment for some motor repairs had been mistakenly entered in the cash book as a debit and posted to the credit of motor vehicles account. Depreciation at 25% per annum (straight line) is charged on motor vehicles, with a full year's charge calculated on the balance at the end of each year.

(g)   The total of the payments side of the cash book had been understated by £1,000. On further investigation it was found that the debit side of the purchases account had also been understated by £1,000.

(h)   George had instructed his bank to credit the interest of £160 on the deposit account maintained for surplus business funds to the current account. This the bank had done on 28 March. George had made an entry on the payments side of the cash book for this £160 and had posted it to the debit of interest payable account.

(i)   George had mistakenly paid an account for £870 for repairs to his house with a cheque drawn on the business account. The entry in the cash book had been debited to repairs on the premises account.

(j)   George had also mistakenly paid £540 to Paul, a trade supplier, to clear his account in the purchases ledger, using a cheque drawn on George's personal bank account. No entries have yet been made for this transaction.

The cash book showed a debit balance of £4,890 before any correcting entries had been made. The balance in the bank statements is to be derived from your answer.

Required

(a)   Prepare an adjusted cash book showing the revised balance which should appear in George's balance sheet at 31 March 20X9.

(b)   Prepare a bank reconciliation statement as at 31 March 20X9.

(c)   Draw up a statement for George showing the effect on his profit of the adjustments necessary to correct the errors found.

17 Bank reconciliations   25 mins

1   Your cash book at 31 December 20X3 shows a bank balance of £565 overdrawn. On comparing this with your bank statement at the same date, you discover the following.

    1   A cheque for £57 drawn by you on 29 December 20X3 has not yet been presented for payment.

    2   A cheque for £92 from a customer, which was paid into the bank on 24 December 20X3, has been dishonoured on 31 December 20X3.

    The correct bank balance to be shown in the balance sheet at 31 December 20X3 is

A	£714 overdrawn	
B	£657 overdrawn	
C	£473 overdrawn	
D	£53 overdrawn	**(2 marks)**

2   The cash book shows a bank balance of £5,675 overdrawn at 31 August 20X5. It is subsequently discovered that a standing order for £125 has been entered twice, and that a dishonoured cheque for £450 has been debited in the cash book instead of credited.

The correct bank balance should be

A	£5,100 overdrawn	
B	£6,000 overdrawn	
C	£6,250 overdrawn	
D	£6,450 overdrawn	**(2 marks)**

3   A business had a balance at the bank of £2,500 at the start of the month. During the following month, it paid for materials invoiced at £1,000 less trade discount of 20% and cash discount of 10%. It received a cheque from a customer in respect of an invoice for £200, subject to cash discount of 5%.

The balance at the bank at the end of the month was

A	£1,970	
B	£1,980	
C	£1,990	
D	£2,000	**(2 marks)**

4   The bank statement on 31 October 20X7 showed an overdraft of £800. On reconciling the bank statement, it was discovered that a cheque drawn by your company for £80 had not been presented for payment, and that a cheque for £130 from a customer had been dishonoured on 30 October 20X7, but that this had not yet been notified to you by the bank.

The correct bank balance to be shown in the balance sheet at 31 October 20X7 is

A	£1,010 overdrawn	
B	£880 overdrawn	
C	£750 overdrawn	
D	£720 overdrawn	**(2 marks)**

5   Your firm's cash book at 30 April 20X8 shows a balance at the bank of £2,490. Comparison with the bank statement at the same date reveals the following differences:

	£
Unpresented cheques	840
Bank charges not in cash book	50
Receipts not yet credited by the bank	470
Dishonoured cheque not in cash book	140

The adjusted bank balance per the cash book at 30 April 20X8 is

A	£1,460	
B	£2,300	
C	£2,580	
D	£3,140	**(2 marks)**

6   The following bank reconciliation statement has been prepared by a trainee accountant:

BANK RECONCILIATION 30 SEPTEMBER 20X2

	£
Balance per bank statement (overdrawn)	36,840
Add: lodgements credited after date	51,240
	88,080
Less: outstanding cheques	43,620
Balance per cash book (credit)	44,460

Assuming the amounts stated for items other than the cash book balance are correct, what should the cash book balance be?

A £44,460 credit as stated
B £60,020 credit
C £29,220 debit
D £29,220 credit

(2 marks)

7 Listed below are some possible causes of difference between the cash book balance and the bank statement balance when preparing a bank reconciliation:

1 Cheque paid in, subsequently dishonoured.
2 Error by bank
3 Bank charges
4 Lodgements credited after date
5 Outstanding cheques not yet presented.

Which of these items require an entry in the cash book?

A 1 and 3 only
B 1, 2, 3, 4 and 5
C 2, 4, and 5 only

(1 mark)

8 In preparing a company's bank reconciliation statement at March 20X3, the following items are causing the difference between the cash book balance and the bank statement balance:

1 Bank charges £380
2 Error by bank £1,000 (cheque incorrectly debited to the account)
3 Lodgements not credited £4,580
4 Outstanding cheques £1,475
5 Direct debit £350
6 Cheque paid in by the company and dishonoured £400

Which of these items will require an entry in the cash book?

A 2, 4 and 6
B 1, 5 and 6
C 3 and 4
D 3 and 5

(2 marks)

9 The following bank reconciliation statement has been prepared by a trainee accountant:

	£
Overdraft per bank statement	3,860
Less: outstanding cheques	9,160
	5,300
Add: deposits credited after date	16,690
Cash at bank as calculated above	21,990

What should be the correct balance per the cash book?

A £21,990 balance at bank as stated
B £3,670 balance at bank
C £11,390 balance at bank
D £3,670 overdrawn

(2 marks)

10 Which of the following statements about bank reconciliations are correct?

1 A difference between the cash book and the bank statement must be corrected by means of a journal entry.

2 In preparing a bank reconciliation, lodgements recorded before date in the cash book but credited by the bank after date should reduce an overdrawn balance in the bank statement.

| 3 | Bank charges not yet entered in the cash book should be dealt with by an adjustment in the bank reconciliation statement. |
| 4 | If a cheque received from a customer is dishonoured after date, a credit entry in the cash book is required. |

A	2 and 4
B	1 and 4
C	2 and 3
D	1 and 3

(2 marks)

(Total = 19 marks)

18 Preparation question: Choctaw (PFS 6/05)

The draft financial statements of Choctaw, a limited company, for the year ended 31 December 20X4 showed a profit of £86,400. The trial balance did not balance, and a suspense account with a credit balance of £3,310 was included in the balance sheet.

In subsequent checking the following errors were found:

(a) Depreciation of motor vehicles at 25 per cent was calculated for the year ended 31 December 20X4 on the reducing balance basis, and should have been calculated on the straight-line basis at 25 per cent. Relevant figures:

Cost of motor vehicles £120,000, net book value at 1 January 20X4, £88,000

(b) Rent received from subletting part of the office accommodation £1,200 had been put into the petty cash box. No debtor balance had been recognised when the rent fell due and no entries had been made in the petty cash book or elsewhere for it. The petty cash float in the trial balance is the amount according to the records, which is £1,200 less than the actual balance in the box.

(c) Irrecoverable debts totalling £8,400 are to be written off.

(d) The opening accrual on the motor repairs account of £3,400, representing repair bills due but not paid at 31 December 20X3, had not been brought down at 1 January 20X4.

(e) The cash discount totals for December 20X4 had not been posted to the discount accounts in the nominal ledger.

The figures were:

	£
Discount allowed	380
Discount received	290

After the necessary entries, the suspense account balanced.

Required

Prepare journal entries, with narratives, to correct the errors found, and prepare a statement showing the necessary adjustments to the profit.

19 Journal entries and suspense accounts I

1   The debit side of a trial balance totals £800 more than the credit side.

Which one of the following errors would fully account for the difference?

A   £400 paid for plant maintenance has been correctly entered in the cash book and credited to the plant asset account.

B   Discount received £400 has been debited to discount allowed account.

C   A receipt of £800 for commission receivable has been omitted from the records.

D   The petty cash balance of £800 has been omitted from the trial balance.   **(2 marks)**

The following information is relevant for question 2 and 3

When Q's trial balance failed to agree, a suspense account was opened for the difference. The trial balance totals were:

	£
Debit	864,390
Credit	860,930

The company does not have control accounts for its sales and purchase ledgers.

The following errors were found:

1   In recording an issue of shares at par, cash received of £333,000 was credited to the ordinary share capital account as £330,000

2   Cash £2,800 paid for plant repairs was correctly accounted for in the cash book but was credited to the plant asset account.

3   The petty cash book balance £500 had been omitted from the trial balance.

4   A cheque for £78,400 paid for the purchase of a motor car was debited to the motor vehicles account as £87,400.

5   A contra between the sales ledger and the purchase ledger for £1,200 which should have been credited in the sales ledger and debited in the purchase ledger was actually debited in the sales ledger and credited in the purchase ledger.

2   Which of these errors will require an entry to the suspense account to correct them?

A   All five items

B   3 and 5 only

C   2, 4 and 5 only

D   1, 2, 3 and 4 only   **(2 marks)**

3   What will the balance on the suspense account be after making the necessary entries to correct the errors affecting the suspense account?

A   £2,440 Debit

B   £15,560 Credit

C   £13,640 Debit

D   £3,440 Debit   **(2 marks)**

4   A company's trial balance totals were:

Debit	£387,642	
Credit		£379,511

A suspense account was opened for the difference.

Which ONE of the following errors would have the effect of reducing the difference when corrected?

A   The petty cash balance of £500 has been omitted from the trial balance

B   £4,000 received for rent of part of the office has been correctly recorded in the cash book and debited to rent account

C   £3,000 paid for repairs to plant has been debited to the plant asset account   **(1 mark)**

---

5   The bookkeeper of Peri made the following mistakes:

Discount allowed £3,840 was credited to discounts received account.
Discount received £2,960 was debited to discounts allowed account.
Discounts were otherwise correctly recorded.

Which of the following journal entries will correct the errors?

		Dr £	Cr £
A	Discount allowed	7,680	
	Discount received		5,920
	Suspense account		1,760
B	Discount allowed	880	
	Discount received	880	
	Suspense account		1,760
C	Discount allowed	6,800	
	Discount received		6,800

(1 mark)

---

6   A company's trial balance failed to agree, the totals being:

Debit	£815,602
Credit	£808,420

Which one of the following errors could fully account for the difference?

A   The omission from the trial balance of the balance on the insurance expense account £7,182 debit

B   Discount allowed £3,591 debited in error to the discount received account

C   No entries made in the records for cash sales totalling £7,182

D   The returns outwards total of £3,591 was included in the trial balance as a debit balance   **(2 marks)**

---

7   Listed below are five potential causes of difference between a company's cash book balance and its bank statement balance as at 30 November 20X3:

1   Cheques recorded and sent to suppliers before 30 November 20X3 but not yet presented for payment.

2   An error by the bank in crediting to another customer's account a lodgement made by the company.

3   Bank charges.

4   Cheques paid in before 30 November 20X3 but not credited by the bank until 3 December 20X3.

5   A cheque recorded and paid in before 30 November 20X3 but dishonoured by the bank.

Which of the following alternatives correctly analyses these items into those requiring an entry in the cash book and those that would feature in the bank reconciliation?

	Cash book entry	Bank reconciliation
A	1, 2, 4	3, 5
B	3, 5	1, 2, 4
C	3, 4	1, 2, 5
D	2, 3, 5	1, 4

(2 marks)

8 A trial balance extracted from a sole trader's records failed to agree, and a suspense account was opened for the difference.

Which of the following errors would require an entry in the suspense account in correcting them?

1 Discount allowed was mistakenly debited to discount received account.

2 Cash received from the sale of a fixed asset was correctly entered in the cash book but was debited to the disposal account.

3 The balance on the rent account was omitted from the trial balance.

4 Goods taken from stock by the proprietor had been recorded by crediting drawings account and debiting purchases account.

A All four items
B 2 and 3 only
C 2 and 4 only
D 1 and 3 only   (2 marks)

---

9 Which of the following journal entries may be accepted as being correct according to their narratives?

		DR £	CR £
1	Wages account	38,000	
	Purchases account	49,000	
	Buildings account		87,000
	Labour and materials used in construction of extension to factory		
2	Directors' personal accounts: A	30,000	
	B	40,000	
	Directors' remuneration		70,000
	Directors' bonuses transferred to their accounts		
3	Suspense account	10,000	
	Sales account		10,000
	Correction of error in addition – total of credit side of sales account £10,000 understated		

A 1 and 3
B 1 and 2
C 3 only
D 2 and 3   (2 marks)

(Total = 16 marks)

---

20 Journal entries and suspense accounts II   24 mins

1 An error of principle would occur if

A plant and machinery purchased was credited to a fixed assets account
B plant and machinery purchased was debited to the purchases account
C plant and machinery purchased was debited to the equipment account   (1 mark)

---

2 An organisation's year end is 30 September. On 1 January 20X6 the organisation took out a loan of £100,000 with annual interest of 12%. The interest is payable in equal instalments on the first day of April, July, October and January in arrears.

How much should be charged to the profit and loss account for the year ended 30 September 20X6, and how much should be accrued on the balance sheet?

	P &L account	Balance sheet
A	£12,000	£3,000
B	£9,000	£3,000
C	£9,000	NIL
D	£6,000	£3,000

(2 marks)

3   A suspense account was opened when a trial balance failed to agree. The following errors were later discovered.

- A gas bill of £420 had been recorded in the gas account as £240
- A discount of £50 given to a customer had been credited to discounts received
- Interest received of £70 had been entered in the bank account only

The original balance on the suspense account was

A   Debit £210
B   Credit £210
C   Debit £160
D   Credit £160

(2 marks)

4   An error of commission is one where

A   a transaction has not been recorded
B   one side of a transaction has been recorded in the wrong account, and that account is of a different class to the correct account
C   one side of a transaction has been recorded in the wrong account, and that account is of the same class as the correct account

(1 mark)

5   Where a transaction is entered into the correct ledger accounts, but the wrong amount is used, the error is known as an error of

A   omission
B   original entry
C   commission
D   principle

(2 marks)

6   A business's bank balance increased by £750,000 during its last financial year. During the same period it issued shares of £1 million and repaid a loan note of £750,000. It purchased fixed assets for £200,000 and charged depreciation of £100,000. Working capital (other than the bank balance) increased by £575,000.

Its profit for the year was

A   £1,175,000
B   £1,275,000
C   £1,325,000
D   £1,375,000

(2 marks)

7   A sole trader's business made a profit of £32,500 during the year ended 31 March 20X8. This figure was after deducting £100 per week wages for himself. In addition, he put his home telephone bill through the business books, amounting to £400 plus VAT at 17.5%. He is registered for VAT and therefore has charged only the net amount to his profit and loss account.

His capital at 1 April 20X7 was £6,500. His capital at 31 March 20X8 was

A   £33,730
B   £33,800
C   £38,930
D   £39,000

(2 marks)

8   The trial balance of Delta, a limited company, did not agree and a suspense account was opened for the difference. The following errors were subsequently found:

1   A cash refund due to customer A was correctly treated in the cash book and then credited to the sales ledger account of customer B.

2   The sale of goods to a director for £300 was recorded by debiting sales account and crediting the director's current account.

3   The total of the discount received column in the cash book had been credited in error to the discount allowed account.

4   Some of the cash received from customers had been used to pay sundry expenses before banking the money.

5   £5,800 paid for plant repairs was correctly treated in the cash book and then credited to plant and equipment asset account.

Which of the above errors would require an entry to the suspense account as part of the process of correcting them?

A   1, 3 and 5
B   1, 2 and 5
C   1 and 5
D   3 and 4   **(2 marks)**

9   A business can make a profit and yet have a reduction in its bank balance. Which ONE of the following might cause this to happen?

A   The sale of fixed assets at a loss.
B   The charging of depreciation in the profit and loss account.
C   The lengthening of the period of credit given to customers.
D   The lengthening of the period of credit taken from suppliers.   **(2 marks)**

10   A manufacturing company receives an invoice on 29 February 20X1 for work done on one of it's machines. £25,500 of the cost is actually for a machine upgrade, which will improve efficiency. The accounts department do not notice and charge the whole amount to maintenance costs. Machinery is depreciated at 25% per annum on a straight-line basis, with a proportional charge in the years of acquisition and disposal. By what amount will the profit for the year to 30 June 20X1 be understated?

A   £19,125
B   £25,500
C   £23,375
D   £21,250   **(2 marks)**

(Total =18 marks)

21 Preparation question: Altese (PFS 6/03)

(a)   The net assets of Altese, a trader, at 1 January 20X2 amounted to £128,000.

De uring the year to 31 December 20X2 Altese introduced a further £50,000 of capital and made drawings of £48,000.

At 31 December 20X2 Altese's net assets totalled £184,000.

Required

Using this information compute Altese's total profit for the year ended 31 December 20X2.

(b)   Senji does not keep proper accounting records, and it is necessary to calculate her total purchases for the year ended 31 January 20X3 from the following information:

	£
Trade payables: 31 January 20X2	130,400
31 January 20X3	171,250
Payment to suppliers	888,400
Cost of goods taken from stock by Senji for her personal use	1,000
Refunds received from suppliers	2,400
Discounts received	11,200

Required

Compute the figure for purchases for inclusion in Senji's financial statements.

(c)   Aluki fixes prices to make a standard gross profit percentage on sales of $33\frac{1}{3}\%$.

The following information for the year ended 31 January 20X3 is available to compute her sales total for the year.

	£
Stock: 1 February 20X2	243,000
31 January 20X3	261,700
Purchases	595,400
Purchases returns	41,200

Required

Calculate the sales figure for the year ended 31 January 20X3.

22 Incomplete records   24 mins

1   A trader's net profit for the year may be computed by using which of the following formulae?

   A   Opening capital + drawings − capital introduced − closing capital
   B   Closing capital + drawings − capital introduced − opening capital
   C   Opening capital − drawings + capital introduced − closing capital   **(1 mark)**

2   The profit earned by a business in 20X7 was £72,500. The proprietor injected new capital of £8,000 during the year and withdrew goods for his private use which had cost £2,200.

   If net assets at the beginning of 20X7 were £101,700, what were the closing net assets?

   A   £35,000
   B   £39,400
   C   £168,400
   D   £180,000   **(2 marks)**

3   The profit made by a business in 20X7 was £35,400. The proprietor injected new capital of £10,200 during the year and withdrew a monthly salary of £500.

   If net assets at the end of 20X7 were £95,100, what was the proprietor's capital at the beginning of the year?

   A   £50,000
   B   £55,500
   C   £63,900
   D   £134,700   **(2 marks)**

4   A business has compiled the following information for the year ended 31 October 20X2:

	£
Opening stock	386,200
Purchases	989,000
Closing stock	422,700

   The gross profit as a percentage of sales is always 40%

Based on these figures, what is the sales turnover for the year?

A   £1,333,500
B   £1,587,500
C   £2,381,250
D   The sales turnover figure cannot be calculated from this information   **(2 marks)**

---

5   Which of the following calculations could produce an acceptable figure for a trader's net profit for a period if no accounting records had been kept?

A   Closing net assets plus drawings minus capital introduced minus opening net assets
B   Closing net assets minus drawings plus capital introduced minus opening net assets
C   Closing net assets minus drawings minus capital introduced minus opening net assets   **(1 mark)**

---

6   A sole trader took some goods costing £800 from stock for his own use. The normal selling price of the goods is £1,600.

Which of the following journal entries would correctly record this?

		Dr £	Cr £
A	Stock account	800	
	Purchases account		800
B	Drawings account	800	
	Purchases account		800
C	Sales account	1,600	
	Drawings account		1,600
D	Drawings account	800	
	Sales account		800

(2 marks)

---

7   A sole trader fixes his prices to achieve a gross profit percentage on sales of 40%. All his sales are for cash. He suspects that one of his sales assistants is stealing cash from sales.

His trading account for the month of June 20X3 is as follows:

	£
Recorded sales	181,600
Cost of sales	114,000
Gross profit	67,600

Assuming that the cost of sales figure is correct, how much cash could the sales assistant have taken?

A   £5,040
B   £8,400
C   £22,000
D   It is not possible to calculate a figure from this information   **(2 marks)**

The following information is relevant for questions 8 and 9

A is a sole trader who does not keep full accounting records. The following details relate to her transactions with credit customers and suppliers for the year ended 30 November 20X3.

	£
Trade debtors, 1 December 20X2	130,000
Trade creditors, 1 December 20X2	60,000
Cash received from customers	686,400
Cash paid to suppliers	302,800
Discounts allowed	1,400
Discounts received	2,960

	£
Irrecoverable debts	4,160
Amount due from a customer who is also a supplier offset against an amount due for goods supplied by him	2,000
Trade debtors, 30 November 20X3	181,000
Trade creditors, 30 November 20X3	84,000

8   Based on the above information, what figure should appear in A's profit and loss account for the year ended 30 November 20X3 for sales?

    A   £748,960
    B   £748,800
    C   £744,960
    D   £743,560   **(2 marks)**

9   Based on the above information, what figure should appear in A's profit and loss account for the year ended 30 November 20X3 for purchases?

    A   £283,760
    B   £325,840
    C   £329,760
    D   £331,760   **(2 marks)**

10   A sole trader fixes her prices by adding 50 per cent to the cost of all goods purchased. On 31 October 20X3 a fire destroyed a considerable part of the stock and all stock records.

Her trading account for the year ended 31 October 20X3 included the following figures:

	£	£
Sales		281,250
Opening stock at cost	183,600	
Purchases	249,200	
	432,800	
Closing stock at cost	204,600	
		228,200
Gross profit		53,050

Using this information, what stock loss has occurred?

    A   £61,050
    B   £87,575
    C   £40,700
    D   £110,850   **(2 marks)**

(Total = 18 marks)

23 Preparation question: PDQ & Co

Profit before appropriation for PDQ & Co in its first year of trading was £72,000.

Drawings were made as follows:-

	£
P	7,200
D	9,600
Q	7,200

P was to receive a salary of £12,960 p.a.

Fixed capital on starting the business was

	£
P	14,400
D	24,000
Q	36,000

Interest was given at 20% in the partnership agreement on fixed capital. Interest was charged at 5% on any drawings made before the year end. Profit sharing was agreed at 10:15:20.

Required

Calculate balances in each partner's current account at the end of the year, using an appropriation account.

24 Preparation question: Leon and Mark (PFS 6/06)

The following balances are in the accounting records of a partnership as at 31 December 20X5:

		£
Capital accounts	Leon, as at 1 January 20X5	400,000
	Mark, introduced 1 July 20X5	200,000
Drawings	Leon	160,000
	Mark	80,000

Notes

(1) Until 30 June 20X5, Leon had run the business as a sole trader. Mark joined him on 1 July 20X5 introducing capital of £200,000.

(2) The following profit-sharing arrangements were agreed from that date:

(i)   Both partners to receive interest on their capital account balances at 5% per year
(ii) Mark to receive a salary of £20,000 per year
(iii) Balance of profit to be shared – Leon 60%, Mark 40%.

(3) The profit for the year ended 31 December 20X5 was £250,000. It was agreed that this profit had accrued one third in the six months ended 30 June 20X5 and two thirds in the six months ended 31 December 20X5, except for an irrecoverable debt of £20,000 charged in arriving at the profit which was to be regarded as occurring in the six months ended 30 June 20X5.

Required

Prepare a statement showing the division of the profit and prepare the partners' current accounts for the year ended 31 December 20X5.

25 Partnerships   32 mins

1   A partnership employs an inexperienced bookkeeper. He has written up the current account of one of the partners as follows.

CURRENT ACCOUNT

	£		£
Interest on capital	2,800	Balance b/f	270
Salary	1,500	Drawings	6,200
Balance c/f	10,870	Net profit	8,700
	15,170		15,170

The balance brought forward is entered correctly and the other entries are all correct in amount. However, the bookkeeper is not very sure of the difference between debits and credits.

What is the corrected balance carried forward?

A   A debit balance of £1,530
B   A debit balance of £6,530
C   A credit balance of £7,070
D   A credit balance of £16,470   **(2 marks)**

2   A partner's private petrol bills have been treated as part of the partnership's motor vehicle expenses. Which of the following entries is necessary to correct the error?

A   *Debit*   Drawings account
    Credit   Motor vehicle expenses account

B   *Debit*   Motor vehicles expenses account
    Credit   Drawings account

C   *Debit*   Motor vehicles expenses account
    Credit   Capital account

D   *Debit*   Capital account
    Credit   Motor vehicle expenses account   **(2 marks)**

3   What double entry is necessary to reflect interest earned on partners' capital account balances?

A   *Debit*   Partners' current accounts
    Credit   Profit and loss appropriation account

B   *Debit*   Profit and loss appropriation account
    Credit   Partners' current accounts

C   *Debit*   Profit and loss appropriation account
    Credit   Cash

D   *Debit*   Profit and loss appropriation account
    Credit   Partners' capital accounts   **(2 marks)**

4   If there is no partnership agreement, the split of profits between the partners is governed by which of the following?

A   Financial Reporting Standards
B   The Partnership Act 1890
C   Must be agreed between the partners   **(1 mark)**

5   What double entry is necessary to reflect interest payable on partners' drawings?

A   *Debit*   Partners' drawings accounts
    Credit   Partners' current accounts

B   *Debit*   Profit and loss appropriation account
    Credit   Partners' drawings accounts

C   *Debit*   Partners' drawings accounts
    Credit   Interest payable account

D   *Debit*   Partners' current accounts
    Credit   Profit and loss appropriation account   **(2 marks)**

6   Faith, Hope and Charity are partners sharing residual profits in the ratio 3:2:1. The partnership agreement provides for interest on capital at the rate of 8% per annum and for a salary for Hope of £8,000 per annum. Net profit for 20X5 was £84,000 and the balances on partners' capital accounts during the year were: Faith £20,000; Hope £15,000; Charity £12,000.

    Calculate Charity's share of residual profits for 20X5.

A	£12,040
B	£12,667
C	£13,000
D	£14,000

(2 marks)

---

7   P and Q are in partnership, sharing profits in the ratio 3:2 and compiling their accounts to 30 June each year.

On 1 January 20X2 R joined the partnership, and from that date the profit-sharing ratio became P 50%, Q 25% and R 25%, after providing for salaries for Q and R as follows:

Q	£20,000 per year
R	£12,000 per year

The partnership profit for the year ended 30 June 20X2 was £480,000, accruing evenly over the year.

What are the partners' total profit shares for the year ended 30 June 20X2?

	P	Q	R
	£	£	£
A	256,000	162,000	62,000
B	248,000	168,000	64,000
C	264,000	166,000	66,000
D	264,000	156,000	60,000

(2 marks)

---

8   A and B are in partnership. They decided to let C join the partnership on 31 December 20X8. On that date the net book value of the net assets is £500,000. The partners agree that the fair value of the net assets is £750,000 at 31 December 20X8. The business is valued at £850,000 by a firm of valuers for the purposes of calculating the amount that C will pay to buy a share in the partnership.

What is the value of goodwill?

A	£350,000
B	£250,000
C	£100,000
D	£850,000

(2 marks)

---

9   P, after having been a sole trader for some years, entered into partnership with Q on 1 July 20X2, sharing profits equally.

The business profit for the year ended 31 December 20X2 was £340,000, accruing evenly over the year, apart from a charge of £20,000 for an irrecoverable debt relating to trading before 1 July 20X2 which it was agreed that P should bear entirely.

How is the profit for the year to be divided between P and Q?

	P	Q
	£'000	£'000
A	245	95
B	250	90
C	270	90
D	255	85

(2 marks)

---

10   G, H and I are in partnership, compiling their accounts for the year to 31 December each year.

The profit-sharing arrangements are as follows:

Until 30 June 20X3

Annual salaries H	£40,000
I	£20,000

	G %	H %	I %
Balance of profit split	60	20	20
From 1 July 20X3			
Salaries to be discontinued, profit to be divided	50	30	20

The profit for the year ended 31 December 20X3 was £400,000 before charging partners' salaries, accruing evenly through the year and after charging an expense of £40,000, which it was agreed related wholly to the first six months of the year.

How should the profit for the year be divided among the partners?

	G £	H £	I £
A	182,000	130,000	88,000
B	200,000	116,000	84,000
C	198,000	118,000	88,000
D	180,000	132,000	88,000

(2 marks)

11   X and Y are in partnership, sharing profits in the ratio 2:1 and compiling their financial statements to 30 June each year.

On 1 January 20X4 Z joined the partnership, and it was agreed that the profit-sharing arrangement should become X 50%, Y 30% and Z 20%.

The profit for the year ended 30 June 20X4 was £540,000, after charging an expense of £30,000 which it was agreed related to the period before 1 January 20X4. The profit otherwise accrued evenly over the year.

What is X's total profit share for the year ended 30 June 20X4?

A   £305,000

B   £312,500

C   £315,000

D   £295,000

(2 marks)

12   Goodwill is calculated as the excess of the price paid over the net book value of the net assets of the business.

Is this statement

A   True

B   False

(1 mark)

13   G, H and I are in partnership, sharing profits in the ratio 3:1:1, after charging salaries of £20,000 per year each for H and I. On 1 January 20X4 they agreed to change the profit-sharing ratio to 3:2:1 and to discontinue H's salary. I's salary continued unchanged. The partnership profit for the year ended 30 June 20X4 was £380,000, accruing evenly over the year.

How should the £380,000 profit be divided among the partners?

	G £	H £	I £
A	192,000	104,000	84,000
B	192,500	103,333	84,167
C	209,000	101,333	69,667
D	209,000	111,333	89,667

(2 marks)

(Total = 24 marks)

26 Preparation question: Bonus issue

Clarke Fringland Ltd

(Extract) Balance Sheet as at 31/12/2003

	£
Share capital (50p)	10,000
Share premium	7,000
Retained profit	8,000
	25,000

Clarke Fringland Ltd has decided on a bonus issue of 1 for 4.

The double entry is   £

Dr

Cr

The adjusted balance sheet extract would be as follows:

                                                    £

Share capital

Share premium

Retained profit

Note: There has been an issue of shares and so share capital must be credited at the **nominal** value only.

---

27 Preparation question: Rights issue

Clarke Fringland Ltd

(Extract) Balance Sheet as at 31/12/2003

	£
Share capital (50p)	8,000
Share premium	7,000
Retained profit	10,000
	25,000

In this instance, Clarke Fringland Ltd decides on a rights issue of 1 for 4 at £1.20.

The double entry is   £

Dr

Cr

Cr

The adjusted balance sheet extract would be as follows:

£

Share capital

Share premium

Retained profit

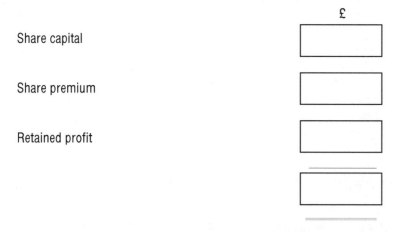

Note: Again here is an issues of shares so share capital must be credited with the **nominal** value of the shares only.

---

28 Preparation question: Shuswap (PFS 6/05)

The draft balance sheet shown below has been prepared for Shuswap, a limited company, as at 31 December 20X4:

	Cost £'000	Accumulated depreciation £'000	Net book value £'000
Fixed assets			
Land and buildings	9,000	1,000	8,000
Plant and equipment	21,000	9,000	12,000
	30,000	10,000	20,000
Current assets			
Stocks		3,000	
Debtors		2,600	
Cash at bank		1,900	
		7,500	
Creditors: amounts falling due within one year			
Trade creditors		2,100	
Net current assets			5,400
			25,400
Creditors: amounts falling due after more than one year			
Debentures (redeemable 20Y0)			2,000
			23,400
Issued share capital (ordinary shares of 50p each)			6,000
Retained profits			12,400
Suspense account			5,000
			23,400

The following further information is available:

1 It has been decided to revalue the land and buildings to £12,000,000 at 31 December 20X4.

2 Trade debtors totalling £200,000 are to be written off.

3 During the year there was a contra settlement of £106,000 in which an amount due to a supplier was set off against the amount due from the same company for goods sold to it. No entry has yet been made to record the set-off.

4 Some stock items included in the draft balance sheet at cost £500,000 were sold after the balance sheet date for £400,000, with selling expenses of £40,000.

5   The suspense account is made up of two items:

(a)   The proceeds of issue of 4,000,000 50p shares at £1.10 per share, credited to the suspense account from the cash book.

(b)   The balance of the account is the proceeds of sale of some plant on 1 January 20X4 with a net book value at the date of sale of £700,000 and which had originally cost £1,400,000. No other accounting entries have yet been made for the disposal apart from the cash book entry for the receipt of the proceeds. Depreciation on plant has been charged at 25% (straight line basis) in preparing the draft balance sheet without allowing for the sale. The depreciation for the year relating to the plant sold should be adjusted for in full.

Required

Prepare the company's balance sheet as at 31 December 20X4, complying as far as possible with the Companies Act.

Details of fixed assets, adjusted appropriately, should appear as they are presented in the question.

29 Company financial statements I   23 mins

1   The issued share capital of Alpha, a limited company, is as follows:

	£
Ordinary shares of 10p each	1,000,000
8% Preference shares of 50p each	500,000

In the year ended 31 October 20X2, the company has paid the preference dividend for the year and an interim dividend of 2p per share on the ordinary shares. A final ordinary dividend of 3p per share was proposed, before the balance sheet date.

What is the total amount of dividends relating to the year ended 31 October 20X2?

A   £580,000
B   £90,000
C   £130,000
D   £540,000   **(2 marks)**

2   When a company makes a rights issue of equity shares which of the following effects will the issue have?

1   Assets are increased
2   Retained earnings are reduced
3   Share premium account is reduced
4   Investments are increased

A   1 only
B   1 and 2
C   3 only
D   1 and 4   **(2 marks)**

3   Which of the following items may appear as current liabilities in a company's balance sheet?

1   Minority interests in subsidiaries.
2   Loan due for repayment within one year.
3   Taxation.
4   Preference dividend payable

A   1, 2 and 3
B   1, 2 and 4
C   1, 3 and 4
D   2, 3 and 4   **(2 marks)**

4   A company made an issue for cash of 1,000,000 50p shares at a premium of 30p per share.

Which of the following journal entries correctly records the issue?

		Debit £	Credit £
A	Share capital	500,000	
	Share premium	300,000	
	Bank		800,000
B	Bank	800,000	
	Share capital		500,000
	Share premium		300,000
C	Bank	1,300,000	
	Share capital		1,000,000
	Share premium		300,000
D	Share capital	1,000,000	
	Share premium		300,000
	Bank		1,300,000

(2 marks)

---

5   Which of the following might appear as an item in a company's statement of movements in reserves?

1   Profit on disposal of properties.
2   Surplus on revaluation of properties
3   Equity dividends proposed after the balance sheet date.
4   Issue of share capital.

A   1, 3 and 4 only
B   2 and 4 only
C   1 and 2 only
D   3 and 4 only

(2 marks)

---

6   At 31 December 20X2 the following matters require inclusion in a company's financial statements:

1   On 1 January 20X2 the company made a loan of £12,000 to an employee, repayable on 30 April 20X3, charging interest at 2 per cent per year. On the due date she repaid the loan and paid the whole of the interest due on the loan to that date.
2   The company has paid insurance £9,000 in 20X2, covering the year ending 31 August 20X3.
3   In January 20X3 the company received rent from a tenant £4,000 covering the six months to 31 December 20X2.

For these items, what total figures should be included in the company's balance sheet at 31 December 20X2?

	Current assets £	Current liabilities £
A	22,000	240
B	22,240	NIL
C	10,240	NIL
D	16,240	6,000

(2 marks)

---

7   At 31 December 20X1 the capital structure of a company was as follows:

	£
Ordinary share capital	
100,000 shares of 50p each	50,000
Share premium account	180,000

During 20X2 the company made a bonus issue of 1 share for every 2 held, using the share premium account for the purpose, and later issued for cash another 60,000 shares at 80p per share.

What is the company's capital structure at 31 December 20X2?

	Ordinary share capital £	Share premium account £
A	130,000	173,000
B	105,000	173,000
C	130,000	137,000
D	105,000	137,000

(2 marks)

8   Which, if any, of the following statements are correct according to FRS 18 *Accounting Policies?*

1   The correction of a fundamental error relating to a past period should be made in the current period. It is not acceptable to make the correction by adjusting the opening balance of retained profits.

2   A change in an accounting policy constitutes a fundamental error and should be accounted for in the current period.

3   The benchmark treatment for a change of accounting policy is normally to apply it retrospectively, with adjustment to the opening balance of retained profits .

A   1 only
B   2 only
C   3 only   (1 mark)

9   If a company changes a material accounting policy, which of the following statements are correct?

1   The notes to the financial statements should disclose the reason for the change and its effect.

2   The effect of the change should be disclosed in the current year's profit and loss account as an extraordinary item.

3   The opening balance of retained profits should be adjusted if practicable, as if the change had been in effect for previous periods.

4   In the financial statements for the current period, comparative figures for the previous period should be adjusted to reflect the change.

A   1, 3 and 4
B   2, 3 and 4
C   1, 2 and 3
D   1, 2 and 4   (2 marks)

(Total = 17 marks)

30 Company financial statements II   24 mins

1   Which of the following statements about company financial statements is/are correct, according to Financial Reporting standards?

1   A material profit or loss on the sale of part of the entity must appear in the profit and loss account as an extraordinary item.

2   Dividends paid and proposed should be included in the profit and loss account.

3   The profit and loss account must show separately any material profit or loss from operations discontinuing during the year.

4   The statement of movements in reserves must not include unrealised gains or losses.

A   1, 2 and 3
B   2 and 4
C   3 only   (1 mark)

2   Which of the following items are required to be disclosed in a limited company's financial statements according to the Companies Act?

1   Authorised share capital
2   Finance costs
3   Staff costs
4   Depreciation and amortisation

A   1, 2 and 3 only
B   2, 3 and 4 only
C   All four items   (1 mark)

---

3   At 30 June 20X2 a company's capital structure was as follows:

	£
Ordinary share capital	
500,000 shares of 25p each	125,000
Share premium account	100,000

In the year ended 30 June 20X3 the company made a rights issue of 1 share for every 2 held at £1 per share and this was taken up in full. Later in the year the company made a bonus issue of 1 share for every 5 held, using the share premium account for the purpose.

What was the company's capital structure at 30 June 20X3?

	Ordinary share capital £	Share premium account £
A	450,000	25,000
B	225,000	250,000
C	225,000	325,000
D	212,500	262,500	(2 marks)

---

4   At 30 June 20X2 a company had £1m 8% debentures in issue, interest being paid half-yearly on 30 June and 31 December.

On 30 September 20X2 the company redeemed £250,000 of these debentures at par, paying interest due to that date.

On 1 April 20X3 the company issued £500,000 7% debentures, interest payable half-yearly on 31 March and 30 September.

What figure should appear in the company's profit and loss account for interest payable in the year ended 30 June 20X3?

A   £88,750
B   £82,500
C   £65,000
D   £73,750   (2 marks)

---

5   Which of the following statements about the financial statements of limited companies are correct according to Financial Reporting Standards?

1   In preparing a cash flow statement, either the direct or the indirect method may be used. Both lead to the same figure for net cash from operating activities.
2   Debentures can be classified as current or long-term liabilities.
3   Financial statements must disclose a company's total expense for staff costs and for depreciation, if material.
4   A company must disclose by note details of all adjusting events allowed for in the financial statements.

A   1, 2 and 3 only
B   2 and 4 only
C   3 and 4 only
D   All four items   (2 marks)

6   Which of the following could appear as separate items in the statement of movements in reserves required
      as part of a company's financial statements?

      1   Gain on revaluation of land.
      2   Loss on sale of investments.
      3   Prior year adjustments.
      4   Proceeds of an issue of ordinary shares.
      5   Dividends proposed after the year end.

      A   1, 3 and 4 only
      B   1, 2 and 4 only
      C   1 and 3 only
      D   All five items   (2 marks)

7   Which of the following must be disclosed in the financial statements of a quoted (listed) company, if
      material?

      1   Total spent on research and development.
      2   An analysis of operating profit into continuing and discontinued activities.
      3   Profit or loss on the disposal of a discontinued operation.
      4   Authorised share capital.
      5   Finance costs.

      A   2, 3 and 4 only
      B   1, 2, 3 and 5 only
      C   1 and 5 only
      D   All five items   (2 marks)

8   A limited company issued 50,000 ordinary shares of 25p each at a premium of 50p per share. The cash
      received was correctly recorded but the full amount was credited to the ordinary share capital account.

      Which of the following journal entries is needed to correct this error?

		Debit £	Credit £
A	Share premium account	25,000	
	Share capital account		25,000
B	Share capital account	25,000	
	Share premium account		25,000
C	Share capital account	37,500	
	Share premium account		37,500
D	Share capital account	25,000	
	Cash		25,000

                                                                                                        (2 marks)

9   Which of the following journal entries could correctly record a bonus (capitalisation) issue of shares?

		Debit £	Credit £
A	Cash	100,000	
	Ordinary share capital		100,000
B	Ordinary share capital	100,000	
	Share premium		100,000
C	Share premium	100,000	
	Ordinary share capital		100,000
D	Investments	100,000	
	Cash		100,000

(2 marks)

10   Which of these statements about limited companies is/are correct?

1   A company might make a bonus (capitalisation) issue to raise funds for expansion.
2   The profit or loss on the disposal of part of a company's operations must be disclosed in the profit and loss account as an extraordinary item if material.
3   Both realised and unrealised gains and losses may be included in the statement of movements in reserves.

A   1 and 3
B   2 and 3
C   1 and 2
D   3 only

(2 marks)

(Total = 18 marks)

31 Events after the balance sheet date   11 mins

1   Which of the following material events after the balance sheet date and before the financial statements are approved by the directors should be adjusted for in those financial statements?

1   A valuation of property providing evidence of impairment in value at the balance sheet date
2   Sale of stock held at the balance sheet date for less than cost
3   Discovery of fraud or error affecting the financial statements
4   The insolvency of a customer with a debt owing at the balance sheet date which is still outstanding

A   All of them
B   1, 2 and 4 only
C   3 and 4 only
D   1, 2 and 3 only

(2 marks)

2   The draft financial statements of a limited company are under consideration. The accounting treatment of the following material events after the balance sheet date needs to be determined.

1   The bankruptcy of a major customer, with a substantial debt outstanding at the balance sheet date.
2   A fire destroying some of the company's stock (the company's going concern status is not affected).
3   An issue of shares to finance expansion.
4   Sale for less than cost of some stock held at the balance sheet date.

According to FRS 21 *Events after the Balance Sheet Date*, which of the above events require an adjustment to the figures in the draft financial statements?

A	1 and 4 only
B	1, 2 and 3 only
C	2 and 3 only
D	2 and 4 only

(2 marks)

3   In finalising the financial statements of a company for the year ended 30 June 20X4, which of the following material matters should be adjusted for?

1   A customer who owed £180,000 at the balance sheet date went bankrupt in July 20X4.

2   The sale in August 20X4 for £400,000 of some stock items valued in the balance sheet at £500,000.

3   A factory with a value of £3,000,000 was seriously damaged by a fire in July 20X4. The factory was back in production by August 20X4 but its value was reduced to £2,000,000.

4   The company issued 1,000,000 ordinary shares in August 20X4.

A	All four items
B	1 and 2 only
C	1 and 4 only
D	2 and 3 only

(2 marks)

4   Which of the following statements about provisions, contingencies and events after the balance sheet date is/are correct?

1   A company expecting future operating losses should make provision for those losses as soon as it becomes probable that they will be incurred.

2   Details of all adjusting events after the balance sheet date must be disclosed by note in a company's financial statements.

3   Contingent assets must be recognised if it is probable that they will arise.

4   Contingent liabilities must be treated as actual liabilities and provided for if it is probable that they will arise.

A	4 only
B	2 and 4 only
C	1 and 2 only
D	All four statements are correct

(2 marks)

(Total = 8 marks)

32 Preparation question: Sioux (PFS 6/05)

The following information is available for Sioux Ltd.

Balance sheets

	31 December			
	20X4		20X3	
	£'000	£'000	£'000	£'000
Fixed assets				
Cost or valuation		11,000		8,000
Accumulated depreciation		(5,600)		(4,800)
Net book value		5,400		3,200
Current assets				
Stock	3,400		3,800	
Debtors	3,800		2,900	
Cash at bank	400		100	
	7,600		6,800	
Current liabilities				
Trade creditors	3,700		3,200	
Taxation	700		600	
	4,400		3,800	
Net current assets		3,200		3,000
		8,600		6,200
Long-term liabilities				
10% Debentures		3,000		2,000
		5,600		4,200
Capital and reserves				
Ordinary share capital		1,000		1,000
Revaluation reserve		1,500		1,000
Retained profits		3,100		2,200
		5,600		4,200

Summarised profit and loss account for the year ended 31 December 20X4

	£'000
Operating profit	2,650
Finance cost (loan note interest)	(300)
	2,350
Taxation	(700)
Net profit for the period	1,650

Notes

1   During the year fixed assets which had cost £800,000, with a net book value of £350,000, were sold for £500,000.
2   The revaluation surplus arose from the revaluation of some land that was not being depreciated.
3   The 20X3 tax liability was settled at the amount provided for at 31 December 20X3.
4   The additional debentures were issued on 1 January 20X4. Interest was paid on 30 June 20X4 and 31 December 20X4.
5   Dividends paid during the year amounted to £750,000.

Required

Prepare the company's cash flow statement for the year ended 31 December 20X4, using the indirect method, adopting the format in FRS 1 *Cash Flow Statements* The reconciliation of net cash flow with movement in net debt not required.

33 Cash flow statements

1   Which of the following items could appear in a company's cash flow statement?

     1   Surplus on revaluation of fixed assets.
     2   Proceeds of issue of shares.
     3   Proposed dividend.
     4   Irrecoverable debts written off.
     5   Dividends received.

     A   1, 2 and 5 only
     B   2, 3, 4, 5 only
     C   2 and 5 only
     D   3 and 4 only   (2 marks)

2   Part of the process of preparing a company's cash flow statement is the calculation of cash inflow from
     operating activities.

     Which of the following statements about that calculation (using the indirect method) are correct?

     1   Loss on sale of operating fixed assets should be deducted from net profit before taxation.
     2   Increase in stock should be deducted from operating profits.
     3   Increase in creditors should be added to operating profits.
     4   Depreciation charges should be added to net profit before taxation.

     A   1, 2 and 3
     B   1, 2 and 4
     C   1, 3 and 4
     D   2, 3 and 4   (2 marks)

3   In the course of preparing a company's cash flow statement, the following figures are to be included in the
     calculation of net cash from operating activities.

	£
Depreciation charges	980,000
Profit on sale of fixed assets	40,000
Increase in stocks	130,000
Decrease in debtors	100,000
Increase in creditors	80,000

     What will the net effect of these items be in the cash flow statement?

		£
A	Addition to operating profit	890,000
B	Subtraction from operating profit	890,000
C	Addition to operating profit	1,070,000
D	Addition to operating profit	990,000

                                                                                             (2 marks)

4   Part of a company's draft cash flow statement is shown below:

	£000
Operating profit	8,640
Depreciation charges	(2,160)
Proceeds of sale of fixed assets	360
Increase in stock	(330)
Increase in creditors	440

     The following criticisms of the above extract have been made:

     1   Depreciation charges should have been added, not deducted.
     2   Increase in stock should have been added, not deducted.
     3   Increase in creditors should have been deducted, not added.
     4   Proceeds of sale of fixed assets should not appear in this part of the cash flow statement.

Which of these criticisms are valid?

A   2 and 3 only
B   1 and 4 only
C   1 and 3 only
D   2 and 4 only   **(2 marks)**

---

5   In preparing a company's cash flow statement complying with FRS 1 *Cash Flow Statements*, which, if any, of
     the following items could form part of the calculation of cash flow from financing activities?

     1   Proceeds of sale of premises
     2   Dividends received
     3   Bonus issue of shares

     A   1 only
     B   2 only
     C   3 only
     D   None of them   **(2 marks)**

---

6   Which of the following assertions about cash flow statements is/are correct?

     1   A cash flow statement prepared using the direct method produces a different figure for operating
          cash flow from that produced if the indirect method is used.
     2   Rights issues of shares do not feature in cash flow statements.
     3   A surplus on revaluation of a fixed asset will not appear as an item in a cash flow statement.
     4   A profit on the sale of a fixed asset will appear as an item under Cash Flows from Investing Activities
          in a cash flow statement.

     A   1 and 4
     B   2 and 3
     C   3 only
     D   2 and 4   **(2 marks)**

---

7   An extract from a cash flow statement prepared by a trainee accountant is shown below.

     Cash flows from operating activities

	£m
Net profit before taxation	28
Adjustments for: Depreciation	(9)
Operating profit before working capital changes	19
Decrease in stocks	13
Increase in debtors	(4)
Increase in creditors	(8)
Cash generated from operations	10

     Which of the following criticisms of this extract are correct?

     1   Depreciation charges should have been added, not deducted
     2   Decrease in stocks should have been deducted, not added.
     3   Increase in debtors should have been added, not deducted.
     4   Increase in creditors should have been added, not deducted

     A   2 and 4
     B   2 and 3
     C   1 and 3
     D   1 and 4   **(2 marks)**

---

8   Which of the following items could appear in a company's cash flow statement?

    1   Proposed dividends
    2   Rights issue of shares
    3   Bonus issue of shares
    4   Repayment of loan

    A   1 and 3
    B   2 and 4
    C   1 and 4
    D   2 and 3   **(2 marks)**

(Total = 16 marks)

34 Mixed bank I   56 mins

1   Who issues Financial Reporting Standards?
    A   The Auditing Practices Board
    B   The stock exchange
    C   The ASB
    D   The government   **(2 marks)**

2   Which of the following is *not* an accounting concept?
    A   Prudence
    B   Consistency
    C   Depreciation
    D   Accruals   **(2 marks)**

3   When preparing financial statements in periods of inflation, directors
    A   Must reduce asset values
    B   Must increase asset values
    C   Must reduce dividends
    D   Need make no adjustments   **(2 marks)**

4   The following information relates to a bank reconciliation.

    (i)   The bank balance in the cashbook before taking the items below into account was £8,970 overdrawn.
    (ii)   Bank charges of £550 on the bank statement have not been entered in the cashbook.
    (iii)   The bank has credited the account in error with £425 which belongs to another customer.
    (iv)   Cheque payments totalling £3,275 have been entered in the cashbook but have not been presented for payment.
    (v)   Cheques totalling £5,380 have been correctly entered on the debit side of the cashbook but have not been paid in at the bank.

    What was the balance as shown by the bank statement *before* taking the items above into account?

    A   £8,970 overdrawn
    B   £11,200 overdrawn
    C   £12,050 overdrawn
    D   £17,750 overdrawn   **(2 marks)**

5   W bought a new printing machine from abroad. The cost of the machine was £80,000. The installation costs were £5,000 and the employees received specific training on how to use this particular machine, at a cost of £2,000. Before using the machine to print customers' orders, a test was undertaken and the paper and ink cost £1,000.

    What should be the cost of the machine in the company's balance sheet?

A	£80,000
B	£85,000
C	£87,000
D	£88,000

(2 marks)

6   The electricity account for the year ended 30 June 20X1 was as follows.

	£
Opening balance for electricity accrued at 1 July 20X0	300
Payments made during the year	
1 August 20X0 for three months to 31 July 20X0	600
1 November 20X0 for three months to 31 October 20X0	720
1 February 20X1 for three months to 31 January 20X1	900
30 June 20X1 for three months to 30 April 20X1	840

Which of the following is the appropriate entry for electricity?

	Accrued At 30 June 20X1	Charge to profit and loss account year ended 30 June 20X1
A	£Nil	£3,060
B	£460	£3,320
C	£560	£3,320
D	£560	£3,420

(2 marks)

7   The year end of M Plc is 30 November 20X0. The company pays for its gas by a standing order of £600 per month. On 1 December 20W9, the statement from the gas supplier showed that M Plc had overpaid by £200. M Plc received gas bills for the four quarters commencing on 1 December 20W9 and ending on 30 November 20X0 for £1,300, £1,400, £2,100 and £2,000 respectively.

Which of the following is the correct charge for gas in M Plc's profit and loss account for the year ended 30 November 20X0.

A	£6,800
B	£7,000
C	£7,200
D	£7,400

(2 marks)

8   S sells three products – Basic, Super and Luxury. The following information was available at the year end.

	Basic £ per unit	Super £ per unit	Luxury £ per unit
Original cost	6	9	18
Estimated selling price	9	12	15
Selling and distribution costs	1	4	5
	units	units	units
Units of stock	200	250	150

The value of stock at the year end should be

A	£4,200
B	£4,700
C	£5,700
D	£6,150

(2 marks)

9   A car was purchased by a newsagent business in May 20W7 for:

	£
Cost	10,000
Road tax	150
Total	10,150

The business adopts a date of 31 December as its year end.

The car was traded in for a replacement vehicle in August 20X0 at an agreed value of £5,000.

It has been depreciated at 25% per annum on the reducing-balance method, charging a full year's depreciation in the year of purchase and none in the year of sale.

What was the profit or loss on disposal of the vehicle during the year ended December 20X0?

A   Profit: £718
B   Profit: £781
C   Profit: £1,788
D   Profit: £1,836   **(2 marks)**

10   A stock record card shows the following details.

February   1   50 units in stock at a cost of £40 per unit
            7   100 units purchased at a cost of £45 per unit
            14   80 units sold
            21   50 units purchased at a cost of £50 per unit
            28   60 units sold

What is the value of stock at 28 February using the FIFO method?

A   £2,450
B   £2,700
C   £2,950
D   £3,000   **(2 marks)**

11   A particular source of finance has the following characteristics: a fixed return, a fixed repayment date, it is secured and the return is classified as an expense.

Is the source of finance

A   Ordinary share
B   Hire purchase
C   Loan stock
D   Preference share   **(2 marks)**

12   Which of the following statements gives the best definition of the objective of accounting?

A   To provide useful information to users
B   To record, categorise and summarise financial transactions
C   To calculate the taxation due to the government
D   To calculate the amount of dividend to pay to shareholders   **(2 marks)**

13   A company has been notified that a debtor has been declared bankrupt. The company had previously made a specific allowance for this debt. Which of the following is the correct double entry?

	DR	CR
A	Irrecoverable debts account	Debtors
B	Debtors	Irrecoverable debts account
C	Allowance for debtors	Debtors
D	Debtors	Allowable for debtors

(2 marks)

14   W is registered for VAT. The managing director has asked four staff in the accounts department why the output tax for the last quarter does not equal 17.5% of sales (17.5% is the rate of tax). Which one of the following four replies she received was *not* correct?

A   The company had some exports that were not liable to VAT
B   The company made some sales of zero-rated products
C   The company made some sales of exempt products
D   The company sold some products to businesses not registered for VAT   **(2 marks)**

15 Which of the following is *not* the purpose of a sales ledger control account?

 A A sales ledger control account provides a check on the arithmetical accuracy of the personal ledger
 B A sales ledger control account helps to locate errors in the trial balance
 C A sales ledger control account ensures that there are no errors in the personal ledger
 D Control accounts deter fraud

(2 marks)

16 The net book value of a company's fixed assets was £200,000 at 1 August 20X0. During the year ended 31 July 20X1, the company sold fixed assets for £25,000 on which it made a loss of £5,000. The depreciation charge of the year was £20,000. What was the net book value of fixed assets at 31 July 20X1?

 A £150,000
 B £155,000
 C £160,000
 D £180,000

(2 marks)

17 According to the ASB *Statement,* which of the following is *not* an objective of financial statements?

 A Providing information regarding the financial position of a business
 B Providing information regarding the performance of a business
 C Enabling users to assess the performance of management to aid decision making
 D Helping to assess the going concern status of a business

(2 marks)

18 The ASB *Statement* identifies user groups. Which of the following is *not* an information need for the 'Investor' group?

 A Assessment of repayment ability of an entity
 B Measuring performance, risk and return
 C Taking decisions regarding holding investments
 D Taking buy/sell decisions

(2 marks)

19 The role of the ASB is to?

 A Oversee the standard setting and regulatory process
 B Formulate accounting standards
 C Review defective accounts
 D Control the accountancy profession

(2 marks)

20 Which of the following items does not appear under the heading 'reserves' on a company balance sheet?

 A Share premium account
 B Retained profits
 C Revaluation surpluses
 D Loan stock

(2 marks)

21 Which of the following statements regarding a limited company profit and loss account is correct?

 A Accounting standards define the expenses which are reported under 'cost of sales'
 B 'Depreciation' appears as a separate heading
 C Interest payable is deducted from profit after taxation
 D Irrecoverable debts will be included under one of the statutory expense headings (usually administrative expenses)

(2 marks)

(Total = 42 marks)

35 Mixed bank II (PFS Pilot Paper)   53 mins

1   In a debtors control account, which of the following lists is composed only of items which would appear on the credit side of the account?

    A   Cash received from customers, sales returns, irrecoverable debts written off, contras against amounts due to suppliers in the purchase ledger

    B   Sales, cash refunds to customers, irrecoverable debts written off, discounts allowed

    C   Cash received from customers, discounts allowed, interest charged on overdue accounts, irrecoverable debts written off

    D   Sales, cash refunds to customers, interest charged on overdue accounts, contras against amounts due to suppliers in the purchase ledger.   **(2 marks)**

2   Y purchased some plant on 1 January 2000 for £38,000. The payment for the plant was correctly entered in the cash book but was entered on the debit side of plant repairs account.

Y charges depreciation on the straight line basis at 20% per year, with a proportionate charge in the year of acquisition and assuming no scrap value at the end of the life of the asset.

How will Y's profit for the year ended 31 March 2000 be affected by the error?

    A   Understated by £30,400
    B   Understated by £36,100
    C   Understated by £38,000
    D   Overstated by £1,900   **(2 marks)**

3   The trial balance of Z failed to agree, the totals being: debit £836,200
                                                  credit £819,700

A suspense account was opened for the amount of the difference and the following errors were found and corrected:

    1   The totals of the cash discount columns in the cash book had not been posted to the discount accounts. The figures were discount allowed £3,900 and discount received £5,100.

    2   A cheque for £19,000 received from a customer was correctly entered in the cash book but was posted to the control account as £9,100.

What will be the remaining balance on the suspense be *after* the correction of these errors?

    A   £25,300 credit
    B   £7,700 credit
    C   £27,700 debit
    D   £5,400 credit   **(2 marks)**

4   The trial balance of C, a limited company, did not agree, and a suspense account was opened for the difference. Checking in the bookkeeping system revealed a number of errors.

    1   £4,600 paid for motor van repairs was correctly treated in the cash book but was credited to motor vehicles asset account

    2   £360 received from B, a customer, was credited in error to the account of BB

    3   £9,500 paid for rent was debited to the rent account as £5,900

    4   The total of the discount allowed column in the cash book had been debited in error to the discounts received account

    5   No entries have been made to record a cash sale of £100.

Which of the errors above would require an entry to the suspense account as part of the process of correcting them?

A   3 and 4
B   1 and 3
C   2 and 5
D   2 and 3   **(2 marks)**

---

5   B acquired a lorry on 1 May 2000 at a cost of £30,000. The lorry has an estimated useful life of four years, and an estimated resale value at the end of that time of £6,000. B charges depreciation on the straight line basis, with a proportionate charge in the period of acquisition.

What will the depreciation charge for the lorry be in B's accounting period to 30 September 2000?

A   £3,000
B   £2,500
C   £2,000
D   £5,000   **(2 marks)**

---

6   SSAP 9 *Stocks* defines the items that may be included in computing the value of a stock of finished goods manufactured by a business.

Which one of the following lists consists only of items which may be included in the balance sheet value of such stocks, according to SSAP 9?

A   Foreman's wages, carriage inwards, carriage outwards, raw materials
B   Raw materials, carriage inwards, costs of storage of finished goods, plant depreciation
C   Plant depreciation, carriage inwards, raw materials, foreman's wages
D   Carriage outwards, raw materials, foreman's wages, plant depreciation   **(2 marks)**

---

7   The closing stock of X amounted to £116,400 *excluding* the following two stock lines:

1   400 items which had cost £4 each. All were sold after the balance sheet date for £3 each, with selling expenses of £200 for the batch.

2   200 different items which had cost £30 each. These items were found to be defective at the balance sheet date. Rectification work after the balance sheet amounted to £1,200, after which they were sold for £35 each, with selling expenses totalling £300.

Which of the following total figures should appear in the balance sheet of X for stock?

A   £122,300
B   £121,900
C   £122,900
D   £123,300   **(2 marks)**

---

8   The ASB's *Statement* gives five qualitative characteristics which make financial information reliable. These five characteristics are:

A   Prudence, consistency, understandability, faithful representation, substance over form
B   Accruals basis, going concern concept, consistency, prudence, true and fair view
C   Faithful representation, neutrality, substance over form, completeness, consistency
D   Substance over form, faithful representation, neutrality, prudence, completeness   **(2 marks)**

---

9   The following attempt at a bank reconciliation statement has been prepared by Q Ltd:

	£
Overdraft per bank statement	38,600
Add: deposits not credited	41,200
	79,800
Less: outstanding cheques	3,300
Overdraft per cash book	76,500

Assuming the bank statement balance of £38,600 to be correct, what *should* the cash book balance be?

A	£76,500 overdrawn, as stated	
B	£5,900 overdrawn	
C	£700 overdrawn	
D	£5,900 cash at bank	**(2 marks)**

10 After checking a business cash book against the bank statement, which of the following items could require an entry in the cash book?

1	Bank charges
2	A cheque from a customer which was dishonoured
3	Cheque not presented
4	Deposits not credited
5	Credit transfer entered in bank statement
6	Standing order entered in bank statement.

A	1, 2, 5 and 6	
B	3 and 4	
C	1, 3, 4 and 6	
D	3, 4, 5 and 6	**(2 marks)**

11 The following information is relevant to the calculation of the sales figure for Alpha, a sole trader who does not keep proper accounting records:

	£
Opening debtors	29,100
Cash received from credit customers and paid into the bank	381,600
Expenses paid out of cash received from credit customers before banking	6,800
Irrecoverable debts written off	7,200
Refunds to credit customers	2,100
Discounts allowed to credit customers	9,400
Cash sales	112,900
Closing debtors	38,600

The figure which should appear in Alpha's trading account for sales is:

A	£525,300	
B	£511,700	
C	£529,500	
D	£510,900	**(2 marks)**

12 A sole trader who does not keep full accounting records wishes to calculate her sales for the year.

The information available is:

1	Opening stock	17,000
2	Closing stock	24,000
3	Purchases	91,000
4	Standard gross profit percentage on sales	40%

Which of the following is the sales figure for the year calculated from these figures?

A	£117,600	
B	£108,000	
C	£210,000	
D	£140,000	**(2 marks)**

13 A business compiling its accounts for the year to 31 January each year pays rent quarterly in advance on 1 January, 1 April, 1 July and 1 October each year. After remaining unchanged for some years, the rent was increased from £24,000 per year to £30,000 per year as from 1 July 2000.

Which of the following figures is the rent expense which should appear in the profit and loss account for year ended 31 January 20X1?

A   £27,500
B   £29,500
C   £28,000
D   £29,000   (2 marks)

14   On 31 December 20X0 the stock of V was completely destroyed by fire. The following information is
      available:

      1   Stock at 1 December 20X0 at cost £28,400
      2   Purchases for December 20X0 £49,600
      3   Sales for December 20X0 £64,800
      4   Standard gross profit percentage on sales revenue 30%

      Based on this information, which of the following is the amount of stock destroyed?

      A   £45,360
      B   £32,640
      C   £40,971
      D   £19,440   (2 marks)

15   Which of the following statements concerning the accounting treatment of research and development
      expenditure are true, according to SSAP 13?

      1   If certain criteria are met, research expenditure may be recognised as an asset.
      2   Research expenditure, other than capital expenditure on research facilities, should be recognised as
           an expense as incurred.
      3   In deciding whether development expenditure qualifies to be recognised as an asset, it is necessary
           to consider whether there will be adequate finance available to complete the project.
      4   Development expenditure recognised as an asset must be amortised over a period not exceeding five
           years.
      5   The financial statements should disclose the total amount of research and development expenditure
           recognised as an expense during the period.

      A   1, 4 and 5
      B   2, 4 and 5
      C   2, 3 and 4
      D   2, 3 and 5   (2 marks)

16   D, E and F are in partnership, sharing profits in the ratio 5:3:2 respectively, after charging salaries for E and F
      of £24,000 each per year.

      On 1 July 20X0 they agreed to change the profit-sharing ratio 3:1:1 and to increase E's salary to £36,000 per
      year, F's salary continuing unchanged.

      For the year ended 31 December 20X0 the partnership profit amounted to £480,000.
      Which of the following correctly states the partners' total profit shares for the year?

           D   E   F
      A   £234,000   £136,800   £109,200
      B   £213,000   £157,800   £109,200
      C   £186,000   £171,600   £122,400
      D   £237,600   £132,000   £110,400

                                                                               (2 marks)

17   At 1 January 20X0 the capital structure of Q, a limited company, was as follows:

                                                                               £
      Issued share capital 1,000,000 ordinary shares of 50p each   500,000
      Share premium account   300,000

On 1 April 20X0 the company made an issue of 200,000 50p shares at £1.30 each, and on 1 July the company made a bonus (capitalisation) issue of one share for every four in issue at the time, using the share premium account for the purpose.

Which of the following correctly states the company's share capital and share premium account at 31 December 20X0?

	Share capital	Share premium account
A	£750,000	£230,000
B	£875,000	£285,000
C	£750,000	£310,000
D	£750,000	£610,000

(2 marks)

18   According to the illustrative financial structure in the Companies Act, dividends paid during the year should be disclosed in:

A   Profit and loss account
B   Statement of movements in reserves
C   Balance sheet
D   None of these   (2 marks)

19   FRS 1 *Cash flow statements* requires the cash flow statement to open with the calculation of net cash from operating activities, arrived at by adjusting net profit before taxation.

Which of the following lists consists only of items which could appear in such a calculation?

A   Depreciation, increase in debtors, decrease in creditors, proceeds from sale of equipment, increase in stocks
B   Increase in creditors, decrease in stocks, profit on sale of plant, depreciation, decrease in debtors
C   Increase in creditors, proceeds from sale of equipment, depreciation, decrease in debtors, increase in stocks
D   Depreciation, interest paid, proceeds from sale of equipment, decrease in stocks   (2 marks)

20   FRS 21 *Events after the balance sheet date* regulates the extent to which events after the balance sheet date should be reflected in financial statements.

Which of the following lists of such events consists only of items that, according to FRS 1, should normally be classified as non-adjusting?

A   Insolvency of a debt which was outstanding at the balance sheet date, issue of shares or debentures, a major merger with another company
B   Issue of shares or debentures, changes in foreign exchange rates, major purchases of fixed assets
C   A major merger with another company, destruction of a major fixed asset by fire, discovery of fraud or error which shows that the financial statements were incorrect
D   Sale of stock, giving evidence about its value at the balance sheet date, issue of shares or debentures, destruction of a major fixed asset by fire   (2 marks)

(Total = 40 marks)

36 Mixed bank III (PFS 6/05)

53 mins

1   B, a limited company, receives rent for subletting part of its office premises to a number of tenants.

In the year ended 31 December 20X4 B received cash of £318,600 from its tenants.

Details of rent in advance and in arrears at the beginning and end of 20X4 are as follows:

	31 December	
	20X4	*20X3*
	£	£
Rent received in advance	28,400	24,600
Rent owing by tenants	18,300	16,900

All rent owing was subsequently received

What figure for rental income should be included in the profit and loss account of B for 20X4?

A	£341,000	
B	£336,400	
C	£300,800	
D	£316,200	**(2 marks)**

2   The following information is available for the year ended 31 December 20X4 for a trader who does not keep proper accounting records:

	£
Stocks at 1 January 20X4	38,000
Stocks at 31 December 20X4	45,000
Purchases	637,000

Gross profit percentage on sales = 30%

Based on this information, what was the trader's sales figure for the year?

A	£900,000	
B	£819,000	
C	£920,000	
D	£837,200	**(2 marks)**

3   The following bank reconciliation statement has been prepared for a company:

	£
Overdraft per bank statement	39,800
Add: Deposits credited after date	64,100
	103,900
Less: Outstanding cheques presented after date	44,200
Overdraft per cash book	59,700

Assuming the amount of the overdraft per the bank statement of £39,800 is correct, what should be the balance in the cash book?

A	£158,100 overdrawn	
B	£19,900 overdrawn	
C	£68,500 overdrawn	
D	£59,700 overdrawn as stated	**(2 marks)**

4 Which, if any, of the following journal entries is correct according to their narratives?

		Debit £	Credit £
1	B sales ledger account	450	
	Irrecoverable debts account		450
	Irrecoverable balance written off		
2	Investments: Q ordinary shares	100,000	
	Share capital		100,000
	80,000 shares of 50p each issued at £1·25 in exchange for shares in Q.		
3	Suspense account	1,000	
	Motor vehicles account		1,000
	Correction of error – debit side of Motor vehicles account undercast by £1,000		

A   None of them
B   1 only
C   2 only
D   3 only   **(2 marks)**

---

5 An entity has made a material change to an accounting policy in preparing its current financial statements.

Which of the following disclosures are required by FRS 18 *Accounting policies* in these financial statements?

1   The reasons for the change.
2   The amount of the consequent adjustment in the current period and in comparative information for prior periods.
3   An estimate of the effect of the change on future periods, where possible.

A   1 and 2 only
B   1 and 3 only
C   2 and 3 only
D   All three items   **(2 marks)**

---

6 At 31 December 20X3 Q, a limited company, owned a building that had cost £800,000 on 1 January 20W4.

It was being depreciated at two per cent per year.

On 31 December 20X3 a revaluation to £1,000,000 was recognised. At this date the building had a remaining useful life of 40 years.

Which of the following pairs of figures correctly reflects the effects of the revaluation?

	Depreciation charge for year ended 31 December 20X4 £	Revaluation reserve as at 31 December 20X3 £
A	25,000	200,000
B	25,000	360,000
C	20,000	200,000
D	20,000	360,000

                                                                       (2 marks)

---

7 The stock value for the financial statements of Q for the year ended 31 December 20X4 was based on a stock count on 4 January 20X5, which gave a total stock value of £836,200.

Between 31 December and 4 January 20X5, the following transactions took place:

	£
Purchases of goods	8,600
Sales of goods (profit margin 30% on sales)	14,000
Goods returned by Q to supplier	700

What adjusted figure should be included in the financial statements for stocks at 31 December 20X4?

A   £838,100
B   £853,900
C   £818,500
D   £834,300   **(2 marks)**

8   P and Q are in partnership, sharing profits in the ratio 2:1. On 1 July 20X4 they admitted P's son R as a partner. P guaranteed that R's profit share would not be less than £25,000 for the six months to 31 December 20X4. The profit sharing arrangements after R's admission were P 50%, Q 30%, R 20%. The profit for the year ended 31 December 20X4 is £240,000, accruing evenly over the year.

What should P's final profit share be for the year ended 31 December 20X4?

A   £140,000
B   £139,000
C   £114,000
D   £139,375   **(2 marks)**

9   Which of the following costs should be included in valuing stocks of finished goods held by a manufacturing company, according to SSAP 9 *Stocks*?

1   Carriage inwards.
2   Carriage outwards.
3   Depreciation of factory plant.
4   Accounts department costs relating to wages for production employees.

A   All four items
B   2 and 3 only
C   1, 3 and 4 only
D   1 and 4 only   **(2 marks)**

10   During 20X4, B, a limited company, paid a total of £60,000 for rent, covering the period from 1 October 20X3 to 31 March 20X5.

What figures should appear in the company's financial statements for the year ended 31 December 20X4?

	P & L account £	Balance sheet £
A	40,000	10,000 Prepayment
B	40,000	15,000 Prepayment
C	50,000	10,000 Accrual
D	50,000	15,000 Accrual

                                                                                (2 marks)

11   Wanda keeps no accounting records. The following information is available about her position and transactions for the year ended 31 December 20X4:

	£
Net assets at 1 January 20X4	210,000
Drawings during 20X4	48,000
Capital introduced during 20X4	100,000
Net assets at 31 December 20X4	400,000

Based on this information, what was Wanda's profit for 20X4?

A   £42,000
B   £242,000
C   £138,000
D   £338,000   **(2 marks)**

12   The following sales ledger control account has been prepared by a trainee accountant:

SALES LEDGER CONTROL ACCOUNT

		£			£
20X5			20X5		
1 Jan	Balance	318,650	31 Jan	Cash from credit customers	181,140
	Credit sales	161,770		Interest charged on overdue	
				accounts	280
	Cash sales	84,260		Irrecoverable debts written off	1,390
	Discounts allowed to			Sales returns from credit	
	credit customers	1,240		customers	3,990
				Balance	379,120
		565,920			565,920

What should the closing balance at 31 January 20X5 be after correcting the errors in the account?

A   £292,380
B   £295,420
C   £292,940
D   £377,200   (2 marks)

---

13   At 31 December 20X4 a company's trade debtors totalled £864,000 and the allowance for debtors was
     £48,000.

It was decided that debts totalling £13,000 were to be written off, and the allowance for debtors adjusted to
five per cent of the debtors.

What figures should appear in the balance sheet for trade debtors (after deducting the allowance) and in the
profit and loss account for the total of irrecoverable debts and movement on debtors allowance?

	P & L account	Balance sheet
	Irrecoverable debts and debtors allowance	Net trade debtors
	£	£
A	8,200	807,800
B	7,550	808,450
C	18,450	808,450
D	55,550	808,450

(2 marks)

---

14   Which of the following statements about accounting concepts and conventions are correct?

1   The entity concept requires that a business is treated as being separate from its owners.
2   The use of historical cost accounting tends to understate assets and profit when prices are rising.
3   The prudence concept means that the lowest possible values should be applied to income and assets
     and the highest possible values to expenses and liabilities.
4   The money measurement concept means that only assets capable of being reliably measured in
     monetary terms can be included in the balance sheet of a business.

A   1 and 2
B   2 and 3
C   3 and 4
D   1 and 4   (2 marks)

---

15   A business profit and loss account for the year ended 31 December 20X4 showed a net profit of £83,600. It
     was later found that £18,000 paid for the purchase of a motor van had been debited to motor expenses
     account. It is the company's policy to depreciate motor vans at 25 per cent per year, with a full year's charge
     in the year of acquisition.

What would the net profit be after adjusting for this error?

A	£106,100
B	£70,100
C	£97,100
D	£101,600	**(2 marks)**

16 How should interest charged on partners' drawings appear in partnership financial statements?

A As income in the profit and loss account
B Added to net profit and charged to partners in the division of profit
C Deducted from net profit and charged to partners in the division of profit
D Deducted from net profit in the division of profit and credited to partners **(2 marks)**

17 Which of the following statements about intangible assets in company financial statements are correct according to financial reporting standards?

1 Internally generated goodwill should not be capitalised.
2 Purchased goodwill should normally be amortised through the profit and loss account.
3 Development expenditure must be capitalised if certain conditions are met.

A 1 and 3 only
B 1 and 2 only
C 2 and 3 only
D All three statements are correct **(2 marks)**

18 Which of the following events occurring after the balance sheet date are classified as adjusting, if material?

1 The sale of stocks valued at cost at the balance sheet date for a figure in excess of cost.
2 A valuation of land and buildings providing evidence of an impairment in value at the year end.
3 The issue of shares and debentures.
4 The insolvency of a customer with a balance outstanding at the year end.

A 1 and 3
B 2 and 4
C 2 and 3
D 1 and 4 **(2 marks)**

19 Which of the following statements about contingent assets and contingent liabilities are correct?

1 A contingent asset should be disclosed by note if an inflow of economic benefits is probable.
2 A contingent liability should be disclosed by note if it is probable that a transfer of economic benefits to settle it will be required, with no provision being made.
3 No disclosure is required for a contingent liability if it is not probable that a transfer of economic benefits to settle it will be required.
4 No disclosure is required for either a contingent liability or a contingent asset if the likelihood of a payment or receipt is remote.

A 1 and 4 only
B 2 and 3 only
C 2, 3 and 4
D 1, 2 and 4 **(2 marks)**

20 Which of the following statements about limited companies' accounting is/are correct?

1 A revaluation reserve arises when a fixed asset is sold at a profit.
2 The authorised share capital of a company is the maximum nominal value of shares and debentures the company may issue.
3 The notes to the financial statements must contain details of all adjusting events as defined in FRS 21 *Events after the Balance Sheet Date*.

A   All three statements
B   1 and 2 only
C   2 and 3 only
D   None of the statements   (2 marks)

(Total = 40 marks)

37 Mixed bank IV (PFS 12/05)   53 mins

1   The following information is available for a sole trader who keeps no accounting records:

	£
Net business assets at 1 July 20X4	186,000
Net business assets at 30 June 20X5	274,000

During the year ended 30 June 20X5:

	£
Cash drawings by proprietor	68,000
Additional capital introduced by proprietor	50,000
Business cash used to buy a car for the proprietor's wife, who takes no part in the business	20,000

Using this information, what is the trader's profit for the year ended 30 June 20X5?

A   £126,000
B   £50,000
C   £86,000
D   £90,000   (2 marks)

2   Evon, a limited company, issued 1,000,000 ordinary shares of 25 pence each at a price of £1.10 per share, all received in cash.

What should be the accounting entries to record this issue?

A	Debit:	Cash	£1,100,000
	Credit:	Share capital	£250,000
		Share premium	£850,000
B	Debit:	Share capital	£250,000
		Share premium	£850,000
	Credit:	Cash	£1,100,000
C	Debit:	Cash	£1,100,000
	Credit:	Share capital	£1,100,000
D	Debit:	Cash	£1,100,000
	Credit	Share capital	£250,000
		Retained profits	£850,000

(2 marks)

3   P and Q are in partnership, sharing profits equally.

On 1 January 20X5, R joined the partnership and it was agreed that from that date all three partners should share equally in the profit.

In the year ended 30 June 20X5 the profit amounted to £300,000, accruing evenly over the year, after charging an irrecoverable debt of £30,000 which it was agreed should be borne equally by P and Q only.

What should be the partners' total profit shares for the year ended 30 June 20X5?

	P	Q	R
	£	£	£
A	95,000	95,000	110,000
B	122,500	122,500	55,000
C	125,000	125,000	50,000
D	110,000	110,000	50,000

(2 marks)

---

4   At 1 July 20X4 a limited company's capital structure was as follows:

	£
Share capital 1,000,000 shares of 50p each	500,000
Share premium account	400,000

In the year ended 30 June 20X5 the company made the following share issues:

1 January 20X5:

A bonus issue of one share for every four in issue at that date, using the share premium account.

1 April 20X5

A rights issue of one share for every ten in issue at that date, at £1.50 per share.

What will be the balances on the company's share capital and share premium accounts at 30 June 20X5 as a result of these issues?

	Share capital	Share premium account
	£	£
A	687,500	650,000
B	675,000	375,000
C	687,500	150,000
D	687,500	400,000

(2 marks)

---

5   Which of the following journal entries are correct, according to their narratives?

		Dr	Cr
		£	£
1	Suspense account	18,000	
	Rent received account		18,000
	Correction of error in posting £24,000 cash received for rent to the rent received account as £42,000		
2	B sales ledger account	22,000	
	A sales ledger account		22,000
	Correction of error: cash received from A wrongly entered to B's account		
3	Share premium account	400,000	
	Share capital account		400,000
	1 for 3 bonus issue on share capital of 1,200,000 50p shares		
4	Shares in X	750,000	
	Share capital account		250,000
	Share premium account		500,000
	500,000 50p shares issued at £1.50 per share in exchange for shares in X.		

A   1 and 3

B   2 and 3

C   1 and 4

D   2 and 4

(2 marks)

---

6   The sales ledger control account below contains several incorrect entries.

SALES LEDGER CONTROL ACCOUNT

	£		£
Opening balance	138,400	Credit sales	80,660
		Contras against credit balances in purchase ledger	1,000
Cash received from credit customers	78,420	Discounts allowed to credit customers	1,950
		Irrecoverable debts written off	3,000
		Dishonoured cheques from credit customers	850
		Closing balance	129,360
	216,820		216,820

What should the closing balance be when all the errors are corrected?

A   £133,840
B   £135,540
C   £137,740
D   £139,840   **(2 marks)**

---

7   A limited company's trial balance does not balance. The totals are:

Debit   £384,030
Credit   £398,580

A suspense account is opened for the difference.

Which of the following pairs of errors could clear the balance on the suspense account when corrected?

A   Debit side of cash book undercast by £10,000; £6,160 paid for rent correctly entered in the cash book but entered in the rent account as £1,610.

B   Debit side of cash book overcast by £10,000; £1,610 paid for rent correctly entered in the cash book but entered in the rent account as £6,160.

C   Debit side of cash book undercast by £10,000; £1,610 paid for rent correctly entered in the cash book but entered in the rent account as £6,160.

D   Debit side of cash book overcast by £10,000; £6,160 paid for rent correctly entered in the cash book but entered in the rent account as £1,610.   **(2 marks)**

---

8   A draft cash flow statement contains the following calculation of cash flows from operating activities:

	£m
Profit before tax	13
Depreciation	2
Decrease in stocks	(3)
Decrease in trade and other debtors	5
Decrease in trade creditors	4
Net cash inflow from operating activities	21

Which of the following corrections need to be made to the calculation?

1   Depreciation should be deducted, not added.
2   Decrease in stocks should be added, not deducted.
3   Decrease in debtors should be deducted, not added.
4   Decrease in creditors should be deducted, not added.

A   1 and 3
B   2 and 3
C   1 and 4
D   2 and 4   **(2 marks)**

---

9   The following information is available for Orset, a sole trader who does not keep full accounting records:

	£
Stock 1 July 20X4	138,600
30 June 20X5	149,100
Purchases made for year ended 30 June 20X5	716,100

Orset makes a standard gross profit of 30 percent on sales.

Based on these figures, what is Orset's sales figure for the year ended 30 June 20X5?

A   £2,352,000
B   £1,038,000
C   £917,280
D   £1,008,000   **(2 marks)**

---

10   At 1 July 20X4 a company had prepaid insurance of £8,200. On 1 January 20X5 the company paid £38,000 for insurance for the year to 30 September 20X5.

What figures should appear for insurance in the company's financial statements for the year ended 30 June 20X5?

	P & L account	Balance sheet
A	£27,200	Prepayment £19,000
B	£39,300	Prepayment £9,500
C	£36,700	Prepayment £9,500
D	£55,700	Prepayment £9,500

(2 marks)

---

11   Which of the following correctly describes the imprest system for operating petty cash?

A   All expenditure out of petty cash must be supported by a properly authorised voucher.
B   A regular equal amount of cash is transferred into petty cash.
C   The exact amount of expenditure out of petty cash is reimbursed at intervals.
D   A budget is fixed for a period which petty cash expenditure must not exceed.   **(2 marks)**

---

12   Alpha buys goods from Beta. At 30 June 20X5 Beta's account in Alpha's records showed £5,700 owing to Beta. Beta submitted a statement to Alpha as at the same date showing a balance due of £5,200.

Which of the following could account fully for the difference?

A   Alpha has sent a cheque to Beta for £500 which has not yet been received by Beta.
B   The credit side of Beta's account in Alpha's records has been undercast by £500.
C   An invoice for £250 from Beta has been treated in Alpha's records as if it had been a credit note.
D   Beta has issued a credit note for £500 to Alpha which Alpha has not yet received.   **(2 marks)**

---

13   Which of the following statements about intangible assets are correct?

1   If certain criteria are met, research expenditure must be recognised as an intangible asset.
2   If certain criteria are met, development expenditure may be capitalised.
3   Intangible assets must be amortised.

A   2 and 3 only
B   1 and 3 only
C   1 and 2 only
D   All three statements are correct.   **(2 marks)**

---

14   Which of the following events between the balance sheet date and the date the financial statements are authorised for issue must be adjusted in the financial statements?

1   Declaration of equity dividends.
2   Decline in market value of investments.
3   The announcement of changes in tax rates.
4   The announcement of a major restructuring.

A	1 only	
B	2 and 4	
C	3 only	
D	None of them	**(2 marks)**

15 A company sublets part of its office accommodation. In the year ended 30 June 20X5 cash received from tenants was £83,700.

Details of rent in arrears and in advance at the beginning and end of the year were:

	In arrears	In advance
	£	£
30 June 20X4	3,800	2,400
30 June 20X5	4,700	3,000

All arrears of rent were subsequently received.

What figure for rental income should be included in the company's profit and loss account for the year ended 30 June 20X5?

A	£84,000	
B	£83,400	
C	£80,600	
D	£85,800	**(2 marks)**

16 At 30 June 20X4 a company's allowance for debtors was £39,000. At 30 June 20X5 trade debtors totalled £517,000. It was decided to write off debts totalling £37,000 and to adjust the allowance for debtors to the equivalent of 5 per cent of the trade debtors based on past events.

What figure should appear in the profit and loss account for these items?

A	£61,000	
B	£22,000	
C	£24,000	
D	£23,850	**(2 marks)**

17 SSAP 9 *Stocks* defines the extent to which overheads are included in the cost of stocks of finished goods.

Which of the following statements about the SSAP 9 requirements in this area are correct?

1 Finished goods stocks may be valued on the basis of labour and materials cost only, without including overheads.

2 Carriage inwards, but not carriage outwards, should be included in overheads when valuing stocks of finished goods.

3 Factory management costs should be included in fixed overheads allocated to stocks of finished goods.

A	All three statements are correct.	
B	1 and 2 only	
C	1 and 3 only	
D	2 and 3 only	**(2 marks)**

18 A limited company sold a building at a profit.

How will this transaction be treated in the company's cash flow statement?

	Proceeds of sale	*Profit on sale*
A	Cash inflow under financing	Add to profit in calculating cash flow from operating activities
B	Cash inflow under capital expenditure	Deducted from profit in calculating cash flow from operating activities
C	Cash inflow under capital expenditure	Added to profit in calculating cash flow from operating activities
D	Cash inflow under financing	Deducted from profit in calculating cash flow from operating activities **(2 marks)**

---

19 Which of the following items may appear in a company's statement of movements in reserves?

1 Unrealised revaluation gains.
2 Dividends paid.
3 Proceeds of equity share issue.
4 Profit for the period.

A 2, 3 and 4 only
B 1, 3 and 4 only
C All four items
D 1, 2 and 4 only **(2 marks)**

---

20 Sigma's bank statement shows an overdrawn balance of £38,600 at 30 June 20X5. A check against the company's cash book revealed the following differences:

1 Bank charges of £200 have not been entered in the cash book.
2 Lodgements recorded on 30 June 20X5 but credited by the bank on 2 July £14,700.
3 Cheque repayments entered in cash book but not presented for payment at 30 June 20X5 £27,800.
4 A cheque payment to a supplier of £4,200 charged to the account in June 20X5 recorded in the cash book as a receipt.

Based on this information, what was the cash book balance **before** any adjustments?

A £43,100 overdrawn
B £16,900 overdrawn
C £60,300 overdrawn
D £34,100 overdrawn **(2 marks)**

(Total = 40 marks)

38 Mixed bank V (PFS 6/06)   51 mins

1 The plant and machinery cost account of a company is shown below. The company's policy is to charge depreciation at 20% on the straight line basis, with proportionate depreciation in years of acquisition and disposal.

Plant and machinery – cost

20X5	£	20X5		£
1 Jan Balance b/f	280,000	30 June	Transfer disposal	14,000
1 Apr Cash	48,000			
1 Sept Cash	36,000	31 Dec	Balance c/f	350,000
	364,000			364,000

What should be the depreciation charge for the year ended 31 December 20X5?

A	£67,000	
B	£70,000	
C	£64,200	
D	£68,600	**(2 marks)**

2   Which of the following are correct?

1   The balance sheet value of stock should be as close as possible to net realisable value.

2   The valuation of finished goods stock must include production overheads.

3   Production overheads included in valuing stock should be calculated by reference to the company's normal level of production during the period.

4   In assessing net realisable value, stock items must be considered separately, or in groups of similar items, not by taking the stock value as a whole.

A	1 and 2 only	
B	3 and 4 only	
C	1 and 3 only	
D	2, 3 and 4	**(2 marks)**

3   A business sublets part of its office accommodation.

The rent is received quarterly in advance on 1 January, 1 April, 1 July and 1 October. The annual rent has been £24,000 for some years, but it was increased to £30,000 from 1 July 20X5.

What amounts for this rent should appear in the company's financial statements for the year ended 31 January 20X6?

	P & L account	Balance sheet
A	£27,500	£5,000 in sundry debtors
B	£27,000	£2,500 in sundry debtors
C	£27,000	£2,500 in sundry creditors
D	£27,500	£5,000 in sundry creditors

(2 marks)

4   A trainee accountant has prepared the following sales ledger control account to calculate the credit sales of a business which does not keep proper accounting records (all sales are on credit):

Sales ledger control account

	£		£
Opening debtors	148,200	Credit sales	870,800
Cash received from customers	819,300		
Discounts allowed to credit customers	16,200		
Irrecoverable debts written off	1,500		
Returns from customers	38,700	Closing debtors	153,100
	1,023,900		1,023,900

The account contains several errors.

What is the sales figure when all the errors have been corrected?

A	£848,200	
B	£877,600	
C	£835,400	
D	£880,600	**(2 marks)**

5   Which of the following events after the balance sheet date would normally qualify as adjusting events according to FRS 21 *Events after the balance* sheet *date*?

1	The bankruptcy of a credit customer with a balance outstanding at the balance sheet date.
2	A decline in the market value of investments.
3	The declaration of an ordinary dividend.
4	The determination of the cost of assets purchased before the balance sheet date.

A   1, 3, and 4
B   1 and 2 only
C   2 and 3 only
D   1 and 4 only   **(2 marks)**

---

6   Ordan received a statement from one of its suppliers, Alta, showing a balance due of £3,980. The amount due according to the purchases ledger account of Alta in Ordan's records was only £230. Comparison of the statement and the ledger account revealed the following differences:

1   A cheque sent by Ordan for £270 has not been allowed for in Alta's statement.

2   Alta has not allowed for goods returned by Ordan £180.

3   Ordan made a contra entry, reducing the amount due to Alta by £3,200, for a balance due from Alta in Ordan's sales ledger. No such entry has been made in Alta's records.

What difference remains between the two companies' records after adjusting for these items?

A   £460
B   £640
C   £6,500
D   £100   **(2 marks)**

---

7   A company's trial balance failed to agree, and a suspense account was opened for the difference.

Subsequent checking revealed that discounts allowed £13,000 had been credited to discounts received account and an entry on the credit side of the cash book for the purchase of some machinery £18,000 had not been posted to the plant and machinery account.

Which two of the following journal entries would correct the errors?

		Debit £	Credit £
(1)	Discounts allowed	13,000	
	Discounts received		13,000
(2)	Discounts allowed	13,000	
	Discounts received	13,000	
	Suspense account		26,000
(3)	Suspense account	26,000	
	Discounts allowed		13,000
	Discounts received		13,000
(4)	Plant and machinery	18,000	
	Suspense account		18,000
(5)	Suspense account	18,000	
	Plant and machinery		18,000

A   1 and 4
B   2 and 5
C   2 and 4
D   3 and 5   **(2 marks)**

The following information is relevant for questions 8 and 9

A company's draft financial statements for 20X5 showed a profit of £630,000. However, the trial balance did not agree, and a suspense account appeared in the company's draft balance sheet. Subsequent checking revealed the following errors:

(1)   The cost of an item of plant £48,000 had been entered in the cash book and in the plant register as £4,800. Depreciation at the rate of 10% per year (£480) had been charged.

(2)   Bank charges of £440 appeared in the bank statement in December 20X5 but had not been entered in the company's records.

(3)   One of the directors of the company paid £800 due to a supplier in the company's purchase ledger by a personal cheque. The bookkeeper recorded a debit in the supplier's ledger account but did not complete the double entry for the transaction. (The company does not maintain a purchase ledger control account).

(4)   The payments side of the cash book had been understated by £10,000.

---

8   Which of the above items would require an entry to the suspense account in correcting them?

  A   All four items
  B   3 and 4 only
  C   2 and 3 only
  D   1, 2 and 4 only   (2 marks)

---

9   What would the company's profit become after the correction of the above errors?

  A   £634,760
  B   £624,760
  C   £624,440
  D   £625,240   (2 marks)

---

10   Which of the following statements are correct?

  1   A company might make a rights issue if it wished to raise more equity capital.
  2   A rights issue might increase the share premium account whereas a bonus issue is likely to reduce it.
  3   A bonus issue will generate cash for a company.
  4   A rights issue will always increase the number of shareholders in a company whereas a bonus issue will not.

  A   1 and 2
  B   1 and 3
  C   2 and 3
  D   2 and 4   (2 marks)

---

11   Which of the following statements are correct?

  1   Contingent assets are included as assets in financial statements if it is probable that they will arise.
  2   Contingent liabilities must be provided for in financial statements if it is probable that they will arise.
  3   Details of all adjusting events after the balance sheet date must be given in notes to the financial statements.
  4   Material non-adjusting events are disclosed by note in the financial statements.

  A   1 and 2
  B   2 and 4
  C   3 and 4
  D   1 and 3   (2 marks)

12   At 1 January 20X5 a company had an allowance for debtors of £18,000

At 31 December 20X5 the company's trade debtors were £458,000.

It was decided:

(a)   To write off debts totalling £28,000 as irrecoverable;

(b)   To adjust the allowance for debtors to the equivalent of 5% of the remaining debtors based on past experience.

What figure should appear in the company's profit and loss account for the total of debts written off as irrecoverable and the movement in the allowance for debtors for the year ended 31 December 20X5?

A   £49,500
B   £31,500
C   £32,900
D   £50,900   **(2 marks)**

---

13   The following purchase ledger control account contains some errors. All goods are purchased on credit

Purchase ledger control account

	£		£
Purchases	963,200	Opening balance	384,600
		Cash paid to suppliers	988,400
Discounts received	12,600	Purchases returns	17,400
Contras with amounts receivable in sales ledger	4,200		
Closing balance	410,400		
	1,390,400		1,390,400

What should the closing balance be when the errors have been corrected?

A   £325,200
B   £350,400
C   £358,800
D   £376,800   **(2 marks)**

---

14   What journal entry is required to record goods taken from stock by the owner of a business?

A   Debit Drawings
      Credit Purchases

B   Debit Sales
      Credit Drawings

C   Debit Drawings
      Credit Stock

D   Debit Purchases
      Credit Drawings   **(2 marks)**

---

15   The following information is available about the transactions of Razil, a sole trader who does not keep proper accounting records:

	£
Opening stock	77,000
Closing stock	84,000
Purchases	763,000
Gross profit as a percentage of sales	30%

Based on this information, what is Razil's sales for the year?

A	£982,800
B	£1,090,000
C	£2,520,000
D	£1,080,000	**(2 marks)**

16   Which of the following statements are correct?

1   All fixed assets must be depreciated.

2   If property is revalued, the revaluation surplus appears in the statement of movements in reserves.

3   If a tangible fixed asset is revalued, all tangible assets of the same class should be revalued.

4   In a company's published balance sheet, tangible assets and intangible assets must be shown separately.

A	1 and 2
B	2 and 3
C	3 and 4
D	1 and 4	**(2 marks)**

17   The following bank reconciliation statement has been prepared by an inexperienced bookkeeper at 31 December 20X5.

Bank reconciliation statement

	£
Balance per bank statement (overdrawn)	38,640
Add: lodgements not credited	19,270
	57,910
Less: unpresented cheques	14,260
Balance per cash book	43,650

What should the final cash book balance be when all the above items have been properly dealt with?

A	£43,650	overdrawn
B	£33,630	overdrawn
C	£5,110	overdrawn
D	£72,170	overdrawn	**(2 marks)**

18   On 1 January 20X5 a company purchased some plant.

The invoice showed

	£
Cost of plant	48,000
Delivery to factory	400
One year warranty covering breakdown during 20X5	800
	49,200

Modifications to the factory building costing £2,200 were necessary to enable the plant to be installed.

What amount should be capitalised for the plant in the company's records?

A	£51,400
B	£48,000
C	£50,600
D	£48,400	**(2 marks)**

19   A business had an opening stock of £180,000 and a closing stock of £220,000 in its financial statements for the year ended 31 December 20X5.

Which of the following entries for these opening and closing stock figures are made when completing the financial records of the business?

		Debit £	Credit £
A	Stock account	180,000	
	P & L account		180,000
	P & L account	220,000	
	Stock account		220,000
B	P & L account	180,000	
	Stock account		180,000
	Stock account	220,000	
	P & L account		220,000
C	Stock account	40,000	
	Purchases account		40,000
D	Purchases account	40,000	
	Stock account		40,000

(2 marks)

(Total = 38 marks)

39 Mixed bank VI (PFS 12/06)   53 mins

1   On 1 September 20X6, a business had a stock of £380,000. During the month, sales totalled £650,000 and purchases £480,000. On 30 September 20X6 a fire destroyed some of the stock. The undamaged stock was valued at £220,000. The business operates with a standard gross profit margin of 30%.

Based on this information, what is the cost of the stock destroyed in the fire?

A   £185,000
B   £140,000
C   £405,000
D   £360,000   (2 marks)

2   A company had the following transactions:

1   Goods in stock that had cost £1,000 were sold for £1,500 cash.
2   A credit customer whose £500 debt had been written off paid the amount in full.
3   The company paid trade creditors £1,000

What will be the combined effect of these transactions on the company's total net current assets (current assets less current liabilities)?

A   Increase of £1,000
B   Net current assets remains unchanged
C   Increase of £2,000
D   Increase of £3,000   (2 marks)

3   Which of the following should appear as items in a company's statement of total recognised gains and losses?

1   Profit for the financial year
2   Income from investments
3   Surplus on revaluation of fixed assets
4   Dividends paid

A	1 and 3 only
B	1 and 4 only
C	2 and 3 only
D	1, 2 and 3	**(2 marks)**

---

4   The following information is available about a company's dividends:

£

20X5

Sept.   Final dividend for the year ended 30 June 20X5 paid (declared August 20X5)   100,000

20X6

March   Interim dividend for the year ended 30 June 20X6 paid   40,000

Sept   Final dividend for the year ended 30 June 20X6 paid (declared August 20X6)   120,000

What figures, if any, should be disclosed in the company's profit and loss account for the year ended 30 June 20X6 and its balance sheet as at that date?

	Profit and loss account for the period	*Balance sheet liability*
A	£160,000 deduction	£120,000
B	£140,000 deduction	nil
C	nil	£120,000
D	nil	nil **(2 marks)**

---

5   A and B are in partnership, sharing profits in the ratio 3:2 and preparing their accounts to 30 June each year. On 1 January 20X6, C joined the partnership and the profit sharing ratio became A 40%, B 30%, and C 30%.

Profits for the year ended 30 June 20X6 were:

£

6 months ended 31 December 20X5   300,000

6 months ended 30 June 20X6   450,000

An irrecoverable debt of £50,000 was written off in the six months to 30 June in computing the £450,000 profit. It was agreed that this expense should be borne by A and B only, in their original profit-sharing ratios.

What is A's total profit share for the year ended 30 June 20X6?

£

A	330,000
B	310,000
C	340,000
D	350,000	**(2 marks)**

---

6   At 1 July 20X5 a company's allowance for debtors was £48,000.

At 30 June 20X6, trade debtors amounted to £838,000. It was decided to write off £72,000 of these debts and adjust the allowance for debtors to £60,000.

What are the final amounts for inclusion in the company's balance sheet at 30 June 20X6?

	Trade debtors	Allowance for debtors	Net balance
	£	£	£
A	838,000	60,000	778,000
B	766,000	60,000	706,000
C	766,000	108,000	658,000
D	838,000	108,000	730,000

(2 marks)

---

7   Which of the following statements about stock valuation for balance sheet purposes are correct?

1   According to SSAP 9 Stocks and long-term contracts, average cost and FIFO (first in and first out) are both acceptable methods of arriving at the cost of stocks.

2   A stock of finished goods may be valued at labour and materials cost only, without including overheads.

3   Stock should be valued at the lowest of cost, net realisable value and replacement cost.

4   It may be acceptable for stock to be valued at selling price less estimated profit margin.

A   1 and 3
B   2 and 3
C   1 and 4
D   2 and 4   **(2 marks)**

8   A business received a delivery of goods on 29 June 20X6, which was included in stock at 30 June 20X6. The invoice for the goods was recorded in July 20X6.

What effect will this have on the business?

1   Profit for the year ended 30 June 20X6 will be overstated.
2   Stock at 30 June 20X6 will be understated.
3   Profit for the year ending 30 June 20X7 will be overstated.
4   Stock at 30 June 20X6 will be overstated.

A   1 and 2
B   2 and 3
C   1 only
D   1 and 4   **(2 marks)**

9   Which of the following statements are correct?

1   A company's authorised share capital must be included in its published balance sheet as part of shareholders' funds.

2   If a company makes a bonus issue of ordinary shares, the total shareholders' interest (share capital plus reserves) remains unchanged.

3   A company's statement of total recognised gains and losses must include the proceeds of any share issue during the period.

4   A company must disclose its significant accounting policies by note to its financial statements.

A   1 and 2
B   1 and 3
C   3 and 4
D   2 and 4   **(2 marks)**

10   Which, if any, of the following statements about intangible assets are correct?

1   Deferred development expenditure must be amortised over a period not exceeding five years.

2   If the conditions specified in SSAP 13 Accounting for research and development are met, development expenditure must be capitalised.

3   Trade investments must appear in a company's balance sheet under the heading of intangible assets.

A   1 and 3
B   1 only
C   2 and 3
D   None of the statements is correct   **(2 marks)**

11 Which of the following characteristics of financial information contribute to reliability, according to the ASB's *Statement of Principles for Financial Reporting*?

    1   Completeness
    2   Prudence
    3   Neutrality
    4   Faithful representation

    A   All four items
    B   1, 2 and 3 only
    C   1, 2 and 4 only
    D   2, 3 and 4 only   **(2 marks)**

12 Details of a company's insurance policy are shown below:

    Premium for year ended 31 March 20X6 paid April 20X5   £10,800
    Premium for year ending 31 March 20X7 paid April 20X6   £12,000

    What figures should be included in the company's financial statements for the year ended 30 June 20X6?

Profit and loss account	*Balance sheet*
£	£
A 11,100	9,000 prepayment (Dr)
B 11,700	9,000 prepayment (Dr)
C 11,100	9,000 accrual (Cr)
D 11,700	9,000 accrual (Cr)

                                                                                           (2 marks)

13 Which of the following statements about bank reconciliations are correct?

    1   In preparing a bank reconciliation, unpresented cheques must be deducted from a balance of cash at bank shown in the bank statement.
    2   A cheque from a customer paid into the bank but dishonoured must be corrected by making a debit entry in the cash book.
    3   An error by the bank must be corrected by an entry in the cash book.
    4   An overdraft is a debit balance in the bank statement.

    A   1 and 3
    B   2 and 3
    C   1 and 4
    D   2 and 4   **(2 marks)**

14 At 30 June 20X5 the capital and reserves of Meredith Limited were:

                                         £m
    Share capital
    Ordinary shares of £1 each   100
    Share premium account   80

    During the year ended 30 June 20X6, the following transactions took place:

    1 September 20X5   A bonus issue of one ordinary share for every two held, using the share premium account.

    1 January 20X6   A fully subscribed rights issue of two ordinary shares for every five held at that date, at £1·50 per share.

    What would the balances on each account be at 30 June 20X6?

	Share capital £m	Share premium account £m
A	210	110
B	210	60
C	240	30
D	240	80

(2 marks)

15   The following items have to be considered in finalising the financial statements of Q Limited:

1   The company gives warranties on its products. The company's statistics show that about 5% of sales give rise to a warranty claim.

2   The company has guaranteed the overdraft of another company. The likelihood of a liability arising under the guarantee is assessed as possible.

What is the correct action to be taken in the financial statements for these items?

	Create a provision	Disclose by note only	No action
A	1	2	
B		1	2
C	1, 2		
D		1, 2	

(2 marks)

16   Which of the following errors would cause a trial balance not to balance?

1   An error in the addition in the cash book.

2   Failure to record a transaction at all.

3   Cost of a motor vehicle debited to motor expenses account. The cash entry was correctly made.

4   Goods taken by the proprietor of a business recorded by debiting purchases and crediting drawings account.

A   1 only
B   1 and 2 only
C   3 and 4 only
D   All four items

(2 marks)

17   How should interest charged on partners' drawings be dealt with in partnership financial statements?

A   Credited as income in the profit and loss account
B   Deducted from profit when appropriating the profit among the partners
C   Added to profit when appropriating the profit among the partners
D   Debited as an expense in the profit and loss account.

(2 marks)

18   All the sales made by a retailer are for cash, and her sale prices are fixed by doubling cost. Details recorded of her transactions for September 20X6 are as follows:

		£
1 Sept.	Stock	40,000
30 Sept.	Purchases for month	60,000
	Cash banked for sales for month	95,000
	Stock	50,000

Which two of the following conclusions could separately be drawn from this information?

1   £5,000 cash has been stolen from the sales revenue prior to banking
2   Stock costing £5,000 has been stolen
3   Stock costing £2,500 has been stolen
4   Some goods costing £2,500 had been sold at cost price

A   1 and 2
B   1 and 3
C   2 and 4
D   3 and 4   **(2 marks)**

19   A company owns a number of properties which are rented to tenants. The following information is available for the year ended 30 June 20X6:

	Rent in advance	Rent in arrears
	£	£
30 June 20X5	134,600	4,800
30 June 20X6	144,400	8,700

Cash received from tenants in the year ended 30 June 2006 was £834,600.

All rent in arrears was subsequently received.

What figure should appear in the company's profit and loss account for rent receivable in the year ended 30 June 20X6?

A   £840,500
B   £1,100,100
C   £569,100
D   £828,700   **(2 marks)**

20   The purchases ledger control account below contains a number of errors:

PURCHASES LEDGER CONTROL ACCOUNT

	£		£
Opening balance (amounts owed to suppliers)	318,600	Purchases	1,268,600
Cash paid to suppliers	1,364,300	Contras against debit balances in sales ledger	48,000
Purchases returns	41,200	Discounts received	8,200
Refunds received from suppliers	2,700	Closing balance	402,000
	£1,726,800		£1,726,800

All items relate to credit purchases.

What should the closing balance be when all the errors are corrected?

A   £128,200
B   £509,000
C   £224,200
D   £144,600   **(2 marks)**

(Total = 40 marks)

40 Mixed bank VII (PFS 6/07)

1   A company issued one million ordinary £1 shares at a premium of 50p per share. The proceeds were correctly recorded in the cash book, but were incorrectly credited to the sales account.

Which of the following journal entries will correct the error?

		Debit £	Credit £
A	Sales	1,500,000	
	Share capital		1,000,000
	Share premium		500,000
B	Share capital	1,000,000	
	Share premium	500,000	
	Sales		1,500,000
C	Sales	1,500,000	
	Share capital		1,500,000
D	Share capital	1,500,000	
	Sales		1,500,000

(2 marks)

2   Where, in a company's financial statements complying with UK accounting standards, should you find dividends paid?

1   Profit and loss account
2   Notes to the financial statements.
3   Cash flow statement
4   Statement of total recognised gains and losses.

A   1 and 3
B   1 and 4
C   3 and 4
D   2 and 3

(2 marks)

3   A property company received cash for rent totalling £838,600 in the year ended 31 December 20X6.

Figures for rent in advance and in arrears at the beginning and end of the year were:

	31 December 20X5 £	31 December 20X6 £
Rent received in advance	102,600	88,700
Rent in arrears (all subsequently received)	42,300	48,400

What amount should appear in the company's profit and loss account for the year ended 31 December 20X6 for rental income?

A   £818,600
B   £738,000
C   £939,200
D   £858,600

(2 marks)

4   Which one of the following journal entries is correct according to its narrative?

		Debit £	Credit £
A	Mr Smith personal account	100,000	
	Directors' remuneration		100,000
	Bonus allocated to account of managing director (Mr Smith)		
B	Purchases	14,000	
	Wages	24,000	
	Repairs to buildings		38,000
	Transferring cost of repairs to buildings carried out by company's own employees and using materials from stock.		
C	Discounts allowed	2,800	
	Discounts received		2,800
	Correction of error: discounts allowed total incorrectly debited to discounts received account		
D	Suspense account	20,000	
	Rent receivable		10,000
	Rent payable		10,000
	Correction of error: rent received credited in error to rent payable account.		

(2 marks)

5   Which of the following items could appear as items in a company's cash flow statement?

1   A bonus issue of shares
2   A rights issue of shares
3   Revaluation of fixed assets
4   Dividends paid

A   All four items
B   1, 3 and 4 only
C   2 and 4 only
D   2 and 3 only

(2 marks)

6   A company has occupied rented premises for some years, paying an annual rent of £120,000. From 1 April 20X6 the rent was increased to £144,000 per year. Rent is paid quarterly in advance on 1 January, 1 April, 1 July and 1 October each year.

What figures should appear for rent in the company's financial statements for the year ended 30 November 20X6?

	Profit and loss account £	Balance sheet £
A	136,000	Prepayment 12,000
B	136,000	Prepayment 24,000
C	138,000	Nil
D	136,000	Accrual 12,000

(2 marks)

7   At 1 January 20X6 a company had an allowance for debtors of £49,000.

    At 31 December 20X6 the company's trade debtors were £863,000 and it was decided to write off debts totaling £23,000 and to adjust the allowance for debtors to the equivalent of 5% of the remaining debtors based on past experience.

    What total figure should appear in the company's profit and loss account for irrecoverable debts and allowance for debtors?

    A   £16,000
    B   £65,000
    C   £30,000
    D   £16,150   **(2 marks)**

8   At 1 January 20X6, a company's capital structure was as follows:

                                                                    £

    Ordinary share capital
            2,000,000 shares of 50p each   1,000,000
            Share premium account   1,400,000

    In January 20X6 the company issued 1,000,000 shares at £1·40 each.

    In September 20X6 the company made a bonus issue of 1 share for every 3 held using the share premium account.

    What were the balances on the company's share capital and share premium accounts after these transactions?

	Share capital	Share premium
	£	£
A	4,000,000	800,000
B	3,200,000	600,000
C	2,000,000	1,800,000
D	2,000,000	1,300,000

                                                                                                (2 marks)

9   Which of the following statements about the treatment of stock and work in progress in financial statements are correct?

    1   Stock should be valued at the lowest of cost, net realisable value and replacement cost.
    2   In valuing work in progress, materials costs, labour costs and variable and fixed production overheads must be included.
    3   Stock items can be valued using either first in, first out (FIFO) or weighted average cost.
    4   A company's financial statements must disclose the accounting policies used in measuring stocks.

    A   All four statements are correct.
    B   1, 2 and 3 only
    C   2, 3 and 4 only
    D   1 and 4 only   **(2 marks)**

10 The plant and equipment account in the records of a company for the year ended 31 December 20X6 is shown below:

PLANT AND EQUIPMENT – COST

20X6		£	20X6		£
1 Jan	Balance	960,000			
1 July	Cash	48,000	30 Sept	Transfer disposal account	84,000
			31 Dec	Balance	924,000
		1,008,000			1,008,000

The company's policy is to charge depreciation on the straight line basis at 20% per year, with proportionate depreciation in the years of purchase and sale.

What should be the charge for depreciation in the company's profit and loss account for the year ended 31 December 20X6?

A £184,800
B £192,600
C £191,400
D £184,200 **(2 marks)**

11 The trial balance of a company did not balance, and a suspense account was opened for the difference.

Which of the following errors would require an entry to the suspense account in correcting them?

(1) A cash payment to purchase a motor van had been correctly entered in the cash book but had been debited to motor expenses account.
(2) The debit side of the wages account had been undercast.
(3) The total of the discounts allowed column in the cash book had been credited to discounts received account.
(4) A cash refund to a customer had been recorded by debiting the cash book and crediting the customer's account.

A 1 and 2
B 2 and 3
C 3 and 4
D 2 and 4 **(2 marks)**

12 A trader took goods that had cost £2,000 from stock for personal use.

Which of the following journal entries would correctly record this?

		Debit £	Credit £
A	Drawings	2,000	
	Stock		2,000
B	Purchases	2,000	
	Drawings		2,000
C	Sales	2,000	
	Drawings		2,000
D	Drawings	2,000	
	Purchases		2,000

(2 marks)

13 Which of the following statements about the requirements of FRS 12 *Provisions, contingent liabilities and contingent assets* are correct?

1 A contingent asset should be disclosed by note if an inflow of economic benefits is probable.
2 No disclosure of a contingent liability is required if the possibility of a transfer of economic benefits arising is remote.
3 Contingent assets must not be recognised in financial statements unless an inflow of economic benefits is virtually certain to arise.

A All three statements are correct
B 1 and 2 only
C 1 and 3 only
D 2 and 3 only **(2 marks)**

14 Which of the following statements are correct, according to FRS 21 *Events after the balance sheet date*?

1 Details of all adjusting events must be disclosed by note to the financial statements.

2 A material loss arising from the sale, after the balance sheet date, of stock valued at cost at the balance sheet date must be reflected in the financial statements.

3 If the market value of investments falls materially after the balance sheet date, the details must be disclosed by note.

4 Events after the balance sheet date are those that occur between the balance sheet date and the date when the financial statements are authorised for issue.

A 1 and 2 only
B 1, 3 and 4
C 2 and 3 only
D 2, 3 and 4

(2 marks)

15 Where in the financial statements should tax on profit on ordinary activities for the current period, and unrealised surplus on revaluation of properties, be separately disclosed?

	Tax on profit on ordinary activities for current period	*Unrealised surplus on revaluation of properties*
A	Profit and loss account	Profit and loss account
B	Statement of total recognised gains and losses	Profit and loss account
C	Profit and loss account	Statement of total recognised gains and losses
D	Statement of total recognised gains and losses	Statement of total recognised gains and losses

(2 marks)

16 Which one of the following statements is correct?

A The prudence concept requires assets to be understated and liabilities to be overstated.

B To comply with the law, the legal form of a transaction must always be reflected in financial statements.

C If a fixed asset initially recognised at cost is revalued, the surplus must be credited in the profit and loss account.

D In times of rising prices, the use of historical cost accounting tends to understate assets and overstate profits.

(2 marks)

17 A draft cash flow statement contains the following calculation of net cash inflow from operating activities:

	£m
Operating profit	22
Depreciation	8
Increase in stocks	(4)
Decrease in debtors	(3)
Increase in creditors	(2)
Net cash inflow from operating activities	21

Which of the following corrections need to be made to the calculation?

1 Depreciation should be deducted, not added

2 Increase in stocks should be added, not deducted

3 Decrease in debtors should be added, not deducted

4 Increase in creditors should be added, not deducted

A	1 and 2
B	1 and 3
C	2 and 4
D	3 and 4	(2 marks)

18 What is the correct treatment of interest charged on partners' drawings in preparing a partnership's financial statements?

A	Credited as income in the profit and loss account
B	Debited as an expense in the profit and loss account
C	Added to total profit in calculating partners' profit shares
D	Deducted from total profit in calculating partners' profit shares.	(2 marks)

19 X and Y are in partnership. They share profits equally after charging a salary £40,000 per year for X and interest on capital at 5% per year.

At 1 January 20X6 their capital balances were:

	£
X	200,000
Y	100,000

On 1 July 20X6 Y introduced a further £100,000 capital, and X's salary was discontinued.

The partnership profit for the year ended 31 December 20X6 was £337,500.

What was X's total profit share for the year ended 31 December 20X6?

	£
A	182,500
B	178,750
C	180,000
D	190,000	(2 marks)

20 Where, in a company's financial statements complying with UK accounting standards, should you find the proceeds of fixed assets sold during the period?

A	Cash flow statement and balance sheet
B	Statement of total recognised gains and losses and balance sheet
C	Profit and loss account and cash flow statement
D	Cash flow statement only	(2 marks)

21 A purchases ledger control account showed a credit balance of £768,420. The purchases ledger balances totalled £781,200.

Which one of the following possible errors could account in full for the difference?

A	A contra against a sales ledger debit balance of £6,390 has been entered on the credit side of the purchases ledger control account.
B	The total of discount allowed £28,400 was entered to the debit of the purchases ledger control account instead of the correct figure for discount received of £15,620.
C	£12,780 cash paid to a supplier was entered on the credit side of the supplier's account in the purchases ledger.
D	The total of discount received £6,390 has been entered on the credit side of the purchases ledger control account.	(2 marks)

(Total = 42 marks)

41 Mixed bank VIII (FA 12/07, FA 6/08)   15 mins

The following questions are taken from the December 2007 and June 2008 exam papers

12/07

1   Jill and John are in partnership sharing profits in the ratio 3:2. During the financial year the partnership earned £28,650 profit. Jill is paid a salary of £5,000 and partners were charged interest on drawings amounting to £200 for Jill and £350 for John. Jill's current account had a credit balance of £15,614 at the beginning of the year.

What is the net increase in Jill's current account during the year?

A   £19,320
B   £34,934
C   £19,720
D   £14,480

(2 marks)

12/07

2   Which of the following provides advice to the Accounting Standards Board (ASB) as well as informing the ASB of the implications of proposed standards for users and preparers of financial statements?

A   Financial Reporting Council
B   The Review Panel

(1 mark)

12/07

3   Samantha has extracted a trial balance and created a suspense account with a credit balance of £759 to make it balance.

Samantha found the following:

1   A sales invoice for £4,569 has not been entered in the accounting records
2   A payment of £1,512 has been posted correctly to the creditors control account but no other entry has been made.
3   A credit sale of £131 has only been credited to the sales account.

What is the remaining balance on the suspense account after these errors have been corrected?

A   £3,810 debit
B   £2,140 credit
C   £890 credit
D   £622 debit

(2 marks)

6/08

4   Charles entered into the following transactions:

1   He sold goods on credit to Cody with a list price of £3,200. He allows a 10% trade discount and a further 2% discount for payment within seven days. Cody paid within two days.
2   He made a credit sale to Mary allowing a 5% trade discount on the list price of £640.
3   He purchased goods for £600 and paid £590, receiving a discount for immediate cash payment.

How much discount should be recorded in the Discount Allowed account as a result of the above transactions?

A   £57.60
B   £10.00
C   £352.00
D   £409.60

(2 marks)

6/08

5   Johnsons use the imprest method of accounting for petty cash.

The petty cash was counted and there was £57.22 in hand. The following petty cash slips were found for the following:

	£
Stamps	16.35
Sale of goods to staff	12.00
Coffee and tea purchase	18.23
Birthday cards for staff	20.20

What is Johnsons' imprest amount?

A   £124
B   £100
C   £112
D   £80

(2 marks)

6/08

6   Joanna has prepared her draft accounts for the year ended 30 April 2008, and needs to adjust them for the following items:

1   Rent of £10,500 was paid and recorded on 2 January 2007 for the period 1 January to 31 December 2007. The landlord has advised that the annual rent for 2008 will be £12,000 although it has not been invoiced or paid yet.

2   Property and contents insurance is paid annually on 1 March. Joanna paid and recorded £6,000 on 1 March 2008 for the year from 1 March 2008 to 28 February 2009.

What should the net effect on profit be in the draft accounts for the year ended 30 April 2008 of adjusting for the above items?

A   £1,000 decrease
B   £1,500 increase
C   £1,000 increase
D   £1,500 decrease

(2 marks)

(Total = 11 marks)

Objective test questions

42 Accounting principles and regulation

15 mins

1   Which *two* of the following statements concerning the Accounting Standards Board is true?

    1   It develops and ultimately issues Financial Reporting Standards (FRSs).

    2   Each new standard issued by the ASB has to be approved by the Consultative Committee of Accountancy Bodies.

    3   The ASB has stronger legal backing than its predecessor the ASC.

    4   Consensus of the Board is required to approve a new standard.

    5   The ASB is accountable to the Accounting Standards Committee (IASC).

(2 marks)

2   According to Chapter 3 'Qualitative characteristics of financial information' of the ASB's *Statement*, which *two* of the following make information reliable?

    1   It is understandable

    2   It is relevant

    3   Use of information that has the ability to influence decisions

    4   Information that is free from material error

(2 marks)

3   A newly-registered company is considering the accounting policies it should adopt.

Policies under consideration are:

    1   Research and development expenditure should be capitalised and amortised over the years in which the resultant product is sold or used.

    2   Stock should be valued at the lower of cost and net realisable value.

    3   Purchased goodwill should be written off immediately it arises against distributable profits.

Which of these possible accounting policies would, if adopted, contravene Financial Reporting Standards?

(2 marks)

4   There are generally agreed to be seven separate user groups for published accounting statements. Six groups are: owner/investors, loan creditor, analyst-advisers, business contact, the government and the public. Which is the missing group?

(1 mark)

5   Which of the following accounting concepts means that similar items should receive a similar accounting statement?

    Going concern

    Accruals

    Prudence

    Consistency

(2 marks)

6   'The shareholder needs a statement of financial prospects, ie an indication of future progress. However, the supplier of goods on credit needs a statement of financial position, ie an indication of the current state of affairs.'

True   ☐
False ☐   (1 mark)

7   You have recently been appointed as assistant accountant of PQR Ltd. You have assisted in preparing a forecast set of final accounts for the company whose year end is 31 December 20X7. The forecast shows that the company is expected to make a loss during the year to 31 December 20X7. This would be the first time that the company has made a loss since it was incorporated twenty years ago.

The managing director is concerned that the company's shareholders would be unhappy to hear that the company had made a loss. He is determined to avoid making a loss if at all possible. He has made the following suggestions in order to remedy the situation.

1   Make no further provision for obsolete stock and consider crediting the profit and loss account with the provision made in previous years.

2   Do not allow for depreciation for the year to 31 December 20X7.

3   Capitalise all research expenditure.

4   Do not make any further allowance for debtors and credit the profit and loss account with the full amount of allowances made in previous years.

Which of these suggestions do you agree with?

☐   (1 mark)

                                                                                   (Total = 11 marks)

43 Preparing financial accounts   50 mins

1   Your organisation sold goods to PQ Ltd for £800 less trade discount of 20% and cash discount of 5% for payment within 14 days. The invoice was settled by cheque five days later. The entries required to record BOTH of these transactions are:

			Debit £	Credit £
☐	A	PQ Ltd	640	
		Sales		640
		Bank	608	
		Discount allowed	32	
		PQ Ltd		640
☐	B	PQ Ltd	640	
		Sales		640
		Bank	600	
		Discount allowed	40	
		PQ Ltd		640
☐	C	PQ Ltd	640	
		Sales		640
		Bank	608	
		Discount received	32	
		PQ Ltd		640

	D	PQ Ltd		800	
		Sales			800
		Bank		608	
		Discount allowed		182	
		PQ Ltd			800

(2 marks)

2   The following totals appear in the day books for March 20X8.

	Goods excluding VAT	VAT
	£	£
Sales day book	40,000	7,000
Purchases day book	20,000	3,500
Returns inwards day book	2,000	350
Returns outward day book	4,000	700

Opening and closing stocks are both £3,000. The gross profit for March 20X8 is

£ [   ]   **(1 mark)**

3   Diesel fuel in stock at 1 November 20X7 was £12,500, and there were invoices awaited for £1,700. During the year to 31 October 20X8, diesel fuel bills of £85,400 were paid, and a delivery worth £1,300 had yet to be invoiced. At 31 October 20X8, the stock of diesel fuel was valued at £9,800. The diesel fuel to be charged to the profit and loss account for the year to 31 October 20X8 is £ [   ]   **(1 mark)**

4   An increase in the allowance for debtors results in

	A	a decrease in current liabilities
	B	an increase in net profit
	C	an increase in working capital
	D	a decrease in working capital

(2 marks)

5   The petty cash imprest is restored to £100 at the end of each week. The following amounts are paid out of petty cash during week 23.

Stationery	£14.10 including VAT at 17.5%
Travelling costs	£25.50
Office refreshments	£12.90
Sundry creditors	£24.00 plus VAT at 17.5%

The amount required to restore the imprest to £100 is £ [   ]   **(1 mark)**

6   A company's telephone bill consists of two elements. One is a quarterly rental charge, payable in advance; the other is a quarterly charge for calls made, payable in arrears. At 1 April 20X9, the previous bill dated 1 March 20X9 had included line rental of £90. Estimated call charges during March 20X9 were £80.

During the following 12 months, bills totalling £2,145 were received on 1 June, 1 September, 1 December 20X9 and 1 March 20Y0, each containing rental of £90 as well as call charges. Estimated call charges for March 20Y0 were £120.

The amount to be charged to the profit and loss account for the year ended 31 March 20Y0 is

£ [   ]   **(1 mark)**

7   Which *three* of the following sets of items all appear on the same side of the trial balance?

1   Sales, interest received and accruals
2   Debtors, drawings and discount received
3   Fixed assets, cost of sales and carriage outwards
4   Capital, trade creditors and other operating expenses
5   Sundry expenses, prepayments and purchases

(2 marks)

---

8   Profit is £1,051 and capital introduced is £100. There is an increase in net assets of £733.

What are drawings? £ [   ]   (1 mark)

---

9   The increase in net assets is £173, drawings are £77 and capital introduced is £45.

What is the net profit for the year? £ [   ]   (1 mark)

---

10   Liabilities of a business are £153, whereas assets are £174.

How much capital is in the business? £ [   ]   (1 mark)

---

11   Capital introduced is £50. Profits brought forward at the beginning of the year amount to £100 and liabilities are £70. Assets are £90.

What is the retained profit for the year? £ [   ]   (1 mark)

---

12   On 1 May 20X9 Marshall's cash book showed a cash balance of £224 and an overdraft of £336. During the week ended 6 May the following transactions took place.

May 1   Sold £160 of goods to P Dixon on credit.
May 1   Withdrew £50 of cash from the bank for business use.
May 2   Purchased goods from A Clarke on credit for £380 less 15% trade discount.
May 2   Repaid a debt of £120 owing to R Hill, taking advantage of a 10% cash discount. The payment was by cheque.
May 3   Sold £45 of goods for cash.
May 4   Sold £80 of goods to M Maguire on credit, offering a 12$\frac{1}{2}$% discount if payment made within 7 days.
May 4   Paid a telephone bill of £210 by cheque.
May 4   Purchased £400 of goods on credit from D Daley.
May 5   Received a cheque from H Larkin for £180. Larkin has taken advantage of a £20 cash discount offered to him.
May 5   Sold £304 of goods to M Donald on credit.
May 5   Purchased £135 of goods from Honour Ltd by cheque.
May 6   Received a cheque from D Randle for £482.
May 6   Purchased £100 of goods on credit from G Perkins.

What are the balances on the following books?

(a)   Sales day book £ [   ]   (1 mark)

(b)   Purchases day book £ [   ]   (1 mark)

(c)   Bank £ [   ]   (1 mark)

13 A debit balance of £1,250 on X's account in the books of Y means that:

- A X owes £1,250 to Y
- B Y owes £1,250 to X
- C X has returned goods worth £1,250 to Y
- D X is owed £1,250 by Y

(2 marks)

14 You are an employee of Exelan Ltd and have been asked to help prepare the end of year statements for the period ended 30 November 20X9 by agreeing the figure for the total debtors.

The following figures, relating to the financial year, have been obtained from the books of original entry.

	£
Purchases for the year	361,947
Sales	472,185
Returns inwards	41,226
Returns outwards	16,979
Irrecoverable debts written off	1,914
Discounts allowed	2,672
Discounts received	1,864
Cheques paid to suppliers	342,791
Cheques received from customers	429,811
Customer cheques dishonoured	626

You discover that at the close of business on 30 November 20X8 the total of the debtors amounted to £50,241. What is the balance on the sales ledger control account at 30 November 20X9?

£ _____ **(1 mark)**

15 Your rather inexperienced colleague, Peter Johnson, has attempted to extract and total the individual balances in the sales ledger. He provides you with the following listing which he has prepared.

	£
Bury Plc	7,500
P Fox & Son (Swindon) Ltd	2,000
Frank Wrendlebury Ltd	4,297
D Richardson Ltd	6,847
Ultra Ltd	783
Lawrenson Ltd	3,765
Walkers Plc	4,091
P Fox & Son (Swindon) Ltd	2,000
Whitchurch Ltd	8,112
Ron Bradbury Ltd	5,910
Anderson Ltd	1,442
	46,347

Subsequent to the drawing up of the list, the following errors have so far been found.

(a) A sales invoice for £267 sent to Whitchurch Ltd had been correctly entered in the day book but had not then been posted to the account for Whitchurch Ltd in the sales ledger.

(b) One of the errors made by Peter Johnson (you suspect that his list may contain others) was to omit the £2,435 balance of Rectofon Ltd from the list.

(c) A credit note for £95 sent to Bury Plc had been correctly entered in the day book but was entered in the account in the sales ledger as £75.

Calculate the revised balance of the sales ledger £ _____ **(1 mark)**

16   At 1 April 20X9, the purchase ledger control account showed a balance of £142,320.

At the end of April the following totals are extracted from the subsidiary books for April:

	£
Purchases day book	183,800
Returns outwards day book	27,490
Returns inwards day book	13,240
Payments to creditors, after deducting £1,430 cash discount	196,360

It is also discovered that:

(a)   the purchase day book figure is net of VAT at 17.5%; the other figures all include VAT.

(b)   a customer's balance of £2,420 has been offset against his balance of £3,650 in the purchases ledger.

(c)   a supplier's account in the purchases ledger, with a debit balance of £800, has been included on the list of creditors as a credit balance.

Calculate the corrected balance on the purchases ledger control account £ [   ]   **(1 mark)**

---

17   On 10 January 20X9, Jane Smith received her monthly bank statement for December 20X8. The statement showed the following.

SOUTHERN BANK PLC

J Smith: Statement of Account				
Date	Particulars	Debits	Credits	Balance
20X8		£	£	£
Dec 1	Balance			1,862
Dec 5	417864	243		1,619
Dec 5	Dividend		26	1,645
Dec 5	Bank Giro Credit		212	1,857
Dec 8	417866	174		1,683
Dec 10	417867	17		1,666
Dec 11	Sundry Credit		185	1,851
Dec 14	Standing Order	32		1,819
Dec 20	417865	307		1,512
Dec 20	Bank Giro Credit		118	1,630
Dec 21	417868	95		1,535
Dec 21	417870	161		1,374
Dec 24	Bank charges	18		1,356
Dec 27	Bank Giro Credit		47	1,403
Dec 28	Direct Debit	88		1,315
Dec 29	417873	12		1,303
Dec 29	Bank Giro Credit		279	1,582
Dec 31	417871	25		1,557

Her cash book for the corresponding period showed:

CASH BOOK

20X8		£	20X8		Cheque no	£
Dec 1	Balance b/d	1,862	Dec 1	Electricity	864	243
Dec 4	J Shannon	212	Dec 2	P Simpson	865	307
Dec 9	M Lipton	185	Dec 5	D Underhill	866	174
Dec 19	G Hurst	118	Dec 6	A Young	867	17
Dec 26	M Evans	47	Dec 10	T Unwin	868	95
Dec 27	J Smith	279	Dec 14	B Oliver	869	71
Dec 29	V Owen	98	Dec 16	Rent	870	161
Dec 30	K Walters	134	Dec 20	M Peters	871	25
			Dec 21	L Philips	872	37
			Dec 22	W Hamilton	873	12
			Dec 31	Balance c/d		1,793
		2,935				2,935

Calculate the revised cash book balance at 31 December 20X8. £ ⬚ **(1 mark)**

---

18   Sandilands Ltd uses a computer package to maintain its accounting records. A printout of its cash book for the month of May 20X3 was extracted on 31 May and is summarised below.

	£		£
Opening balance	546	Payments	335,966
Receipts	336,293	Closing balance	873
	336,839		336,839

The company's chief accountant provides you with the following information.

(a)   The company's bank statement for May was received on 1 June and showed an overdrawn balance of £2,954 at the end of May.

(b)   Cheques paid to various creditors totalling £7,470 have not yet been presented to the bank.

(c)   Cheques received by Sandilands Ltd totalling £6,816 were paid into the bank on 31 May but not credited by the bank until 2 June.

(d)   Bank charges of £630 shown on the bank statement have not been entered in the company's cash book.

(e)   Three standing orders entered on the bank statement have not been recorded in the company's cash book: a subscription for trade journals of £52, an insurance premium of £360 and a business rates payment of £2,172.

(f)   A cheque drawn by Sandilands Ltd for £693 and presented to the bank on 26 May has been incorrectly entered in the cash book as £936.

(g)   A cheque for £510 has been charged to the company's bank account in error by the bank. The cheque relates to Sandford plc and should not have appeared on Sandilands Ltd's statement.

(h)   A monthly direct debit payable to a leasing company for £1,000 was wrongly paid twice by the bank.

Prepare a bank reconciliation statement as at 31 May 20X3, and state the revised cash book figure.

£ ⬚ **(2 marks)**

---

19   An organisation restores its petty cash balance to £250 at the end of each month. During October, the total expenditure column in the petty cash book was calculated as being £210, and the imprest was restored by this amount. The analysis columns posted to the nominal ledger totalled only £200.

This error would result in:

☐   A   the trial balance being £10 higher on the debit side

☐   B   the trial balance being £10 higher on the credit side

☐   C   no imbalance in the trial balance

☐   D   the petty cash balance being £10 lower than it should be   **(2 marks)**

20   You work for Perin Products as a bookkeeper and one of your duties is to enter appropriate transactions into the Journal. During the week ended 20 October 20X9 the following details are passed to you for your attention.

October 18   It comes to light that during the previous week motor vehicle servicing costs of £124 were debited to the Motor Vehicles Account.

October 18   A payment by cheque to A Brigham for £20 made earlier in the week was debited to the Bank Account and credited to A Brigham.

October 20   It is discovered that an invoice for £425 relating to goods received from EFI Co on 30 September was filed away and not entered anywhere in the books of Perin Products.

Required

Show the journal entries that you would have made during the week. Narratives are not required.

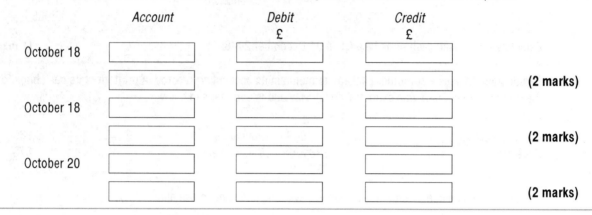

	Account	Debit £	Credit £	
October 18				
				(2 marks)
October 18				
				(2 marks)
October 20				
				(2 marks)

21   A trial balance has an excess of debits over credits of £14,000 and a suspense account has been opened to make it balance. It is later discovered that:

(a)   The discounts allowed balance of £3,000 and the discounts received balance of £7,000 have both been entered on the wrong side of the trial balance.

(b)   The purchases control account balance of £233,786 had been included in the trial balance as £237,386.

(c)   An item of £500 had been omitted from the sales records (ie from the sales day book).

(d)   The balance on the current account with the senior partner's wife had been omitted from the trial balance. This item when corrected removes the suspense account altogether.

Calculate the amount to be entered in the suspense account for item (d) above.

£ [   ] debit/credit (delete as appropriate)   **(1 mark)**

22   Accounting packages, such as Sage, are specifically tailored to each organisation's needs.

True   [ ]
False [ ]   **(1 mark)**

23   What is the name for a collection of information stored on a computer, which can be used in a number of ways?

[   ]   **(1 mark)**

                                                                          (Total = 36 marks)

44 Accounting conventions and standards

1   A machine cost £9,000. It has an expected useful life of six years, and an expected residual value of £1,000. It is to be depreciated at 30% per annum on the reducing balance basis. A full year's depreciation is charged in the year of purchase, with none in the year of sale. During year 4, it is sold for £3,000.

The profit or loss on disposal is £ [   ] profit/loss *(delete as appropriate)*.   **(1 mark)**

2   The most appropriate definition of depreciation is a means of determining the decrease in market value of an asset over time.

True   [   ]

False   [   ]   **(1 mark)**

3   The accounting concept which dictates that fixed assets should be valued at cost, less accumulated depreciation, rather than their enforced saleable value, is called which concept? [   ] **(1 mark)**

4   A fixed asset was disposed of for £2,200 during the last accounting year. It had been purchased exactly three years earlier for £5,000, with an expected residual value of £500, and had been depreciated on the reducing balance basis, at 20% per annum.

The profit or loss on disposal was £ [   ] profit/loss *(delete as appropriate)*.   **(1 mark)**

5   By charging depreciation in the accounts, a business aims to ensure that:

[   ] A   the cost of fixed assets is spread over the accounting periods which benefit from their use

[   ] B   there are sufficient funds set aside to replace the assets when necessary

[   ] C   its profits are not understated

[   ] D   the assets are shown at their real value   **(2 marks)**

6   A machine was purchased in 20X6 for £64,000. It was expected to last for 5 years and to have a residual value of £2,000. Depreciation was charged at 50% per annum on the reducing balance method, with a full year's charge in the year of purchase. No depreciation is charged in the year of disposal. The company's year end is 31 December. The machine was sold on 3 April 20Y0 for £2,500. The profit or loss on sale is

£ [   ] profit/loss *(delete as appropriate)*.   **(1 mark)**

7   The asset register shows a net book value of £271,200. However the fixed asset account in the nominal ledger shows a net book value of £251,200.

The difference could be due to not having removed a disposed asset from the register, which had:

[   ] A   disposal proceeds of £30,000 and a profit on disposal of £10,000
[   ] B   disposal proceeds of £30,000 and a net book value of £10,000
[   ] C   disposal proceeds of £30,000 and a loss on disposal of £10,000
[   ] D   disposal proceeds of £10,000 and a net book value of £10,000   **(2 marks)**

8   The reducing balance method of depreciating fixed assets is more appropriate than the straight-line methods when

[   ] A   the expected life of the asset is short
[   ] B   the asset is expected to decrease in value by a fixed percentage of cost each year
[   ] C   the expected life of the asset is not capable of being estimated accurately
[   ] D   the asset is expected to decrease in value less in later years than in the early years of its life
                                                                                              (2 marks)

9   On 1 January 20X1 a business purchased a laser printer costing £1,800. The printer has an estimated life of 4 years after which it will have no residual value.

Required

Calculate the annual depreciation charge for 20X1 on the laser printer on the following bases.

(a)   The straight line basis £ [   ]   **(1 mark)**

(b)   The reducing balance method at 60% per annum £ [   ]   **(1 mark)**

---

10   Suppose that in 20X4 the laser printer in question 9 were to be sold on 1 July for £200 and that the business had chosen to depreciate it at 60% per annum using the reducing balance method applied on a month for month basis.

Calculate the profit or loss on disposal. £ [   ] profit/loss *(delete as appropriate)*.   **(1 mark)**

---

11   ABC Ltd had the following balances on its motor vehicles accounts at 30 September 20X0.

	£
Motor vehicles at cost	10,000
Provision for depreciation of motor vehicles	4,000

During the year to 30 September 20X1, the following transactions occurred.

31 January 20X1	Bought a motor van (plant number MV11) costing £9,000.
24 April 20X1	Sold a motor van (plant number MV05) for £500 which had originally cost £4,000 in January 19W8.

During the year to 30 September 20X2, the following transactions occurred.

20 February 20X2	Bought a motor van (plant number MV12) costing £12,000.
31 August 20X2	Traded in van bought on 31 January 20X1 (plant number MV11) for a new van (plant number MV13) costing £14,000. The trade-in allowance was £7,400.

ABC Ltd provides for depreciation on its motor vehicles at a rate of 25% per annum using the reducing balance method. It is company policy to make a full year's charge against all assets held at the end of its financial year (30 September).

(a)   Calculate the profit or loss on disposal at 30 September 20X1.

£ [   ] profit/loss *(delete as appropriate)*.   **(1 mark)**

(b)   Calculate the profit or loss on disposal at 30 September 20X2.

£ [   ] profit/loss *(delete as appropriate)*.   **(1 mark)**

---

12   Griffin Ltd maintains an asset register which contained the following details at 1 April 20X7.

	Cost/valuation at 1 April 20X7	Accumulated depreciation at 1 April 20X7
	£	£
Building	80,000	18,000
Plant: Machine A	60,000	27,000
Machine B	40,000	24,000
Machine C	26,000	11,700
Machine D	18,000	13,500

Buildings are depreciated at 2.5% per annum on cost. Plant is depreciated at 7.5% per annum on cost.

During the year ended 31 March 20X8, the following transactions occurred:

(a)   Machine E was purchased by cheque for £17,000.

(b)   Machine C was sold for £13,000 to A Jones, on credit.

(c)   Machine F was purchased by cheque for £42,300 including VAT at 17.5%. The purchase price included delivery and installation of £1,200 plus VAT, and a one-year maintenance contract of £2,000 plus VAT.

Notes

(1)   Ignore VAT on all items except for those in transaction (c).
(2)   The organisation's policy is to charge a full year's depreciation in the year of purchase.

For the year ended 31 March 20X8, calculate each of the following.

(a)   Buildings depreciation £ [   ]   **(1 mark)**

(b)   Plant depreciation £ [   ]   **(1 mark)**

(c)   Profit or loss on disposal of plant. £ [   ] profit/loss *(delete as appropriate).*   **(1 mark)**

---

13   A firm has the following transactions with its product R

Year 1
Opening stock: nil
Buys 10 units at £300 per unit
Buys 12 units at £250 per unit
Sells 8 units at £400 per unit
Buys 6 units at £200 per unit
Sells 12 units at £400 per unit

Year 2
Buys 10 units at £200 per unit
Sells 5 units at £400 per unit
Buys 12 units at £150 per unit
Sells 25 units at £400 per unit

Using FIFO:

At the end of the year 1, calculate closing stock. £ [   ]   **(1 mark)**

At the end of the year 2, calculate cost of sales. £ [   ]   **(1 mark)**

---

14   The directors of a company are reviewing the company's most recent draft financial statements and the following points have been raised for discussion.

(a)   **Events after the balance sheet date**

Shortly after the balance sheet date a major customer of the company with a balance outstanding went into liquidation because of heavy trading losses and it is expected that little or nothing will be recoverable for the debt.

In the financial statements the debt has been written off, but one of the directors has pointed out that, as an event after the balance sheet date, the debt should not in fact be written off but disclosure should be made by note to this year's financial statements, and the debt written off next year.

True   [   ]
False   [   ]   **(1 mark)**

(b)   **Contingency**

An ex-director of the company has commenced an action against the company claiming substantial damages for wrongful dismissal. The company's solicitors have advised that the ex-director is unlikely to succeed with his claim. The solicitors' estimates of the company's potential liabilities are:

	£
Legal costs (to be incurred whether the claim is successful or not)	50,000
Settlement of claim if successful	500,000
	550,000

At present there is no provision or note for this contingency. Is this the correct treatment?

Yes ☐

No ☐ **(1 mark)**

15 The accounts of Exposure Plc for the year ended 31 December 20X1 are to be approved on 31 March 20X2.

On 14 February 20X2 the directors decided to close down its northern branch which had been making losses for some years.

Are the directors correct in believing that the 20X1 accounts should be adjusted to reflect this decision under the provisions of FRS 21 *Events after the balance sheet date*?

Yes ☐

No ☐ **(1 mark)**

(Total = 24 marks)

45 Final accounts and cash flow statements   32 mins

1 Halberd runs a fish shop. He buys supplies daily from the wholesale market paying immediately by cheque. Most of his sales are for cash, except for sales to three local restaurants, which are supplied on monthly credit terms.

Halberd keeps only partial accounting records, and he has asked for your help in preparing his financial statements for the year ended 30 June 20X7. In previous years he has been assisted by a friend who is now ill and unable to continue or give any information.

Halberd's balance sheet at 30 June 20X6 was as follows.

	Reference notes	Cost £	Aggregate depreciation £	Net book value £
Fixed assets				
Refrigeration equipment		8,400	2,520	5,880
Shop fittings		3,720	2,090	1,630
Van		9,200	4,600	4,600
		21,320	9,210	12,110
Current assets				
Stock			680	
Trade debtors			4,270	
Prepayments	1		1,150	
Cash at bank			3,240	
Cash in till			100	
			9,440	
Current liabilities				
Accrued expenses	2		440	
				9,000
Net current assets				21,110
Capital @ 30 June 20X6				21,110

Notes

1 *Prepayments at 30 June 20X6*

	£
Insurance: paid in advance to 30 September 20X6	300
Business rates: paid in advance to 31 March 20X7	850
	1,150

2   *Accrued expenses owing at 30 June 20X6*

	£
Van expenses	320
Miscellaneous expenses	120
	440

Halberd has prepared an analysis of his bank transactions for the year to 30 June 20X7 and this is summarised below.

	£	£
Balance per balance sheet 30 June 20X6		3,240
Receipts		
Cash sales banked	108,600	
Receipts from credit customers (the restaurants)	28,440	
Loan received 1 January 20X7 carrying interest at 10% per annum and repayable in 20Y2	10,000	
		147,040
		150,280
Payments		
Purchases of fish for sale	81,470	
Rent of shop	8,600	
Staff wages	21,400	
Drawings	20,600	
Insurance	1,400	
Van expenses	3,270	
Miscellaneous expenses	3,600	
Purchase of new shop fittings	1,570	
		141,910
Balance at 30 June 20X7		8,370

The following further information is available.

(a)   Depreciation is to be provided as follows:

Refrigeration equipment: 10% on cost (straight line)
Shop fittings: 15% (reducing balance)
Van: 25% on cost (straight line)

A full year's depreciation is to be taken for the shop fittings purchased during the year.

(b)   At 30 June 20X7 the following assets and liabilities existed.

	Assets	Liabilities
	£	£
Stock of fish for sale	810	
Trade debtors (see note c)	6,190	
Prepayments: Insurance	350	
Rent	1,000	
Amounts owing for miscellaneous expenses		200

(c)   Halberd is worried about the amount owing by one of the restaurants. The account is three months in arrears and a provision for the full amount due of £1,860 is to be made.

(d)   In addition to the drawings of £20,600 shown in the bank statement summary, Halberd always takes £300 per week (£15,600 for the year) out of the takings before banking them. He also estimates that he has had fish costing £400 from stock for his own use during the year.

(e)   Halberd had a balance of cash in his till of £150 at 30 June 20X7.

Calculate the following figures for the year ended 30 June 20X7.

(a)   What is the sales figure for the year?   £ [   ]   **(1 mark)**

(b)   What is cost of sales for the year?   £ [   ]   **(1 mark)**

(c)   What is the charge to P & L for insurance?   £ [＿＿＿＿＿＿＿]   **(1 mark)**

(d)   What is the depreciation charge for the year?   £ [＿＿＿＿＿＿＿]   **(1 mark)**

---

2   You are given the following information about a sole trader.

TRIAL BALANCE 31 DECEMBER 20X8

	£'000	£'000
Bank	53	
Capital		300
Land and buildings	320	
Plant and machinery: cost	200	
Depreciation		80
Closing stock	100	
Sales		1,000
Cost of sales	600	
Operating expenses (including depreciation of £20,000)	140	
Irrecoverable debt written off	2	
Debtors	100	
Accruals		5
Creditors		130
	1,515	1,515

	£'000
Cash receipts (year to 31 December 20X8)	
Sales	950
Cash payments (year to 31 December 20X8)	
Purchases	560
Plant (1 January 20X8)	90
Operating items	130
Drawings	20

The creditors figure has doubled since 1 January 20X8.

Calculate the following figures in the *opening* balance sheet at 1 January 20X8.

(a)   Stock   £ [＿＿＿＿＿＿]   **(1 mark)**

(b)   Debtors   £ [＿＿＿＿＿＿]   **(1 mark)**

(c)   Bank   £ [＿＿＿＿＿＿]   **(1 mark)**

---

3   Ganatri and Lucifer are in partnership sharing profits and losses in the ratio 7:3 respectively.

The following information has been taken from the partnership records for the financial year ended 31 May 20X9.

Partners' capital account balances:

Ganatri	£200,000
Lucifer	£140,000

Partners' current accounts, balances as at 1 June 20X8:

Ganatri	£15,000 Cr
Lucifer	£13,000 Cr

During the year ended 31 May 20X9 the partners made the following drawings from the partnership bank account.

Ganatri	£10,000 on 31 August 20X8
	£10,000 on 30 November 20X8
	£10,000 on 28 February 20X9
	£10,000 on 31 May 20X9
Lucifer	£7,000 on 31 August 20X8
	£7,000 on 30 November 20X8
	£7,000 on 28 February 20X9
	£7,000 on 31 May 20X9

Interest is to be charged on drawings at the rate of 12% per annum. Interest is allowed on capital accounts and credit balances on current accounts at the rate of 12% per annum.

Lucifer is to be allowed a salary of £15,000 per annum.

The net profit of the partnership for the year ended 31 May 20X9 is £102,940.

(a) Calculate the total interest chargeable on the partner's drawings for the year ended 31 May 20X9.

£ [   ]   **(1 mark)**

(b) Calculate the profit share for each partner for the year ended 31 May 20X9.

Ganatri £ [   ]   **(1 mark)**

Lucifer £ [   ]   **(1 mark)**

(c) A computation of the balance on each partner's current account as at 31 May 20X9.

Ganatri £ [   ] debit/credit *(delete as appropriate)*.   **(1 mark)**

Lucifer £ [   ] debit/credit *(delete as appropriate)*.   **(1 mark)**

---

4   The trial balance of Zed Ltd at 1 January 20X3 contains the following items.

	£'000
Bank overdraft	7
Building: cost	80
depreciation	5
Creditors: trade	28
operating expenses	2
16% Debentures	50
Debtors	24
Land at valuation	125
Machinery: cost	90
depreciation	43
Ordinary shares, £1 each	100
10% preference shares, £1 each	40
Retained profits	34
Revaluation reserve	45
Stocks	35

Summarised transactions and events for the year to 31 December 20X3 are as follows.

(a)

	£'000
Sales	920
Purchases	500
Irrecoverable debts written off	5
Contras between debtors and creditors accounts	8
Operating expenses paid	360

(b) 30,000 £1 ordinary shares were issued at £2.00 per share on 1 January 20X3; this transaction was not reflected in the trial balance above.

(c) Debenture interest and the preference dividend for the year were all paid on 31 December. An ordinary dividend of 20p per share was paid on 31 December.

(d) The land is revalued at 31 December 20X3 at £130,000. The machinery is to be depreciated at 10% on cost and the buildings are to be depreciated on the straight line basis over eighty years.

(e) At 31 December 20X3:

	£'000
Additional operating expenses owing are	10
Closing stock is	40
Closing debtors are	35
Closing trade creditors are	25

Calculate the following items as at 31 December 20X3.

(a) Dividends paid: ordinary   £ [   ]   **(1 mark)**

preference   £ [   ]   **(1 mark)**

(b) The balance on the share premium account   £ [   ]   **(1 mark)**

(c) The balance on the revaluation reserve   £ [   ]   **(1 mark)**

---

5   The following balances existed in the accounting records of Koppa Ltd, at 31 December 20X7.

	£'000
Development costs capitalised, 1 January 20X7	180
Research and development expenditure for the year	162

In preparing the company's profit and loss account and balance sheet at 31 December 20X7 the following further information is relevant.

(a) The £180,000 total for development costs as at 1 January 20X7 relates to two projects:

	£'000
Project 836: completed project:	82
(balance being amortised over the period expected to benefit from it.	
Amount to be amortised in 20X7: £20,000)	
Project 910: in progress	98
	180

(b) The research and development expenditure for the year is made up of:

	£'000
Research expenditure	103
Development costs on Project 910 which continues to satisfy the	
requirements in SSAP 13 for capitalisation	59
	162

Calculate the research and development costs to be disclosed:

(a) In the profit and loss account   £ [   ]   **(1 mark)**

(b) In the balance sheet   £ [   ]   **(1 mark)**

---

6 The balance sheets of Rapier Ltd at 30 September 20X6 and 30 September 20X7 are given below.

BALANCE SHEETS AS AT 30 SEPTEMBER

	20X6		20X7	
	£'000	£'000	£'000	£'000
Fixed assets (see note 1)				
Cost	600		730	
Aggregate depreciation	220		240	
		380		490
Current assets				
Stock	81		90	
Debtors	90		86	
Cash	4		7	
	175		183	
Current liabilities				
Trade creditors	48		50	
Bank overdraft	13		18	
Dividends	18		22	
	79		90	
Net current assets		96		93
Long-term liabilities		476		583
10% debentures (see note 2)		100		50
		376		533
Capital and reserves				
Called up share capital				
Ordinary shares of £1 each (see note 3)		150		200
Share premium account		50		80
Revaluation reserve		–		50
Retained profit		176		203
		376		533

Notes

1 *Fixed assets*

   During the year fixed assets which had cost £100,000, and which had a book value at 30 September 20X6 of £20,000, were sold for £25,000.

2 *Debentures*

   Interest is due half-yearly on 31 March and 30 September and was paid on the due dates.

   £50,000 of the 10% debentures were repaid on 30 September 20X7.

3 *Share capital*

   The increase in share capital took place on 1 January 20X7.

4 An interim dividend of 5 pence per share was paid on 6 May 20X7 to holders of all the shares in issue at that date.

5 Taxation has not been allowed for and is to be ignored in your answer.

Required

(a) Calculate the net cash inflow from operating activities at 30 September 20X7.

   £ [   ]   **(1 mark)**

(b) Calculate capital expenditure for the year. £ [   ]   **(1 mark)**

7   Set out below are the financial statements of Emma Ltd.

EMMA Ltd
PROFIT AND LOSS ACCOUNT FOR THE YEAR ENDED 31 DECEMBER 20X2

	£'000
Turnover	2,553
Cost of sales	1,814
Gross profit	739
Distribution costs	125
Administrative expenses	264
Interest received	25
Interest paid	75
Profit before taxation	300
Taxation	140
Profit for the period	160

EMMA Ltd
BALANCE SHEETS AS AT 31 DECEMBER

	20X2 £'000	20X1 £'000
Fixed assets		
Tangible assets	380	305
Intangible assets	250	200
Investments	–	25
	630	530
Current assets		
Stocks	150	102
Debtors	390	315
Short-term investments	50	–
Cash in hand	2	1
	592	418
	1,222	948
Current liabilities		
Trade creditors	127	119
Bank overdraft	85	98
Taxation	120	110
Dividends proposed	100	80
	432	407
Long-term liabilities		
Long-term loan	100	–
Deferred taxation	70	50
	170	50
Total net assets	620	491
Share capital and reserves	200	150
Share capital (£1 ordinary shares)		
Share premium account	160	150
Revaluation reserve	100	91
Retained profits	160	100
	620	491

The following information is available.

(a)   The proceeds of the sale of fixed asset investments amounted to £30,000.

(b)   Fixtures and fittings, with an original cost of £85,000 and a net book value of £45,000, were sold for £32,000 during the year.

(c)   The current asset investments fall within the definition of liquid resources under FRS 1.

(d) The following information relates to fixed assets.

	31 December 20X2 £000	31 December 20X1 £000
Cost	720	595
Accumulated depreciation	340	290
Net book value	380	305

(e) 50,000 £ ordinary shares were issued during the year at a premium of 20p per share.

(f) The dividends were declared before the year end.

Required

Prepare the following elements in the cash flow statement for the year to 31 December 20X2.

(a) Taxation £ _____ **(1 mark)**

(b) Net cash from operating activities £ _____ **(1 mark)**

(c) Net cash flow from investing activities £ _____ **(1 mark)**

(d) Net cash flow from financing activities £ _____ **(1 mark)**

(Total = 24 marks)

Answers to multiple choice questions

1 Preparation question: Accounting concepts

Top tips. There are plenty of accounting concepts to choose from. We give six here, although only four were required. But make sure you answer the question – explain how each of your concepts contributes to fair presentation.

Going concern

Under the going concern concept, users of financial statements are entitled to assume that the business will continue for the foreseeable future, and the financial statements are prepared on this basis. If this concept does not apply, this must be made clear in the financial statements and it will affect some items such as the valuation of assets.

Accruals

Under the accruals concept, transactions are recognised in the financial statements in the period in which they occur, rather than in the period in which any related cash is received or paid. This enables users to see the true trading position, undistorted by any cash management issues, and also gives them valuable information regarding outstanding assets and liabilities.

Reliability

Information in financial statements must be reliable if it is to be useful to users. It can be said to be reliable when it is free from material error or bias. This is not always so easy to achieve, but financial statements must seek to represent faithfully the transactions which have taken place during the year.

Prudence

Prudence is important when dealing with estimates and uncertainties in financial information. Under this concept, preparers of financial statements must exercise a degree of caution when making judgements under conditions of uncertainty.

Neutrality

Information in financial statements must be neutral, or free from bias. Users need to know that they are not being given a distorted view of the entity's performance or position. This is not the case if, for instance, accounting policies are selected which will give the most favourable impression of an entity's results.

Comparability

Users must be able to compare an entity's results to its results in previous years and to the results of other entities. In order for this to be possible, accounting policies must be applied consistently both within the financial statements and from one period to the next. Users must be informed of any changes of accounting policy or accounting estimate and must be able to see the effects of such changes.

Note: Only four concepts were required.

2 Accounting concepts I

1	A	Fails to take account of changing price levels over time.
2	B	Remember you were asked for the main aim.
3	D	The historical cost convention.
4	B	The going concern concept.
5	C	Assets less liabilities = opening capital plus profits less drawings
		Therefore, assets less liabilities less opening capital plus drawings = profit
6	D	The separate entity concept.
7	B	Historical cost
8	C	The accruals concept.

9	C	The prudence concept.
10	A	The realisation concept.

3 Accounting concepts II

1	A	Neutrality, prudence and completeness.
2	C	The prudence concept does not require the understating of assets or the overstating of liabilities.
3	A	(a) Materiality concerns whether an item in the financial statements can influence users decisions
		(b) Substance over form means that the commercial effect should be recognised not the strict legal form
4	A	The application of a degree of caution in exercising judgement under conditions of uncertainty.
5	C	Profit will be overstated due to depreciation based on understated assets and cost of sales based on understated stock.
6	D	Statements 1,3 and 4 are all incorrect.
7	B	The use of a degree of caution in making estimates required under conditions of uncertainty.
8	D	None of these statements is correct.

4 Preparation question: Sampi

> **Top tips.** This is a short question testing a topic that is more likely to appear in an MCQ in the exam. Note that as LIFO is no longer examinable you are more likely to be tested on weighted average.

Weighted average cost

Date	Narrative	No. of units	Unit cost £	Value £
28 Feb	Stock b/f	4,000	13.00	52,000
8 Mar	Issues	3,800	15.00	57,000
12 Mar	Sale	(5,000)	13.97	(69,850)
18 Mar	Sale	(2,000)	13.97	(27,940)
	Balance	800	14.01	11,210
22 Mar	Issues	6,000	18.00	108,000
24 Mar	Sale	(3,000)	17.53	(52,590)
28 Mar	Sale	(2,000)	17.53	(35,060)
28 Mar	Balance	1,800	17.53	31,560

Note: You would only need to enter a value total on the final line.

5 Stocks

1	D		£
		Opening stock	318,000
		Purchases	412,000
		Closing stock	(214,000)
			516,000
		Notional cost of sales (612,000 x 75%)	(459,000)
		Stock lost	57,000

2	C	Carriage outwards and storage are distribution costs.

114   Answers to multiple choice questions

BPP
LEARNING MEDIA

3   A
		£
Original value		284,700
Coats – Cost 400 × £80		(32,000)
– NRV (£75 × 95%) × 400		28,500
		281,200

At 31 January 20X3 the skirts were correctly valued at costs incurred to date of £20 per skirt which was lower than the NRV of £22. Therefore no adjustment required.

4   A
	£
50 @ £190	9,500
500 @ £220	110,000
300 @ £230	69,000
	188,500

5   C   Statement 1) stock should be valued at the lower of cost and NRV not the higher
Statement 2) production overheads based on a normal level of production should be included

6   D
	£
Stock check balance	483,700
Less: goods from suppliers	(38,400)
Add: goods sold	14,800
Less: goods returned	(400)
Add: goods returned to supplier	1,800
	461,500

7   C   If closing stock is understated, cost of sales will be overstated. Next year opening stock will be understated and cost of sales will be understated.

8   A
	£	£
Original balance		386,400
Item 1) Cost	(18,000)	
NRV 15,000 – 800	14,200	
Write down		(3,800)
Stock value		382,600

9   C   2 is a distribution cost, 4 is administrative expenses.

6 Preparation question: Riffon

Top tips. This requires six ledger accounts. Draw them all up, leave plenty of space and enter the opening balances. Then you can just methodically post the transactions.

(a)

OFFICE BUILDING AT COST/VALUATION

			£'000				£'000
20X2				*20X3*			
1 July	Balance		1,600	30 June	Balance c/d		2,000
1 July	Revaluation		400				
			2,000				2,000

OFFICE BUILDING – ACCUMULATED DEPRECIATION

		£'000				£'000
20X2			*20X2*			
1 July	Revaluation	320	1 July	Balance		320
20X3			*20X3*			
30 June	Balance c/d	50	30 June	Profit & loss account		
				(2,000,000/40)		50
		370				370

REVALUATION RESERVE

		£'000				£'000
20X3			*20X2*			
30 June	Balance c/d	720	1 July	Cost		400
			1 July	Depreciation		320
		720				720

(b)

PLANT AND MACHINERY AT COST

		£'000				£'000
20X2			*20X3*			
30 June	Balance	840	1 April	Disposal		240
1 Oct	Additions	200	30 June	Balance c/d		800
		1,040				1,040

PLANT AND MACHINERY – ACCUMULATED DEPRECIATION

		£'000			£'000
20X3			*20X2*		
1 April	Disposal	180	30 June	Balance	306
30 June	Balance c/d	326	*20X3*		
			30 June	Profit & loss account	
				(800,000 x 25%)	200
		506			506

PLANT AND MACHINERY – DISPOSAL

		£'000			£'000
20X3			*20X3*		
1 April	Cost	240	1 April	Depreciation	180
30 June	Profit & loss account profit	10		Proceeds	70
		250			250

7 Tangible fixed assets

1 **A** It is **never** B as funds are not set aside; nor C, this is revaluation.

2 **D** (£5,000 – £1,000)/4 = £1,000 depreciation per annum ∴ NBV = £2,000.

3 **D**

	£
Balance b/d	67,460
Less: NBV of fixed asset sold	
(4,000 + 1,250)	5,250
	62,210

4 **A** If disposal proceeds were £15,000 and profit on disposal is £5,000, then net book value must be £10,000, the difference between the asset register figure and the fixed asset account in the nominal ledger.

5 **A** An expense has been posted as a fixed asset.

6 **D**

	£
December addition – 18,000 × 20% × 10/12	3,000
June disposal – 36,000 × 20% × 8/12	4,800
Balance – 345,200 × 20%	69,040
	76,840

7 **C**

	£
Valuation	210,000
Net book value (170,000 × 16/20)	(136,000)
Revaluation reserve	74,000

8	A		£
		Repairs cost overstated	20,000
		Depreciation understated ((20,000 – 4,000) × 20% 6/12)	(1,600)
		Profit understated	18,400

9	A		£
		Plant held all year (200,000 – 40,000) × 20%	32,000
		Disposal 40,000 × 20% × 9/12	6,000
		Additions 50,000 × 20% × 6/12	5,000
			43,000

10	D		£
		Plant held all year (240,000 – 60,000) × 20%	36,000
		Addition 160,000 × 20% × 6/12	16,000
		Disposal 60,000 × 20% × 3/12	3,000
			55,000

8 Intangible fixed assets

1 B There is no requirement that development expenditure should be amortised over a period not exceeding five years.

2 A 3 There is no time scale given by SSAP 13 for amortisation

3 C Development costs are amortised over the useful life of the project. This is not confined to five years.

4 B 2 and 3 only.

5 D Goodwill is an **intangible** non-current asset shown on the **balance sheet** and internally generated goodwill is never recognised.

9 Preparation question: XY ledger accounts

> **Top tips.** Questions asking you to prepare four ledger accounts are relatively uncommon. This question tests both in theory and in practice, whether you fully understand accruals and prepayments.

(a)

RENT PAYABLE ACCOUNT

		£			£
20X5			*20X6*		
1 Oct	Bal b/fwd	1,000	30 Sep	Charge to P & L	6,000
30 Nov	Bank	1,500	30 Sep	Rent prepaid c/fwd	1,000
20X6					
29 Feb	Bank	1,500			
31 May	Bank	1,500			
31 Aug	Bank	1,500			
		7,000			7,000
1 Oct	Rent prepaid b/fwd	1,000			

(b)

ELECTRICITY ACCOUNT

		£			£
20X5			*20X5*		
5.11.X5	Bank	1,000	1 Oct	Bal b/fwd	800
20X6			*20X6*		
10 Feb	Bank	1,300	30 Sep	Charge to P & L	5,000
8 May	Bank	1,500			
7 Aug	Bank	1,100			
30 Sep	Accrual c/fwd	900			
		5,800			5,800
			1 Oct	Balance b/fwd	900

(c)

INTEREST RECEIVABLE ACCOUNT

		£			£
20X5			*20X5*		
1 Oct	Bal b/fwd	300	2 Oct	Bank	250
20X6			*20X6*		
30 Sep	Transfer to I/S	850	3 Apr	Bank	600
			30 Sep	Accrual c/fwd	300
		1,150			1,150
1 Oct	Balance b/fwd	300			

(d)

ALLOWANCE FOR DEBTORS

		£			£
20X6			*20X5*		
30 Sep	Bal c/fwd (125,000 × 5%)	6,250	1 Oct	Bal b/fwd	4,800
			20X6		
			30 Sep	Charge to P & L	1,450
		6,250			6,250
			1 Oct	Balance b/fwd	6,250

10 Preparation question: Kate's Coffee House

Electricity expense (P & L)   £1,317

Insurance expense (P & L)   £950

Workings

	£
Electricity paid:	309
	320
	340
	321
Add: closing accrual	
$(321 \times \frac{1}{3})$	107
Less: opening accrual	(80)
	1,317

	£
Insurance paid:	1,000
Less: closing prepayment	
$(1,000 \times \frac{6}{12})$	(500)
Add: opening prepayment	450
	950

These can be shown in "T" account form:

Electricity Expense

	£		£
Bank (Qtr – 31.8.X0)	309	Accrual – reversal	80
Bank (Qtr – 30.11.X0)	320	∴ P & L	1,317
Bank (Qtr – 28.2.X1)	340		
Bank (Qtr – 31.5.X1	321		
Accrual ($\frac{1}{3} \times 321$)	107		
	1,397		1,397

Insurance Expense

	£		£
Prepayment – reversal	450	∴ P & L	950
Bank	1,000	Prepayment ($1,000 \times \frac{6}{12}$)	500
	1,450		1,450

11 Preparation question: Irrecoverable debts

Trade debtors

	£		£
B/d	76,000		
		Irrecoverable debts expense (a)	3,000
		C/d	73,000
	76,000		76,000

Irrecoverable Debt expense a/c

	£		£
Trade debtors	3,000	P & L	6,200
Allowance for debtors:			
– specific	3,000		
– general	200		
	6,200		6,200

	£		£
		B/d	4,000
C/d allowance		Allowance	
– specific	3,000	expense a/c	
– general	4,200	– specific	700
		– specific	2,300
		Increase in general allowance (4,200 – 4,000)	200
	7,200		7,200

General allowance:

	£
Revised trade debtors balance	73,000
Less: trade debtors specifically provided for	(3,000)
Trade debtors on which to calculate allowance	70,000
General allowance required	4,200
(6% × 70,000)	
General allowance opening balance	(4,000)
Increase required	200

12 Adjustments to accounts

1 D

RENT RECEIVABLE

	£		£
Opening balance	21,200	Opening balance	28,700
Closing balance	31,200	Cash received	481,200
20X2 income	475,900	Closing balance	18,400
	528,300		528,300

2 C

	£
Receipt	
1 October 20X1 (£7,500 × 1/3)	2,500
30 December 20X1	7,500
4 April 20X2	9,000
1 July 20X2	9,000
1 October 20X2 (9,000 × 2/3)	6,000 Credit accrual 3,000
Credit to profit and loss account	34,000

3 B

	£
February to March 20X2 (22,500 × 2/3)	15,000
April to June	22,500
July to September	22,500
October to December	30,000
January 20X3 (30,000 x 1/3)	10,000
Rent for the year	100,000

Accrual 30,000 × 1/3 = 10,000

			£
4	D		
		Payments made	34,600
		Add: opening balance	8,200
		Less: opening accrual	(3,600)
		Less: closing balance	(9,300)
		Add: closing accrual	3,200
			33,100

			£
5	D		
		Closing allowance required (400,000 − 38,000) × 10%	36,200
		Opening allowance	50,000
		Decrease in allowance	(13,800)
		Irrecoverable debts written off	38,000
		Profit and loss account charge	24,200

			£
6	A		
		Irrecoverable debts written off	14,600
		Reduction in allowance	(2,000)
			12,600

			£
7	B		
		Profit and loss account	
		December to June 8,400 × 7/12	4,900
		July to November 12,000 × 5/12	5,000
			9,900
		Sundry creditors 12,000 × 1/12 = 1,000 (December rent received in advance)	

			£
8	D		
		Irrecoverable debt written off	28,500
		Increase in allowance ((868,500 − 28,500) x 5% − 38,000)	4,000
			32,500

9	C	£146,000 + (£218,000 − £83,000) = £281,000

			£
10	C		
		August to September 60,000 × 2/12	10,000
		October to July 72,000 × 10/12	60,000
			70,000

13 Preparation Question: Scimitar

Top tips. If you find yourself running out of time, do not bother to close off the accounts. There are no points allocated to straightforward opening and closing balances; in this question the only such balance for which a mark was allocated was the closing credit balance on the sales ledger control account.

With ledger control accounts questions, make sure that you have the figures on the correct side.

SALES LEDGER CONTROL ACCOUNT

20X7		£	20X7		£
1 Sep	Balance b/f	188,360	1 Sep	Balance b/f	2,140
30 Sep	Sales (W1)	102,620	30 Sep	Sales returns	9,160
	Cash refunds	300		Cash received	91,270
	Petty cash refund	20		Cash discounts	1,430
	Balance c/f (W2)	3,320		Irrecoverable debts written off	460
				Contras	980
				Balance c/f	189,180
		294,620			294,620
1 Oct	Balance b/f	189,180	1 Oct	Balance b/f	3,320

PURCHASE LEDGER CONTROL ACCOUNT

20X7		£	20X7		£
1 Sep	Balance b/f	120	1 Sep	Balance b/f	89,410
30 Sep	Purchases returns	4,280	30 Sep	Purchases (W3)	67,060
	Cash to suppliers	71,840		Balance c/f	90
	Cash discounts	880			
	Contras	980			
	Balance c/f	78,460			
		156,560			156,560
1 Oct	Balance b/f	90	1 Oct	Balance b/f	78,460

Workings

1   Debtors

	£
Credit sales	101,260
Error (c)	1,360
	102,620

2   Sales ledger control account closing balance

	£
Sales ledger balance given in question	2,680
Error (a)	680
Error (d)	(40)
	3,320

3   Purchases

	£
Credit purchases	68,420
Error (c)	(1,360)
	67,060

14 Control accounts

1   C   Credit sales = £80,000 – £10,000 + £9,000 = £79,000.

2   B   A, C and D would make the supplier's statement £150 *higher*.

3   C   Debits total £32,750 + £125,000 + £1,300 = £159,050.
Credits total £1,275 + £122,500 + £550 = £124,325.
Therefore, net balance = £34,725 debit.

4   A   B and C would make the credit side £50 higher. D would have no effect.

5   A   £8,500 – (2 × £400) = £7,700.

6   A   Sales and refunds are posted on the *debit* side, changes in the allowance for debtors do not appear in the control account.

7   B

SALES LEDGER CONTROL ACCOUNT

	£		£
Opening balance	180,000	Cash from credit customers	228,000
Credit sales	190,000	Irrecoverable debts written off	1,500
Cash refunds	3,300	Sales returns	8,000
		Discount allowed	4,200
		Contras	2,400
		Closing balance	129,200
	373,300		373,300

8   C

SALES LEDGER CONTROL ACCOUNT

	£		£
Opening balance	284,680	Cash received	179,790
Credit sales	189,120	Discounts allowed	3,660
		Irrecoverable debts written off	1,800
		Sales returns	4,920
		Contras	800
		Closing balance	282,830
	473,800		473,800

9   C

SALES LEDGER CONTROL ACCOUNT

	£		£
Opening balance	308,600	Cash received	147,200
Credit sales	154,200	Discounts allowed	1,400
Interest charged	2,400	Contra	4,600
		Irrecoverable debts	4,900
		Closing balance	307,100
	465,200		465,200

10 A

SALES LEDGER CONTROL ACCOUNT

	£		£
Opening balance	614,000	Cash from customers	311,000
Credit sales	301,000	Discounts allowed	3,400
Interest charged on overdue		Irrecoverable debts written off	32,000
accounts	1,600	Contras	8,650
		Closing balance	561,550
	916,600		916,600

15 Preparation question: Cain

Top tips. This is quite a tough question. It is more realistic than many bank reconciliations given in examinations, because you have to *detect* the errors as well as *correct* them. Some are obvious, such as the omission of the standing order, bank giro credit etc from the cash book, but others will only be spotted by careful attention to the question: for example, did you notice that the overdraft has been brought down as a debit balance? Or that the casting of the first December credits is wrong? Or the transposition error in recording cheque number 7655?

	£	£	£		Note
Jan-Nov receipts		39,500.54	7,000.12	Overdraft	(i)
Balance at 30/11		2,499.92	35,000.34	Jan-Nov payments	(ii)
		42,000.46	42,000.46		
Dec receipts	178.19		2,499.92	Brought down 1/12	
	121.27				
	14.92			Cheques	
	16.88		37.14	7654	
		331.26	129.79	7655	(iii), (iv)
			5,000.00	7656	
Dec receipt	3,100.00		123.45	7657	
	171.23		678.90	7658	
	1,198.17		1.47	7659	
		4,469.40	19.84	7660	
Dec receipt		117.98	10.66	7661	
			80.00	Charges	
Balance		3,712.53	50.00	Standing order	
		8,631.17	8,631.17		

(a) The trainee had entered the overdraft to the wrong side of the cash book.
(b) Discounts should not be entered in the cash book.
(c) The receipt had been miscast in the draft cash book as £329.26.
(d) There was a transposition error in recording the cheque in the cash book.

BANK RECONCILIATION AT 31 DECEMBER

	£	£
Balance per bank statement (overdraft)		3,472.34
Unpresented cheques 7660	19.84	
7657	123.45	
		143.29
		3,615.63
Balance as per cash book		3,712.53
Remaining difference		96.90

16 Preparation question: George

> **Top tips.** Watch the preparation of the bank reconciliation. This is the area where most candidates slip up in the actual exam. You must be clear which adjustments are made in the cash book.

(a) *Cash book*

		£
Opening balance		4,890
(3)	Bank charges	(320)
(4)	Mistake on cheque recorded	(10,000)
(5)	Dishonoured cheque	(980)
(6)	Misposted cheque payment	(4,800)
(7)	Miscasting	(1,000)
(8)	Misposting of interest received	320
Adjusted cash book balance as at 31 March 20X9		(11,890)

(b)   *Bank reconciliation*

		£
Balance from cash book (from part (a))		(11,890)
Add: (1) unpresented cheque		1,000
(5) dishonoured cheque		980
Less: uncleared lodgement		(2,890)
Balance per bank statement		(12,800)

(c)   *Profit adjustment*

		£
Original profit figure		81,208
(3)	Bank charges	(320)
(4)	Additional depreciation [(12,900 − 2,900)@ 10%]	(1,000)
(5)	Irrecoverable debt	(980)
(6)	Motor repairs	(2,400)
(6)	Depreciation adjustment	(600)
(7)	Purchases	(1,000)
(8)	Interest received	320
(9)	Home repairs	870
Adjusted profit		76,098

17 Bank reconciliations

1   B   £(565)o/d − £92 dishonoured cheque = £(657) o/d

2   D

	£
Balance b/d	5,675 o/d
Less: standing order	(125)
Add: dishonoured cheque (450 × 2)	900
	6,450 o/d

3   A

	£
Opening bank balance	2,500
Payment (£1,000 − £200) × 90%	(720)
Receipt (£200 − £10)	190
Closing bank balance	1,970

4   B

	£
Balance per bank statement	(800)
Unpresented cheque	(80)
Dishonoured cheque (affects cash book only)	–
	(880)

5   B

	£
Original cash book figure	2,490
Adjustment re charges	(50)
Adjustment re dishonoured cheque	(140)
Adjusted cash book figure	2,300

6   D

	£
Bank statement	(36,840)
Lodgements credited after date	51,240
Outstanding cheques	(43,620)
Balance per cash book (o/d)	(29,220)

7   A   Dishonoured cheques and bank charges must be entered in the cash book.

8   B   Bank charges, direct debits and dishonoured cheques will all be written into the cash book.

9	B		£
		Overdraft	(3,860)
		Outstanding cheques	(9,160)
			(13,020)
		Deposits	16,690
		Cash at bank	3,670

10 A Bank charges not entered in the cash book can be entered, and the cash book balance adjusted.

18 Preparation question: Choctaw

Top tips. The first point to note is that not all of these errors will have affected the suspense account. Otherwise, this is a standard bookkeeping question. If you need to do any workings, make sure they are legible.

Journal entries

		Debit £	Credit £
(a)	Depreciation expense- motor vehicles (W)	8,000	
	Accumulated depreciation – motor vehicles		8,000
	Being change of depreciation calculation from reducing balance to straight line		
(b)	Petty cash	1,200	
	Rent receivable		1,200
	Being rent received but omitted from the records		
(c)	Irrecoverable debts expense	8,400	
	Sales ledger control		8,400
	Being irrecoverable debts written off		
(d)	Suspense account	3,400	
	Motor repairs		3,400
	Being correction of omission of opening balance		
(e)	Discount allowed	380	
	Discount received		290
	Suspense account		90
	Being posting of discounts omitted from ledgers.		

Statement of profit adjustments

	£
Draft profit	86,400
Additional depreciation	(8,000)
Rental income	1,200
Irrecoverable debts written off	(8,400)
Motor repairs	3,400
Discounts allowed	(380)
Discounts received	290
Adjusted profit	74,510

Top tips. It was not a necessary part of the question to show how the suspense account was cleared but it is a useful check that the journal entries relating to the suspense account are correct.

SUSPENSE ACCOUNT

	£		£
Motor repairs	3,400	Opening balance	3,310
		Discounts	90
	3,400		3,400

Working

Depreciation adjustment

	£
Reducing balance (88 x 25%)	22,000
Straight line (120 x 25%)	30,000
Additional depreciation	8,000

19 Journal entries and suspense accounts I

1   B   The discount received should have been *credited* to discounts received, so the effect is doubled.

2   D   Error (5) will not cause a trial balance imbalance.

3   A   SUSPENSE ACCOUNT

	£		£
Share capital	3,000	Opening balance	3,460
Motor vehicles	9,000	Plant asset (2,800 × 2)	5,600
		Petty cash (TB)	500
		Closing balance	2,440
	12,000		12,000

4   B   This results in a debit to the suspense account therefore reducing the balance.

Option A results in a credit to the suspense account and options C and D do not affect the suspense account at all.

5   B   Star by posting the adjustment in full:

	Debit	Credit
	£	£
Discount allowed	3,840	2,960
Discount received	3,840	2,960
Suspense account		1,760

6   D   Option A would be a further credit entry in the suspense account
Option B and C do not affect the suspense account

7   B   Cash book 3, 5: bank reconciliation 1, 2, 4

8   B   (1)   This entry has been correctly debited but to the wrong account – no effect on trial balance
(4)   Double entry has been carried out although the wrong way round – no effect on trial balance

9   C   Journal entries 1 and 2 should both be reversed.

20 Journal entries and suspense accounts II

1   B   This has debited a non current asset to cost of sales.

2   B   £9,000 is payable (P & L), but only £6,000 paid (April and July).

3   A   SUSPENSE ACCOUNT

	£		£
Balance b/d	210	Gas bill (420 – 240)	180
Interest	70	Discount (2 × 500)	100
	280		280

4	C	A transaction has been posted to the wrong account, but not the wrong class of account.
5	B	This is an error of original entry.

6   A

	£'000
Profit for the year	1,175
Add back depreciation	100
	1,275
Add: issue of shares	1,000
Less: repayment of debentures	(750)
Less: purchase of fixed assets	(200)
	1,325
Less: increase in working capital	(575)
Increase in bank balance	750

7   C

	£
Capital at 1 April 20X7	6,500
Add: profit (after drawings)	32,500
Less: VAT element	(70)
Capital at 31 March 20X8	38,930

8	C	The transactions in 1 and 5 should both have been **debited.**
9	C	This will mean less cash coming into the bank.
10	C	Cost less 4 months depreciation = 25,500 – 2,125 = £23,375

21 Preparation question: Altese

> **Top tips.** These are three small incomplete records calculations. Read them carefully and set out your workings very clearly.

(a)   Increase in net assets = Capital introduced + profit – drawings

184,000 – 128,000 = 50,000 + profit – 48,000

Profit = 56,000 – 50,000 + 48,000
       = £54,000

(b)
PURCHASES CONTROL ACCOUNT

	£		£
Payments to suppliers	888,400	Opening balance	130,400
Discounts received	11,200	Goods taken	1,000
Closing balance	171,250	Refunds received	2,400
		Purchases (bal fig)	937,050
	1,070,850		1,070,850

(c)   *Cost of sales*

	£
Opening stock	243,000
Purchases	595,400
Less: purchases returns	(41,200)
	797,200
Less: closing stock	(261,700)
	535,500

Sales = 535,500 × 3/2 = £803,250

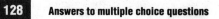

22 Incomplete records

1   B   Closing capital – opening capital = increase (I) in net assets. This means that option B is equivalent to:

$P = I + D - C_i$

This is the correct form of the business equation.

2   D $I = P + C_i - D$
        $= £(72,500 + 8,000 - 2,200)$
        $= £78,300$

Therefore, closing net assets = £(101,700 + 78,300) = £180,000.

3   B $I = P + C_i - D$
        $= £(35,400 - 6,000 + 10,200)$
        $= £39,600$

Therefore, opening capital = opening net assets = £(95,100 – 39,600) = £55,500.

4   B

	£
Opening stock	386,200
Purchases	989,000
Closing stock	(422,700)
Cost of sales	952,500

952,500 × 100/60 = 1,587,500

5   A   Closing net assets plus drawings minus capital introduced minus opening net assets.

6   B   The selling price is not relevant to this adjustment.

7   B   Cost of sales = £114,000

Therefore sales should be = £114,000 × 100/60 = £190,000

Theft = £190,000 – 181 600 = £8,400

8   C

TOTAL DEBTORS ACCOUNT

	£		£
Opening balance	130,000	Cash received	686,400
Sales (balancing figure)	744,960	Discounts allowed	1,400
		Irrecoverable debts	4,160
		Contra	2,000
		Closing balance	181,000
	874,960		874,960

9   D

TOTAL CREDITORS ACCOUNT

	£		£
Cash paid	302,800	Opening balance	60,000
Discounts received	2,960	Purchases (balancing figure)	331,760
Contra	2,000		
Closing balance	84,000		
	391,760		391,760

10   C   Cost of sales = £281,250 × 2/3 = £187,500
        Loss of stock = £228,200 – 187,500 = £40,700

23 Preparation question: PDQ & Co

Appropriation of profits:

Appropriation Account

	£		£
		Profit before appropriation	72,000
Salary:	12,960		
Interest on capital: P	2,880	Interest on drawings: P	360
D	4,800	D	480
Q	7,200	Q	360
Profit: P	10,080		
D	15,120		
Q	20,160		
	73,200		73,200

Current Account

	P £	D £	Q £		P £	D £	Q £
Drawings	7,200	9,600	7,200				
				Salary	12,960		
				Interest on capital	2,880	4,800	7,200
Interest on drawings	360	480	360				
				Profit	10,080	15,120	20,160
c/d	18,360	9,840	19,800				
	25,920	19,920	27,360		25,920	19,920	27,360

24 Preparation question: Leon and Mark

> **Top tips.** Note that Mark joins half way through the year. So the profit needs to be divided between Leon as a sole trader and the partnership.

Division of profit

(a) **Six months to 30 June 20X5**

	£
Profit accrual ($\frac{1}{3} \times (250{,}000 + 20{,}000) - 20{,}000$)	70,000

All goes to Leon

(b) **Six months to 31 December 20X5**

	£	£
Profit accrual ($2/3 \times (250{,}000 + 20{,}000)$)		180,000
Interest on capital – Leon ($5\% \times 400{,}000 \times \frac{1}{2}$)	10,000	
– Mark ($5\% \times 200{,}000 \times \frac{1}{2}$)	5,000	
		(15,000)
Salary – Mark ($20{,}000 \times \frac{1}{2}$)		(10,000)
		155,000
Balance of profit – Leon (60%)	93,000	
– Mark (40%)	62,000	
		155,000

(c)

CURRENT ACCOUNTS

	Leon £	Mark £		Leon £	Mark £
Drawings	160,000	80,000	Profit to 30.6.X5	70,000	–
			Profit to 31.12.X5:		
			Interest	10,000	5,000
			Salary	–	10,000
			Balance of profit	93,000	62,000
Balance	13,000	–	Balance c/f	–	3,000
	173,000	80,000		173,000	80,000

25 Partnerships

1   C   The corrected account looks like this.

CURRENT ACCOUNT

	£		£
Drawings	6,200	Balance b/f	270
Balance c/f	7,070	Interest on capital	2,800
		Salary	1,500
		Net profit	8,700
	13,270		13,270

2   A   The petrol bills have been debited to motor vehicle expenses. This is incorrect and should be revised (so credit motor vehicles expenses). Because they are private expenses of the expenses of the partner they should be debited to his drawing account.

3   B   Interest on partners' capital is an appropriation of profit (debit appropriation account). Since partners have earned the money by their investment in the business, their current accounts should be credited with it. (option D would be theoretically possible, but most firms maintain current accounts separately from capital accounts in order to record such items.)

4   B   There is no FRS on partnerships. All UK partnerships are subject to the Partnership Act.

5   D   Interest payable by partners increases the amounts of profits available for appropriation (credit appropriation account). It must be charged against the partners (debit partners' current accounts).

6   A   The appropriations earned by each partner are shown below.

	Faith £	Hope £	Charity £	Total £
Interest on capital	1,600	1,200	960	3,760
Salary		8,000		8,000
	1,600	9,200	960	11,760
Residual profit (3:2:1)	36,120	24,080	12,040	72,240
	37,720	33,280	13,000	84,000

7   A

		P £	Q £	R £
Profit to 30 December	240,00	144,000	96,000	
Salaries	16,000		10,000	6,000
Balance of profit	224,000	112,000	56,000	56,000
	480,000	256,000	162,000	62,000

8   C   Goodwill   =   price payable – fair value of net assets.
           =   £850,000 – £750,000
           =   £100,000

9   B

	P £	Q £
January to June (340 – (360/2))	160	
July to December (180/2)	90	90
	250	90

10   B

	G £	H £	I £	Total £
To 30 June				
Salaries		20,000	10,000	30,000
Profit (220 – 40 – 30)	90,000	30,000	30,000	150,000
To 31 Dec (220)	110,000	66,000	44,000	220,000
	200,000	116,000	84,000	400,000

$$\text{Profit for each half year} = \frac{(400 + 40)}{2}$$

$$= 220$$

11   B

	£
Profit for July to Dec (570,000/2 – 30,000)	255,000
Profit for Jan to June (570,000/2)	285,000
X profit share July to Dec 255,000 × 2/3	170,000
X profit share Jan to June 285,000 × 50%	142,500
	312,500

12   B   False. Goodwill is the excess of purchase price over the **fair value** of the net assets.

13   A

	G £	H £	I £	Total £
July to December – salaries		10,000	10,000	20,000
Profit share (380/2 – 20)	102,000	34,000	34,000	170,000
January to June – salary			10,000	10,000
Profit share (380/2 – 10)	90,000	60,000	30,000	180,000
	192,000	104,000	84,000	380,000

26 Preparation question: Bonus issue

The double entry is   £

Dr	Share premium*	2,500	(£10,000 ÷ 50c x ¼ x 50c)

Cr	Share capital	2,500	

* or retained profit

Adjusted Balance Sheet

	£
Share capital (50p)	12,500
Share premium	4,500
Retained profit	8,000
	25,000

27 Preparation question: Rights issue

The double entry is		£	
Dr	Bank	4,800	(£8,000 ÷ 50p x ¼ x £1.20)
Cr	Share capital	2,000	(£8,000 ÷ 50p x ¼ x 50p)
Cr	Share premium	2,800	

Adjusted Balance Sheet

	£
Share capital	10,000
Share premium	9,800
Retained profit	10,000
	29,800

28 Preparation question: Shuswap

Top tips. This question is not difficult but requires an organised approach. Most of the adjustments can be annotated against the figures in the question paper. You will have to do a working for property, plant and equipment and retained profit, so do them neatly so that they can be presented as part of your answer.

Shuswap – Balance sheet as at 31 December 20X4

	Cost or valuation £'000	Accumulated depreciation £'000	Net book value £'000
Fixed Assets			
Land and buildings	12,000	–	12,000
Plant and equipment (W1)	19,600	7,950	11,650
			23,650
Current assets			
Stock (3,000 –140)			2,860
Debtors (2,600 – 200 – 106)			2,294
Cash at bank			1,900
			7,054
Creditors: amounts falling due within one year			
Trade creditors (2,100 – 106)			1,994
Net current assets			5,060
			28,710
Creditors: amounts falling due after more than one year			
Debentures			2,000
			26,710
Share capital and reserves			
Issued share capital (6,000 + 2,000)			8,000
Share premium (4,000 x 0.60)			2,400
Revaluation reserve (3,000 + 1,000)			4,000
Retained profits (W2)			12,310
			26,710

Workings

1. Plant and equipment

	£'000
Disposal – Cost	1,400
– Depreciation	(700)
– NBV	700
Proceeds (W3)	(600)
Loss on sale	100

Cost adjustment 21,000 – 1,400 = 19,600

Accumulated depreciation adjustment (9,000 – 700 – (1,400 × 25%)) = 7,950

2. Retained profits

	£'000
Per draft balance sheet	12,400
Irrecoverable debts	(200)
Stock write down (500 – 360)	(140)
Loss on disposal of plant (W1)	(100)
Depreciation adjustment (1,400 x 25%) (W1)	350
	12,310

3. Suspense account

	£'000
Proceeds of issue of 4m shares at £1.10	4,400
Proceeds of sale of plant (balance)	600
	5,000

29 Company financial statements I

1 D

		£
Preference shares 500,000 × 8%		40,000
Ordinary shares 10m × 5p		500,000
		540,000

2 A A rights issue will increase cash and therefore assets. Retained earnings remain the same and the share premium account will be increased.

3 D Minority interest is not a current liability.

4 B Share capital will be credited with the nominal value of the shares – the balance goes to share premium.

5 B Profit on disposal of properties will be included in profit in the profit and loss account.
Equity dividends proposed after the balance sheet date are disclosed by note.

6 B

	£
Current assets	
Insurance 9,000 × 8/12	6,000
Loan	12,000
Interest due 12,000 × 2%	240
Rent due	4,000
	22,240

7 B

	£
Ordinary shares at start of year	50,000
Add: bonus issue 50,000 × 50p	25,000
Add: new issue 60,000 × 50p	30,000
	105,000
Share premium at start of year	180,000
Less: bonus issue 50,000 × 50p	(25,000)
Add: new issue 60,000 × 30p	18,000
	173,000

8 C Statement 3 is the correct treatment for a change of accounting policy or the correction of a prior period error.

9 A Changes of accounting policy require retrospective adjustment.

30 Company financial statements II

1 C Only statement 3 is correct. Extraordinary items are now prohibited.

2 C All of these items are disclosed, either in the financial statements or in the notes.

3 B

		£
Ordinary shares		
Opening balance		125,000
Rights issue	250,000 × 25p	62,500
Bonus issue	150,000 × 25p	37,500
		225,000
Share premium		
Opening balance		100,000
Rights issue	250,000 × 75p	187,500
Bonus issue	150,000 × 25p	(37,500)
		250,000

4	D			£
		July – September	1,000,000 × 8% × 3/12	20,000
		October – March	750,000 × 8% × 6/12	30,000
		April – June	750,000 × 8% × 3/12	15,000
			500,000 × 7% × 3/12	8,750
				73,750

5   A   Adjusting events after the balance sheet date should be adjusted for, not just disclosed.

6   A   The loss on sale of investments will have been recognised in the profit and loss account

7   D   All of these items must be disclosed.

8   B   This is the transfer of the premium to the share premium account.

9   C   A bonus issue does not involve cash but can be financed from the share premium account.

10   D   A bonus issue does not raise any funds and items are no longer classified as extraordinary.

31 Events after the balance sheet date

1   A   All of these events are indicative of conditions that existed at the balance sheet date.

2   A   2 and 3 do not affect the company's position at the balance sheet date.

3   B   These affect valuation of debtors and stock at the balance sheet date.

4   A   1   Future operating losses must not be provided for

             2   Adjusting events must be adjusted in the financial statements. It is non-adjusting events that should be disclosed

             3   Contingent assets must be disclosed, not recognised, if they are probable

32 Preparation question: Sioux

Top tips. This is a basic cash flow question. Make sure you know the format and the working for net cash flow from operating activities using the indirect method. The only working required is for fixed assets – do not forget to allow for the revaluation.

Sioux

Cash flow statement for the year ended 31 December 20X4

Reconciliation of operating profit to net cash inflow from operating activities	£'000	£'000
Operating profit	2,650	
Add: depreciation (W)	1,250	
Less: profit on disposal (500 – 350)	(150)	
Decrease in stocks	400	
Increase in debtors	(900)	
Increase in creditors	500	
	3,750	

Cash flow statement		
Net cash inflow from operating activities		3,750
Interest paid (3,000 × 10%)		(300)
Taxation paid		(600)
Capital expenditure		
Payments to acquire fixed assets (W)	(3,300)	
Proceeds from sale of fixed assets	500	
		(2,800)
		50
Dividends paid		(750)
Financing		
Proceeds from issue of debentures (3,000 – 2,000)		1,000
Increase in cash		300

Workings

Fixed assets

FIXED ASSETS AT COST

	£		£
Opening balance	8,000	Disposal	800
Revaluation	500	Closing balance	11,000
Additions (balance figure)	3,300		
	11,800		11,800

FIXED ASSETS – ACCUMULATED DEPRECIATION

	£		£
Disposal (800 – 350)	450	Opening balance	4,800
Closing balance	5,600	Charge for year (balance figure)	1,250
	6,050		6,050

33 Cash flow statements

1   C   Only the proceeds of a share issue and dividends received involve the movement of cash.

2   D   Loss on sale of fixed assets should be added back to net profit before tax.

3   D

	£
Add: depreciation charge	980,000
Less: profit on sale of assets	(40,000)
Less: increase in stocks	(130,000)
Add: decrease in debtors	100,000
Add: increase in creditors	80,000
Addition to operating profit	990,000

4   B   Depreciation should be added back as it not a cash flow and proceeds of sale of fixed assets appears under 'investing' cash flows.

5	D	1	Proceeds from sale of premises appears under investing activities
		2	Dividends received appears under operating or investing activities
		3	A bonus issue of shares is not a cash flow.
6	C	1	The direct and indirect methods will give the same figure
		2	A rights issue of shares is a cash flow
		4	The profit on sale of a fixed asset appears as an adjustment to profit in order to reach net cash flow from operations
7	D		The depreciation charge and the increase in creditors should both have been added.
8	B		Neither a proposed dividend nor a bonus issue of shares involve the movement of cash.

34 Mixed bank I

1   C

2   C

3   D

4   B

Cash book	£	Bank statement	£
Balance	(8,970)	Balance	(11,200)
Bank charges	(550)	Credit in error	(425)
		Unpresented cheques	(3,275)
		Outstanding deposits	5,380
	(9,520)		(9,520)

5   D

	£
Cost of machine	80,000
Installation	5,000
Training	2,000
Testing	1,000
	88,000

6   C   ELECTRICITY ACCOUNT

		£			£
			Balance b/fwd		300
20X0:					
1 August	Paid bank	600			
1 November	Paid bank	720			
20X1:					
1 February	Paid bank	900			
30 June	Paid bank	840			
30 June	Accrual c/d				
	£840 × ²/₃	560	P & L account		3,320
		3,620			3,620

7   A   GAS SUPPLIER ACCOUNT

	£			£
Balance b/fwd	200			
Bank £600 x 12	7,200	28 February	invoice	1,300
		31 May	invoice	1,400
		31 August	invoice	2,100
		30 November	invoice	2,000
		30 November	bal. c/d	600
	7,400			7,400

GAS ACCOUNT

		£			£
28 February	invoice	1,300			
31 May	invoice	1,400			
31 August	invoice	2,100			
30 November	invoice	2,000	30 November	P & L account	6,800
		6,800			6,800

8   B

	Cost	Net realisable value	Lower of cost & NRV	Units	Value
	£	£	£		£
Basic	6	8	6	200	1,200
Super	9	8	8	250	2,000
Luxury	18	10	10	150	1,500
					4,700

9   B

	£
Cost	10,000
20W7 Depreciation	2,500
	7,500
20W8 Depreciation	1,875
	5,625
20W9 Depreciation	1,406
	4,219
20X0 Part exchange	5,000
Profit	781

10   C

11   C

12   A

13   C

14   D

15   C

16   A

	£	£
Net book value at 1st August 20X0		200,000
Less depreciation		(20,000)
Proceeds	25,000	
Loss	5,000	
Therefore net book value		(30,000)
		150,000

17   D   Correct. This is not an objective from the *Statement*. Additional data is required to assess this.

     A   This is a primary objective.
     B   Again, a major objective.
     C   All Classes of users require information for decision making.

18   A   This information is needed by lenders

19   B

20   D   Loan stock is a long-term liability.

     A   This is statutory reserve.
     B   Otherwise known as the revenue reserve.
     C   This is an unrealised reserve.

21	D	Correct, company will usually include this under distribution costs or administrative expenses.
	A	Incorrect, the contents of cost of sales are not defined by any FRS.
	B	Depreciation will be included under the relevant statutory expense heading (eg office equipment depreciation will go into administrative expenses).
	C	Incorrect, net profit is calculated after interest.

35 Mixed bank II

1 A

2 B

DEBIT	Property, plant and equipment	£38,000	
CREDIT	Plant repairs		£38,000
DEBIT	Dep'n expense	£1,900	
CREDIT	Accumulated dep'n		£1,900

Profit is understated by £38,000 – £1,900 = £36,100

3 D

	£
Suspense account	
Opening balance	16,500 credit
Discount allowed (debit discount allowed)	3,900 credit
Discount received (credit discount received)	(5,100) debit
Transposition of cash received (credit RLCA)	(9,900) debit
	5,400 credit

4 B   Only errors 1 and 3 involve a suspense account entry to correct them.

5 B $\dfrac{£30,000 - £6,000}{4 \text{ years}} \times \dfrac{5 \text{ months}}{12 \text{ months}} = £2,500$

6 C

7 C

	£
	116,400
Line 1: (400 × £3) – £200	1,000
Line 2: (200 × £35) – £300 – £1,200	5,500
	122,900

8 D

9 C   The bank is overdrawn.

	£
Overdraft	(38,600)
Deposits	41,200
	2,600
Unpresented cheques	(3,300)
Overdraft	(700)

10 A   The other two items are part of the bank reconciliation.

11 A

RLCA			
	£		£
Opening balance	29,100	Cash from credit customers	381,600
Refunds	2,100	Cash sales	112,900
Sales (balancing figure)	525,300	Expenses paid out of cash	6,800
		Irrecoverable debts w/off	7,200
		Discounts allowed	9,400
		Closing balance	38,600
	556,500		556,500

12   D   Cost of sales: £17,000 + £91,000 − £24,000 = £84,000

Sales	100%
Cost of sales	60%
Gross profit	40%

Sales: $\dfrac{£84,000}{60\%}$ = £140,000

13   A $\dfrac{5 \text{ months}}{12 \text{ months}}$ × £24,000 = £10,000

$\dfrac{7 \text{ months}}{12 \text{ months}}$ × £30,000 = £17,500

Total rent: £10,000 + £17,500 = £27,500

14   B

	£
Sales (100%)	64,800
Cost of sales (70%)	45,360
Gross profit (30%)	19,440
Opening stock	28,400
Purchases	49,600
	78,000
Calculated closing stock (balancing figure)	(32,640)
Cost of sales	45,360
Calculated closing stock	32,680
Actual closing stock	–
Destroyed by fire	32,640

15   D   Research expenditure is never capitalised

16   A

	D £	E £	F £	Total £
Salaries (see note)	–	30,000	24,000	54,000
PSR to 1.7.20X0 (240,000 − 24,000) 5:3:2	108,000	64,800	43,200	216,000
PSR to 31.12.20X0 (240,000 − 30,000) 3:1:1	126,000	42,000	42,000	210,000
	234,000	136,800	109,200	480,000

Note: F's salary is £24,000 for the year (£12,000 each ½ year). E's salary is ½ × £24,000 for the first 6 months and ½ × £36,000 for the second six months (£12,000 + £18,000).

17   C

	£
Share capital @ 1.1.20X0	500,000
Issue on 1.4.20X0 (200,000 @ 50p)	100,000
Bonus issue (1.2m ÷ 4) @ 50p	150,000
Share capital as at 31.12.20X0	750,000
Share premium @ 1.1.20X0	300,000
1.4.20X0 200,000 shares @ (130p − 50p)	160,000
Bonus issue (as above)	(150,000)
	310,000

18   B   The statement of movements in reserves

19   B   Proceeds from sale of equipment are included in capital expenditure.

20   B

36 Mixed bank III

1 D RENTAL INCOME ACCOUNT

	£		£
Opening rent owing	16,900	Opening rent in advance	24,600
Rent income (balance figure)	316,200	Cash received	318,600
Closing rent in advance	28,400	Closing rent owing	18,300
	361,500		361,500

2 A

	£
Cost of sales	
Opening stock	38,000
Purchases	637,000
Less: closing stock	(45,000)
	630,000

Sales 630,000 × 100/70 = £900,000

3 B

	£
Overdraft per bank statement	39,800
Less: deposits credited	(64,100)
Add: outstanding cheques	44,200
Overdraft per cash book	19,900

4 A All three are incorrect. In 1 and 3 the debit and credit entries should be reversed and 2 should show a credit of £60,000 to the share premium account.

5 A A change of accounting policy should be adjusted retrospectively. Estimates of impact on future periods are not required.

6 B Revaluation reserve – (1,000,000 – (800,000 – (800,000 × 2% × 10)) = £360,000
Depreciation charge – (1,000,000/40) = £25,000

7 A

	£
Stock count value	836,200
Less: purchases	(8,600)
Add: sales (14,000 x 70/100)	9,800
Add: goods returned	700
Stock figure	838,100

8 B

	P	Q	R
	£	£	£
Profit share January to June (120,000)	80,000	40,000	
Profit share July to December (120,000)	60,000	36,000	24,000
Guarantee amount	(1,000)		1,000
	139,000	76,000	25,000

9 C Carriage outwards is a distribution expense.

10 A Profit and loss account = £60,000 × 12/18 = £40,000
Balance sheet = £60,000 × 3/18 prepayment = £10,000

11 C

Opening net assets	+ Profit +	Capital introduced	– Drawings	= Closing net assets
210,000	+ Profit +	100,000	– 48,000	= 400,000

Profit = £138,000

SALES LEDGER CONTROL ACCOUNT

	£		£
Opening balance	318,650	Cash from customers	181,140
Credit sales	161,770	Discounts allowed	1,240
Interest on overdue accounts	280	Irrecoverable debts written off	1,390
		Sales returns	3,990
		Closing balance	292,940
	480,700		480,700

13 B

	£
Allowance required 5% × (864,000 − 13,000)	42,550
Existing allowance	(48,000)
Reduction in allowance	(5,450)
Irrecoverable debts written off	13,000
Profit and loss account charge	7,550

Net trade debtors = £864,000 − 13,000 − 42,550
= £808,450

14 D 1 and 4

15 C

	£
Draft net profit	83,600
Add: purchase price	18,000
Less: additional depreciation (18,000 × 25%)	(4,500)
Adjusted profit	97,100

16 B Interest charged to partners is part of the profit share calculation, not an item in the profit and loss account.

17 A Purchased goodwill is now retained in the balance sheet subject to an impairment review.

18 B 2 and 4 both affect the valuation of assets at the balance sheet date.

19 A A possible transfer of economic benefits should be disclosed. Where transfer is probable a provision should be made.

20 D A revaluation reserve arises when a fixed asset is **revalued**. Debentures are not part of share capital. Adjusting events lead to adjustment in the accounts, not disclosure in the notes.

37 Mixed bank IV

1 A

	£
Increase in net assets	88,000
Capital introduced	(50,000)
Drawings (68,000 + 20,000)	88,000
Profit for the year	126,000

2 A

	£
Debit cash	1,100,000
Credit share capital	250,000
Credit share premium	850,000

3 B

	P	Q	R	Total
Irrecoverable debt	(15,000)	(15,000)	–	(30,000)
Profit to 30 December (330,000/2)	82,500	82,500	–	165,000
Profit to 30 June (330,000/2)	55,000	55,000	55,000	165,000
Total	122,500	122,500	55,000	300,000

			Share capital £	Share premium £
4	D	1 July 20X4	500,000	400,000
		1 January 20X5 – bonus issue (250,000 × 50c)	125,000	(125,000)
		1 April 20X5 – rights issue	62,500	125,000
			687,500	400,000

5 D 2 and 4. Journal entry 1 has debits and credits transposed and journal entry 3 uses the wrong amount.

6 B

SALES LEDGER CONTROL ACCOUNT

	£		£
Opening balance	138,400	Cash received	78,420
Credit sales	80,660	Creditors contra	1,000
Dishonoured cheques	850	Discounts allowed	1,950
		Irrecoverable debts written off	3,000
		Closing balance	135,540
	219,910		219,910

7 A

SUSPENSE ACCOUNT

	£		£
Opening balance	14,550	To cash account	10,000
		To rent account	4,550

8 D 2 and 4. Decrease in stocks should be added, decrease in creditors should be deducted.

9 D

	£
Opening stock	138,600
Purchases	716,100
Closing stock	(149,100)
Cost of sales	705,600

Sales = 705,600 × 100/70 = 1,008,000

10 C

	Profit and loss account £	Balance sheet £
Prepaid insurance	8,200	
Payment January 20X5	38,000	
Prepayment July-Sept 20X5	(9,500)	9,500
	36,700	9,500

11 C The exact amount of expenditure out of petty cash is reimbursed at intervals.

12 D Beta has issued a credit note for £500 to Alpha which Alpha has not yet received.

13 A Research expenditure is never capitalised.

14 D None of these events require adjustment in the financial statements.

15 A

RENT RECEIVED

	£		£
Arrears b/f	3,800	In advance b/f	2,400
Rent in advance	3,000	Cash received	83,700
Balance c/f	84,000	In arrears	4,700
	90,800		90,800

16 B

	£
Allowance for debtors ((517,000 – 37,000) × 5%)	24,000
Previous allowance	(39,000)
Reduction	(15,000)
Debts written off	37,000
Charge to profit and loss account	22,000

17 D   2 and 3 only. Attributable overheads should be included in finished goods stocks.

18 B   The proceeds will appear under *investing activities* and any profit will be deducted under *operating activities*.

19 C   All four items will appear in the statement of movements in reserves.

20 A

	£
Balance per bank statement	(38,600)
Bank charges	200
Lodgements	14,700
Cheque payments	(27,800)
Cheque payment misposted	8,400
Balance per cash book	(43,100)

38 Mixed bank V

1 C

	£
Balance b/f ((28,000 - 14,000)× 20%)	53,200
Addition 1 April (48,000 × 20% × $\frac{9}{12}$)	7,200
Addition 1 Sept (36,000 × 20% × $\frac{4}{12}$)	2,400
	62,800
Sale (14,000 × 20% × $\frac{1}{2}$)	1,400
	64,200

2 D   Item 1 is wrong, as stock should be valued at the **lower** of cost and net realisable value.

Items 2, 3 and 4 are all correct.

3 D

Rent receivable

	£			£
31.1.X6 Profit and loss account	27,500	1.2.X5 Balance b/f ($\frac{2}{3}$ × £6,000)		4,000
		1.4.X5 Received		6,000
		1.7.X5 Received		7,500
		1.10.X5 Received		7,500
31.1. X6 Balance c/f ($\frac{2}{3}$ × £7,500)	5,000	1.1.X6 Received		7,500
	32,500			32,500

4	D	Sales ledger control account				

Sales ledger control account

	£		£
Opening debtors	148,200	Cash received from customers	819,300
Credit sales (bal. fig.)	880,600	Discounts allowed	16,200
		Irrecoverable debts w/off	1,500
		Returns from customers	38,700
		Closing debtors	153,100
	1,028,800		1,028,800

5   D   Items 1 and 4 are adjusting events. Item 2 is a non-adjusting event but might be disclosed by way of note if material. Item 3 is a non-adjusting event that is disclosed by way of note.

6   D

	£
Balance per Alta	3,980
Cheque not yet received	(270)
Goods returned	(180)
Contra entry	(3,200)
Revised balance per Alta	330
Balance per Ordan	(230)
Remaining difference	100

7   C   For discounts, we need to debit the discounts received account £13,000 to reverse the entry and debit the discounts allowed account £13,000 to record the entry correctly. The credit of £26,000 will be to suspense. So journal 2 is correct.

For machinery, we need to debit plant and machinery £18,000 and credit suspense £18,000. So journal 4 is correct.

8   B   Item (1), as the plant register is not part of the double entry system, the adjustment does not go through the suspense account.

Item (2), the transaction has been completely omitted from the records.

Therefore only items (3) and (4) affect the suspense account.

9   D

	£
Initial profit	630,000
Item (1) – increase in depreciation (4,800 – 480)	(4,320)
Item (2) – bank charges	(440)
Item (3) – no effect on P & L	–
Item (4) – no effect on P & L	–
Revised profit	625,240

10   A   Statements 1 and 2 are correct.

11   B   Only statements 2 and 4 are correct.

12   B

	£
Closing debtors	458,000
Irrecoverable debts w/off	(28,000)
	430,000
Allowance required (5% × 430,000)	21,500
Existing allowance	(18,000)
Increase required	3,500
Charge to profit and loss account (28,000 + 3,500)	31,500

13 A

Purchase ledger control account

	£		£
Cash paid to suppliers	988,400	Opening balance	384,600
Discounts received	12,600	Purchases	963,200
Purchases returns	17,400		
Contras	4,200		
Closing balance	325,200		
	1,347,800		1,347,800

14 A We need to increase drawings (debit) and reduce purchases (credit). Therefore journal A is the correct answer. Remember that we only adjust stock at the year end.

15 D

	£	£
Sales (balancing figure)		1,080,000
Opening stock	77,000	
Purchases	763,000	
	840,000	
Closing stock	84,000	
Cost of sales (70%)		756,000
Gross profit ($\frac{30}{70}$ × 756,000)		324,000

16 C Statements (3) and (4) are correct. Statement (1) is incorrect because land is not usually depreciated.

17 B *Bank reconciliation statement*

	£
Balance per bank (overdrawn)	(38,640)
Add: outstanding lodgements	19,270
	(19,370)
Less: unpresented cheques	(14,260)
Balance per cash book (overdrawn)	(33,630)

18 C 48,000 + 400 + 2,200 = 50,600

19 B Opening stock: debit profit and loss account, credit stock account

Closing stock: debit stock account, credit profit and loss account

Remember that stock is part of cost of sales, which is included in the profit and loss account.

39 Mixed bank VI

1 A

Cost of sales

	£
Sales (100%)	650,000
Cost of sales (70%)	455,000
Gross profit (30%)	195,000

Stock destroyed

	£
Opening stock	380,000
Purchases	480,000
	860,000
Closing stock (bal. fig.)	(405,000)
Cost of sales	455,000
Calculated closing stock	405,000
Remaining stock	(220,000)
Stock destroyed	185,000

2 A

Transaction	£
1	+500
2	+500
3	–
	+1,000

3 A Income from investments goes to the profit and loss account and dividends paid are shown in the statement of movements on reserves.

4 D The dividends paid go through the statement of movements on reserves. The final dividend was declared after the year end and so is not accrued for in the balance sheet.

5 D

6 months to 31/12/X5

	£	£
Profit share (3/5 × 300,000)		180,000
6 months to 30/6/X6		
Profit share ((450,000 + 50,000) × 40%)	200,000	
Share of irrecoverable debt (3/5 × 50,000)	(30,000)	
		170,000
		350,000

6 B

Trade debtors	838,000
Irrecoverable debts w/off	(72,000)
	766,000
Allowance for debtors	(60,000)
Net balance	706,000

7 C Stock should be valued at the lower of cost and net realisable value.

8 C The closing stock figure is correct. However the invoice will not have been included in purchases. Therefore cost of sales is understated and so profit for 20X6 is overstated.

9 D Authorised share capital is not included in the balance sheet, instead **issued** share capital is shown. Proceeds of a share issue goes into the statement of movements on reserves.

10 D None of the statements is correct.

11 A All four items contribute to reliability.

12 A

INSURANCE

	£		£
Prepayment b/f (9/12 ×10,800)	8,100	P&L A/C	11,100
4/X6 Paid	12,000	Prepayment c/f (9/12 × 12,000)	9,000
	20,100		20,100

13 C Statements 2 and 3 are incorrect. A dishonoured cheque received is a credit entry in the cash book and bank errors do not go through the cash book at all.

14 B

SHARE CAPITAL

	£m		£m
		Bal b/f	100
		1/9/X5 Bonus issue	50
		1/1/X6 Rights issue	60
Bal c/f	210	(2/5 × 150m)	
	210		210

SHARE PREMIUM

	£m		£m
1/9/X5 Bonus issue	50	Bal b/f	80
(1/2 × 100m)		1/1/X6 Rights issues	30
Bal c/f	60	(90m - 60m)	
	110		110

15 A Item 1 is a provision. However item 2 is a contingent liability.

16 A Errors 2,3 and 4 are either completely omitted or a double entry has been made. Only error 1 will result in the trial balance not balancing.

17 C Interest charged increases the funds available to be appropriated.

18 B

Cost of sale $=$ $40,000 + 60,000 - 50,000$
$=$ $50,000$

Sales $=$ $50,000 \times 2$
$=$ $100,000$

Therefore 1 is possible, 2 is incorrect and 4 is incorrect. If stock costing £2,500 had been stolen, the cost of sales would be £47,500, giving the sales figure of £95,000 and so option 3 is also possible.

19 D
RENT RECEIVABLE

	£		£
Opening accruals	4,800	Opening prepayments	134,600
P&L	828,700	Cash received	834,600
Closing prepayments	144,400	Closing accruals	8,700
	977,900		977,900

20 A
PLCA

	£		£
Purchase returns	41,200	Opening balance	218,600
Cash paid	1,364,300	Purchases	1,268,600
Contras	48,000	Refunds	2,700
Discounts received	8,200		
Closing balance	128,200		
	1,589,900		1,589,900

40 Mixed bank VII

1 A You need to remove the entry from the sales account (debit sales £1,500,000). The credits will then be to share capital (£1,000,000) and share premium (£500,000).

2 D Dividends paid do not go through the profit and loss account or STRGL. Instead they are shown in the statement of movements on reserves (notes to the financial statements) and the cash flow statement.

3 D
RENTAL INCOME

	£		£
Accruals b/f	42,300	Prepayments b/f	102,600
P&L	858,600	Cash received	838,600
Prepayment c/f	88,700	Arrears c/f	48,400
	989,600		989,600

4 C In A and B the entries are reversed. D should not involve the use of a suspense account.

5 C Only items involving cash appear in a cash flow statement. Items 1 and 3 do not involve cash.

6	A	Rent from 1/12/X5 to 31/3/X6	$=\dfrac{120,000}{12}\times4$
			$=40,000$
		Rent from 1/4/X6 to 30/11/X6	$=\dfrac{144,000}{12}\times8$
			$=96,000$

$\therefore$ P&L $= 40,000 + 96,000$
$= \underline{136,000}$

Prepayment $= \dfrac{1}{12} \times £144,000 = \underline{£12,000}$

7   A

	£
Trade debtors	863,000
Irrecoverable debts w/off	(23,000)
	840,000
Allowance for debtors (5% × 840,000)	42,000
Existing allowance	49,000
$\therefore$ decrease required	(7,000)

Charge to P&L = 23,000 - 7,000
= 16,000

8   C

SHARE CAPITAL

	£		£
		Balance b/f	1,000,000
		New issue	500,000
Balance c/f	2,000,000	Bonus issue (1/3 × 3m)	500,000
	2,000,000		2,000,000

SHARE PREMIUM

	£		£
Bonus issue	500,000	Balance b/f	1,400,000
Balance c/f	1,800,000	New issue	900,000
	2,300,000		2,300,000

New issue

1,000,000 shares of 50p each = £500,000 share capital. Proceeds of £1,400,000 received, so share premium = £900,000.

Bonus issue

1,000,000 share of 50p each = £500,000

9   C   Statement 1 is incorrect. Stock is valued at the lower of cost and net realisable value.

10   B

	£
Held all year ((960,000 - 84,000) × 20%)	175,200
Purchase 1/7/X6 (48,000 × 20% × ½)	4,800
Sale 30/9/X6 (84,000 × 20% × ¾)	12,600
	192,600

11   B   Errors 2 and 3 will result in the trial balance not balancing and so will require a suspense account entry.

12   D   The debit is to drawings and the credit (at cost price) is to purchases.

13   A   All three statements are correct.

14   D   All adjusting events are reflected in the financial statements and so do not need to be disclosed by note.

15	C	The tax charge goes through the P&L account, while the unrealised surplus on revaluation goes through the STRGL.
16	D	Only D is correct.
17	D	The decrease in debtors should be added and the increase in creditors should also be added.
18	C	Interest charged on partners' drawings increases the profits available for appropriation.
19	C	

	£
Salary (40,000 × ½)	20,000
Interest on capital (200,000 × 5%)	10,000
Profit share ((337,500 - 20,000 - 10,000 – 7,500) × ½)	150,000
	180,000

20	D	Only in the cash flow statement.
21	B	Difference is £12,780 credit. Only B accounts for this correctly.

41 Mixed bank VIII

1

A

	Jill £	John £	Total £
Net profit	–	–	28,650
Interest on drawings	(200)	(350)	550
Salary	5,000	–	(5,000)
Adjusted profit			24,200
PSR (3:2)	14,520	9,680	
	19,320	9,330	

2

A

3

D

SUSPENSE ACCOUNT

	£		£
Cash	1,512	Bal b/f	759
		Receivables	131
		Bal c/f	622
	1,512		1,512

4

A   Selling price = £3,200 × 90% = £2,880. Early settlement discount = 2% × £2,880 = £57.60.

5

B

PETTY CASH ACCOUNT

	£		£
Bal b/f	100.00	Stamps	16.35
Staff sales	12.00	Coffee and tea	18.23
		Birthday cards for staff	20.20
		Bal c/f	57.22
	112.00		112.00

6

> **Examiner's comments**. The correct answer is C although only 30% of students who answered this question correctly selected this answer. The remaining responses were evenly spread across the other three answers. This suggests that students have problems dealing with the effect of accruals and prepayments.
>
> The actual calculation of the accrual and prepayment is straightforward as reading the information carefully should enable students to arrive at an accrual for rent and a prepayment for insurance. It is very important to read the dates carefully to avoid unnecessary errors.
>
> The question asks for the net effect on the profit for the year, so once the accrual and prepayment have been calculated the last step should be very easy and it is worrying that so many students failed to work this out. An accrual is an additional expense and hence will reduce profit, whereas a prepayment is an expense paid in advance so when adjusted will increase profit.
>
> This is a key area in this paper and questions will often go beyond the simple calculation of an accrual and prepayment to ask for the effect on profit or assets / liabilities so students must ensure they are prepared for this.

C

	£
Rent accruals (4/12 × £12,000)	(4,000)
Insurance prepayment (10/12 × £6,000)	5,000
Net increase in profit	1,000

Answers to objective test questions

42 Accounting principles and regulation

1   1 and 3

2   1 and 4

3   1 and 3. Policy 1 because research expenditure should be written off to P & L and 3 since purchased goodwill is shown as an asset and written down when impaired.

4   The employee group

5   ☑   Consistency

6   ☑   False. Although the shareholder needs to know the future prospects, he also needs to know that the current position of the company is secure. Similarly the supplier needs to know the future prospects to ensure that he will be paid.

7   None. All of the suggestions are flawed. Obsolete stock should be provided for under the concepts of prudence and consistency. If no depreciation is allowed for, this assumes that there is no reduction in useful life over the past year (which is very unlikely). Therefore not to allow for depreciation is inconsistent and imprudent. Accounting standards require research costs to be written off in the year they are incurred. To discontinue the allowance for debtors would break the principles of matching, prudence and consistency.

43 Preparing financial accounts

1   ☑   A

		Debit	Credit	£
	Sales price			800
	Less: 20% trade discount			120
	Sale	PQ Ltd	Sales	640
	Cash discount 5%	Discount allowed		32
	Cash payment	Bank		608
			PQ Ltd	640

2   £22,000

Reconstruction of the trading account

	£	£
Sales		40,000
Returns inwards		(2,000)
		38,000
Opening stock	3,000	
Purchases	20,000	
Returns outwards	(4,000)	
Closing stock	(3,000)	
		(16,000)
Gross profit		22,000

3   £87,700

Diesel fuel payable account	£	Cost of fuel used	£
Balance b/fwd	(1,700)	Opening stock	12,500
Payments	85,400	Purchases	85,000
Balance c/fwd	1,300	Closing stock	(9,800)
Purchases	85,000	Transfer to P & L	87,700

4   ☑   D. It reduces debtors.

5   £80.70

Stationery	14.10
Travel	25.50
Refreshments	12.90
Sundry creditors (£24 × 1.175)	28.20
	80.70

£

6   £2,185. Prepayment b/f £60 (2/3 × 90) + £2,145 – prepayment c/f £60 – accrual b/f £80 + accrual c/f £120 = £2,185.

7   1, 3 and 5. In option 2, debtors and drawings are debits but discount received is a credit. In option 4, capital and trade creditors are credits but operating expenses are debits.

8   £418

Profit £1,051 = Drawings + £733 – £100
£1,051 - £733 + £100   = Drawings = £418

9   £205

Profit = Drawings + Increase in net assets – Capital introduced
        = £77 + £173 – £45
        = £205

10   £21

Capital + Liabilities = Assets
Capital + £153 = £174
Therefore, Capital = £21

11   £130 loss

Capital = Assets - Liabilities
£50 + £100 + profit for the year = £90 – £70
£150 + profit for the year = £20
Therefore, the profit for the year is in fact a *loss* of £130.

12   (a)   £544

SALES BOOK

20X9		£
1 May	P Dixon	160
4 May	M Maguire	80
5 May	M Donald	304
		544

(b)   £823

PURCHASES BOOK

20X9		£
2 May	A Clarke (W1)	323
4 May	D Daley	400
6 May	G Perkins	100
		823

(c) £177 overdraft

CASH BOOK

20X9		Bank £	Cash £	Dis-count £	20X9		Bank £	Cash £	Dis-count £
1 May	Balance b/d		224		1 May	Balance b/d	336		
1 May	Cash withdrawal		50		1 May	Cash withdrawal	50		
3 May	Cash sales		45		2 May	R Hill (W2)	108		12
5 May	H Larkin	180		20	4 May	Telephone bill	210		
6 May	D Randle	482			5 May	Honour Ltd	135		
6 May	Balance c/d	177			6 May	Balance c/d		319	
		839	319	20			839	319	12
7 May	Balance b/d		319		7 May	Balance b/d	177		

Workings

1    $£380 \times \dfrac{85}{100} = £323$

2    $£120 \times \dfrac{100-10}{100} = £108$

13   [✓]   A   X is a debtors of Y.

14   £47,429

SALES LEDGER CONTROL

20X8		£	20X8		£
1 Dec	Balance b/d	50,241		Returns inwards	41,226
	Sales	472,185		Irrecoverable debts written off	1,914
	Cheques dishonoured	626		Discounts allowed	2,672
				Cheques received	429,811
			30 Nov	Balance c/d	47,429
		523,052			523,052

15   £47,429

	£	£
Balance per P Johnson		46,347
Add: Whitchurch Ltd invoice, previously omitted from ledger	267	
Rectofen Ltd balance, previously omitted from list	2,435	
Casting error in list total (£46,747, not £46,347)	400	
		3,102
		49,449
Less: Error on posting of Bury Plc's credit note to ledger	20	
P Fox & Son (Swindon) Ltd's balance included twice	2,000	
		2,020
Balance per sales ledger control account		47,429

16   £130,585

PURCHASE LEDGER CONTROL ACCOUNT

	£		£
Returns outwards	27,490	Balance b/f	142,320
Payments to creditors	196,360	Credit purchases (183,800 × 1.175)	215,965
Discount received	1,430		
Contra	2,420		
Balance c/f	130,585		
	358,285		358,285
		Balance b/f	130,585

17   £1,681

CASH BOOK

20X8		£	20X8		£
31 Dec	Balance b/d	1,793	31 Dec	Bank charges	18
31 Dec	Dividend	26		Standing order	32
				Direct debit	88
				Balance c/d	1,681
		1,819			1,819

18   £2,098

BANK RECONCILIATION

	£	£
Balance per bank statement		(2,954)
Add: outstanding lodgements	6,816	
cheque debited in error	510	
direct debit paid in error	1,000	
		8,326
		5,372
Less: unpresented cheques		(7,470)
Balance per cash book		(2,098)

Although the question does not ask you to prepare the revised cash book, this is shown below to prove the above figure.

CASH BOOK

20X3		£	20X3		£
31 May	Balance b/d	873	31 May	Bank charges	630
	Error £(936 – 693)	243		Trade journals	52
	Balance c/d	2,098		Insurance	360
				Business rates	2,172
		3,214			3,214
			1 May	Balance b/d	2,098

19   ✓   B   The cash book was credited with £210 reimbursement of petty cash. However, the nominal ledger was posted with only £200 of expenditure debits. Therefore the credits are £10 higher than the debits.

		Debit £	Credit £
Date			
18 October	Motor vehicle servicing costs	124	
	Motor vehicles at cost		124
	Purchase ledger control	40	
	Bank		40

(**Note.** You must both correct the misposting and post the entry correctly - so the bank balance is credited by 2 × £20, not just £20.)

October 20	Purchases	425	
	Purchase ledger control		425

21   £9,600 debit

SUSPENSE ACCOUNT

	£		£
		Balance b/d	14,000
Discounts received	14,000	Discounts allowed	6,000
Current a/c – partner's wife	9,600	Creditors control a/c	3,600
	23,600		23,600

22   ✓   False. Accounting packages are generally **ready made programs** written to maintain a business accounting system. They are not usually tailored to individual businesses.

23   Database

44 Accounting conventions and standards

1   £87 loss

	£
NBV: 9,000 × 0.7 × 0.7 × 0.7	3,087
Proceeds of sale	(3,000)
Loss on disposal	87

2   ✓   False. Depreciation is a means of allocating the cost of an asset over its useful life.

3   Going concern concept

4   £360 loss

	£
NBV (£5,000 × 0.8 × 0.8 × 0.8)*	2,560
Proceeds	(2,200)
Loss on disposal	360

* Remember this is the reducing balance method, the residual value is included in the 20% rate.

5   ✓   A   Depreciation is an application of the accruals principle.

6   £1,500 loss

	£
NBV (£64,000 × 0.5 × 0.5 × 0.5 × 0.5)	4,000
Proceeds	(2,500)
Loss	1,500

7   ✓   A   ie NBV £20,000

8   ✓   D   The reducing balance method charges more depreciation in earlier years.

9   (a)   £450

$$\text{Annual depreciation} = \frac{\text{Cost minus residual value}}{\text{Estimated economic life}}$$

$$= \frac{£1,800 - £0}{4 \text{ years}}$$

$$= £450$$

(b)   £1,080

The reducing balance method at 60% per annum involves the following calculations.

	£
Cost at 1.1.20X1	1,800
Depreciation 20X1 (60% × £1,800)	1,080
Book value 1.1.20X2	720

10 £113 profit

	£
Received from sale of laser printer	200
Net book value at date of disposal (see below)	87
Profit on disposal	113

	£
Cost at 1.1. 20X1	1,800
Depreciation 20X1 (£1,800 × 60%)	1,080
	720
Depreciation 20X2 (£720 × 60%)	432
	288
Depreciation 20X3 (288 × 60%)	173
	115
Depreciation 20X4 (£115 × 6/12 ×60%)	35
Net book value	80

11 (a)   £1,187 loss

(b)   £650 profit

MOTOR VEHICLES AT COST

		£			£
01.10.X0	Balance b/f	10,000	24.04.X1	Disposals (MV05)	4,000
31.01.X1	Motor van (MV11)	9,000	30.09.X1	Balance c/f	15,000
		19,000			19,000
01.10.X1	Balance b/f	15,000	31.08.X2	Disposals (MV11)	9,000
20.02.X2	Motor van (MV12)	12,000	30.09.X2	Balance c/f	32,000
31.08.X2	Motor van (MV13)	14,000			
		41,000			41,000
01.10.X2	Balance b/f	32,000			

ALLOWANCE FOR DEPRECIATION OF MOTOR VEHICLES

		£			£
24.04.X1	Disposals (W1)	2,313	01.10.X0	b/f	4,000
30.09.X1	c/f	5,015	30.01.X1	Allowance (W2)	3,328
		7,328			7,328
31.08.X2	Disposals (W3)	2,250	01.10.X1	b/f	5,015
30.09.X2	c/f	10,074	30.09.X2	Allowance (W4)	7,309
		12,324			12,324

DISPOSALS

		£			£
24.04.X1	MV05	4,000	24.04.X1	Depreciation (MV05)	2,313
			24.04.X1	Cash	500
			30.09.X1	I/S	1,187
		4,000			4,000
31.08.X2	MV11	9,000	31.08.X2	Depreciation (MV11)	2,250
31.09.X2	I/S	650		Trade-in allowance	7,400
		9,650			9,650

Workings

1   *Depreciation on motor van MV05*

	Net book value £	Depreciation £
Cost (January 20W8)	4,000	
Depreciation – September 20W8 (25%)	(1,000)	1,000
	3,000	
Depreciation – September 20W9 (25%)	(750)	750
	2,250	
Depreciation – September 20X0 (25%)	(563)	563
	1,687	2,313

2   *Depreciation allowance 20X1*

	£
Cost at year end	15,000
Depreciation provision (4,000 – 2,313)	(1,687)
	13,313

Depreciation charge at 25% = 3,328

3   *Depreciation on motor van MV11*

	Net book value £	£
Cost – January 20X1	9,000	
Depreciation – September 20X1 (25%)	(2,250)	2,250
	6,750	2,250

4   *Depreciation allowance 20X2*

	£
Cost at year end	32,000
Accumulated depreciation (5,015 – 2,250)	(2,765)
	29,235

Depreciation charge at 25% = 7,309

12   (a)   £2,000

(b)   £12,675

(c)   £1,300 loss

BUILDINGS (COST) ACCOUNT

		£
1.4.X7	Balance b/f	80,000

PLANT (COST) ACCOUNT

		£			£
1.4.X7	Balance b/f	144,000		Disposal account	26,000
	Bank	17,000	31.3.X8	Balance c/f	169,000
	Bank (W1)	34,000			
		195,000			195,000
1.4.X8	Balance b/f	169,000			

BUILDINGS DEPRECIATION ACCOUNT

		£			£
31.3.X8	Balance c/f	20,000	1.4.X7	Balance b/f	18,000
			31.3.X8	P & L (W2)	2,000
		20,000			20,000
			1.4.X8	Balance b/f	20,000

PLANT DEPRECIATION ACCOUNT

		£			£
31.3.X8	Disposal a/c	11,700	1.4.X7	Balance b/f	76,200
31.3.X8	Balance c/f	77,175	31.3.X8	P & L (W2)	12,675
		88,875			88,875
			1.4.X8	Balance b/f	77,175

Workings

1 £

Machine F

	£
Cost	42,300
Less: VAT $\left(\dfrac{42,300}{1.175} \times 0.175\right)$	(6,300)
	36,000
Less maintenance	(2,000)
	34,000

2 Buildings depreciation: £80,000 × 2.5% = £2,000
   Plant depreciation: £169,000 × 7.5% = £12,675

FIXED ASSET DISPOSAL ACCOUNT

		£			£
31.3.X8	Plant	26,000	31.3.X8	Plant depreciation a/c	11,700
				A Jones	13,000
				Loss on disposal	1,300
		26,000			26,000

13 *FIFO*

Closing stock £1,700

Year 1

Purchases units	Sales units	Balance units	Stock value £	Unit cost £	Cost of sales £	Sales £
10		10	3,000	300		
12			3,000	250		
		22	6,000			
	8		(2,400)		2,400	3,200
		14	3,600			
6			1,200	200		
		20	4,800			
	12		(3,100)*		3,100	4,800
		8	1,700		5,500	8,000

* 2 @ £300 + 10 @ £250 = £3,100

Cost of sales £5,500

Year 2

Purchases units	Sales units	Balance units	Stock value £	Unit cost £	Cost of sales £	Sales £
B/f		8	1,700			
10			2,000	200		
		18	3,700			
	5		(1,100)*		1,100	2,000
		13	2,600			
12		25	1,800	150		
			4,400			
25			(4,400)**		4,400	10,000
		0	0		5,500	12,000

* 2 @ £250 + 3 @ £200 = £1,100
** 13 @ £200 + 12 @ £150 = £4,400

14 (a) **Events after the balance sheet date**

☑ False

These are defined in FRS 21 as 'those events, both favourable and unfavourable, that occur between the balance sheet date and the date when the financial statements are authorised for issue.' Events after the balance sheet date may be either adjusting or non-adjusting in nature.

An appendix to FRS 21 cites a number of events after the balance sheet date which normally should be classified as adjusting events. The insolvency of a receivable is specifically included, since it is an event which provides additional evidence of a condition existing at the balance sheet date.

Under the requirements of FRS 21 a provision for this irrecoverable debt should be made in the financial statements.

  (b) **Contingency**

☑ No

FRS 12, states that an entity should never recognise a contingent liability. The FRS requires a contingent liability to be disclosed by way of note, unless the possibility of any outflow of economic benefits to settle it is remote.

The FRS also states that a provision should be recognised only when an entity has an obligation that requires the transfer of economic benefits in settlement which can be measured sufficiently reliably.

As the claim is unlikely to succeed, the potential settlement of £500,000 should be disclosed as a contingent liability note. However, given that the legal costs of £50,000 must be paid whether the claim is successful or not, this amount should be provided for in the company's financial statements.

15   ✓ No

FRS 21 makes a distinction between

(i)   **Adjusting events**, that provide evidence of conditions that existed at balance sheet date (eg receipt of money from a customer whose debt had been regarded as an irrecoverable debt).

(ii) **Non-adjusting events**, that are indicative of conditions that arose after the balance sheet date (eg a new issue of shares).

FRS 21 requires that:

(i)   If there is an **adjusting event** which materially affects the view of conditions existing at the balance sheet date the amounts to be included in the financial statements should be amended to reflect the event.

(ii) If there is a **non-adjusting** event which is of such material significance that not to report it would prevent users of the financial statements from reaching a proper understanding of the financial position, it should be disclosed by way of note to the accounts. The note should describe the nature of the event and an estimate of its financial effect (or a statement that it is not practicable to make such an estimate).

It would appear that the directors are treating a non-adjusting event as an adjusting event. The decision to close the branch was not made until after the year end.

If, however, the branch was so material to the company as a whole that its closure meant that the company was no longer a going concern, it would have to be treated as an adjusting event.

45 Final accounts and cash flow statements

1   (a)   £154,610 (W1)
     (b)   £80,940 (W3)
     (c)   £1,350 (W5)
     (d)   £3,620 (W6)

Workings

1   *Sales*
	£
Cash sales banked	108,600
Taken as drawings	15,600
Credit sales (per W2)	30,360
Increase in cash balance (150 – 100)	50
	154,610

2   *Credit sales*

SALES LEDGER CONTROL ACCOUNT

	£		£
Opening debtors	4,270	Cash from customers	28,440
Sales	30,360	Closing debtors	6,190
	34,630		34,630

3   *Cost of sales*

	£
Opening stock	680
Purchases (W4)	81,070
	81,750
Closing stock	810
	80,940

4   Purchases

		£
Purchases – per bank summary		81,470
Less: personal consumption		400
		81,070

5   Insurance

		£
Balance b/f @ 1.7.X6		300
Paid in year		1,400
Balance c/f @ 30.6.X7		(350)
Profit and loss account		1,350

6   Depreciation

	£
Refrigeration equipment (10% × £8,400)	840
Shop fittings ((1,630 + 1,570) × 15%)	480
Van (25% × £9,200)	2,300
	3,620

2 (a) £75,000 (W2)
    (b) £52,000 (W3)
    (c) £97,000 overdrawn (W4)

Workings

1   CREDITORS

	£'000		£'000
Bank	560	Balance b/d (£130,000 ÷ 2)	65
Balance c/d	130	∴ Purchases	625
	690		690

2   COST OF SALES

	£'000		£'000
∴ Opening stock	75	Closing stock	100
Purchases (W1)	625	P & L	600
	700		700

3   DEBTORS

	£'000		£'000
∴ Balance b/d	52	Bank	950
Sales	1,000	Irrecoverable debts written off	2
		Balance c/d	100
	1,052		1,052

4   BANK

	£'000		£'000
Debtors	950	Opening balance	97
		Creditors	560
		Plant and machinery – cost	90
		Operating expenses	130
		Drawings	20
		Balance c/d	53
	950		950

3   (a)   Interest on partners' drawings for the year ended 31 May 20X9

	Ganatri		£
	31.8.X8	£10,000 × 12% × $\frac{9}{12}$	900
	30.11.X8	£10,000 × 12% × $\frac{6}{12}$	600
	28.2.X9	£10,000 × 12% × $\frac{3}{12}$	300
			1,800

	Lucifer		£
	31.8.X8	£7,000 × 12% × $\frac{9}{12}$	630
	30.11.X8	£7,000 × 12% × $\frac{6}{12}$	420
	28.2.X9	£7,000 × 12% × $\frac{3}{12}$	210
			1,260

	Total	3,060

(b)   GANATRI AND LUCIFER
APPROPRIATION ACCOUNT
FOR THE YEAR ENDED 31 MAY 20X9

	£	£
Net profit b/d		102,940
Add: interest on drawings paid to partnership		3,060
		106,000
Less: salary – Lucifer		15,000
Less: interest on capital and current accounts		
– Ganatri (12% × £215,000)	25,800	
– Lucifer (12% × £153,000)	18,360	
		44,160
		46,840
Profit share:		
Ganatri (7/10)	32,788	
Lucifer (3/10)	14,052	
		46,840

(c)   PARTNERS' CURRENT ACCOUNTS

	Ganatri £	Lucifer £		Ganatri £	Lucifer £
Drawings	40,000	28,000	Balances b/d	15,000	13,000
Interest on			Salary	–	15,000
drawings	1,800	1,260	Interest on capital		
Balances c/d	31,788	31,152	and current		
			accounts	25,800	18,360
			Profit share	32,788	14,052
	73,588	60,412		73,588	60,412
			Balance b/f	31,788	31,152

4   (a)   Ordinary: £26,000 (W1)
           Preference: £4,000 (W2)

     (b)   £30,000 (W3)

     (c)   £50,000 (W4)

Workings

1   *Ordinary dividend*

     Shares: 100,000 + 30,000 = £130,000

     Dividend at 20p per share = £26,000

2   *Preference dividend*

£40,000 @ 10% = <u>4,000</u>

3   *Share premium account*

30,000 £1 ordinary shares issued at £2 per share, therefore, share premium = £1 per share.

4   *Revaluation reserve*

	£
Bal b/f	45,000
Revaluation of land (£130,000 – £125,000)	<u>5,000</u>
	<u>50,000</u>

5   (a)   £123,000. Research expenditure £103,000 + depreciation of development costs £20,000.

      (b)   £219,000. Development costs b/f £180,000 + additions on project 910 £59,000 – depreciation £20,000.

6   (a)   Net cash inflow from operating activities £151,000 (note)

      (b)   *Capital expenditure*

	£
Purchase of fixed assets (W2)	180,000
Proceeds of sale of fixed assets	<u>(25,000)</u>
	<u>155,000</u>

Note. Reconciliation of profit before tax to net cash inflow from operating activities.

	£'000
Profit before taxation (W1)	59
Depreciation (W2)	100
Interest expense	10
Profit on sale of fixed assets	(5)
Interest paid	(10)
Increase in stock	(9)
Decrease in debtors	4
Increase in creditors	<u>2</u>
Net cash inflow from operating activities	<u>151</u>

Workings

1   *Profit before taxation*

	£'000
Retained profit for year (203 – 176)	27
Interim dividend	10
Final dividend	<u>22</u>
Profit before taxation	<u>59</u>

2   *Movements in fixed assets*

FIXED ASSETS – COST

	£'000		£'000
Balance b/f	600	Disposal – transfer	100
Revaluation	50	Balance c/f	730
New assets purchased (bal fig)	180		
	<u>830</u>		<u>830</u>

FIXED ASSETS – DEPRECIATION

	£'000		£'000
Disposal – transfer	80	Balance b/f	220
Balance c/f	<u>240</u>	Profit and loss account (bal fig)	<u>100</u>
	<u>320</u>		<u>320</u>

FIXED ASSETS – DISPOSAL

	£'000		£'000
Cost	100	Depreciation	80
Profit and loss account (bal fig)	5	Proceeds of sales	25
	105		105

			£'000
7	(a)	Taxation (W1)	(110)
	(b)	Net cash inflow from operating activities (W2)	223
	(c)	Net cash flow from investing activities (W3)	(20)
	(d)	Net cash flow from financing activities (W4)	160

Workings

1 *Tax paid*

TAX

	£'000			£'000
Tax paid	110	1.1.X2	Balance b/d	110
			Profit and loss account	
			140 – (70 – 50)*	120
31.12.X2 Balance c/d	120			
	230			230

* The taxation charge in the profit and loss account includes the increase in deferred taxation provision. This must be excluded when calculating the amount of tax paid.

2 *Reconciliation of profit before tax to net cash from operating activities*

	£'000
Profit before tax	300
Depreciation charge (W5)	90
Interest expense	50
Loss on sale of tangible fixed assets (45 – 32)	13
Profit on sale of investments	(5)
Increase/decrease in stocks	(48)
Increase/decrease in debtors	(75)
Increase/decrease in creditors	8
Cash generated from operations	333
Interest paid	(75)
Tax paid	(110)
Net cash from operating activities	148

3 *Net cash flow from investing activities*

	£'000
Interest received	25
Proceeds of sale of fixed asset investments	30
	55

4 *Net cash flow from financing activities*

Issue of ordinary share capital	60	
Issue of long-term loan	100	
		160

5 *Depreciation charge*

	£'000	£'000
Depreciation at 31 December 20X2		340
Depreciation 31 December 20X1	290	
Depreciation on assets sold (85 – 45)	(40)	
		250
Charge for the year		90

Mock exams

ACCA Fundamentals Level
Paper F3 (UK)
Financial Accounting

Mock Examination 1

Question Paper	
Time allowed	2 hours
ALL FIFTY questions are compulsory and MUST be attempted	

DO NOT OPEN THIS PAPER UNTIL YOU ARE READY TO START UNDER EXAMINATION CONDITIONS

ALL FIFTY questions are compulsory and MUST be attempted

1   The following information was disclosed in the financial statements of Highfield Ltd for the year ended 31/12/20X2

	20X1 £	20X2 £
Plant & Equipment cost	255,000	235,000
Accumulated depreciation	(100,000)	(110,000)

During 20X2, the following occurred in respect of Plant & Equipment:

	£
Purchases of P&E	10,000
Depreciation charged on P&E	25,000
Loss on disposal of P&E	8,000

What were the sales proceeds received on disposal of the P&E?

A   £7,000
B   £15,000
C   £25,000
D   £8,000   (2 marks)

2   The debit side of a trial balance totals £400 more than the credit side.

Which one of the following errors would fully account for the difference?

A   £200 paid for building repairs has been correctly entered in the cashbook and credited to the building fixed asset account.

B   Discount received £200 has been debited to the discount allowed account

C   A receipt of £400 for commission receivable has been omitted from the records.   (1 mark)

3   Under the Companies Act, which of the following **must** be disclosed on the *face* of the profit and loss account:

A   Profit before tax
B   Gross profit
C   Sales
D   Dividends.   (2 marks)

4   Rory and Tony have traded as partners for a number of years. Their balance sheet as at 30 June 20X2 shows:

	£	£
Capital accounts		
Rory		45,000
Tony		37,000
		82,000
Current accounts		
Rory	19,214	
Tony	8,632	
		27,846
		109,846

During the year the business made a profit of £41,320, the partners took drawings of £12,000 each and fixed assets were revalued upwards by £25,000. The net asset total as at 1 July 20X1 was

A   £67,526
B   £92,526
C   £127,166
D   £152,166   (2 marks)

5   The following bank reconciliation has been prepared:

	£
Balance per bank statement (overdrawn)	73,680
Add: Outstanding lodgements	102,480
Less: Outstanding cheques	(87,240)
Balance per cash book (credit)	88,920

Assuming the amounts stated for items other than the cash book balance are correct, what should the cash book balance be?

A   £88,920 credit (as stated)
B   £120,040 credit
C   £58,440 debit
D   £58,440 credit   **(2 marks)**

6   In relation to cash flow statements, which, if any, of the following are correct?

1   The direct method of calculating net cash from operating activities leads to a different figure from that produced by the indirect method, but this is balanced elsewhere in the cash flow statement.

2   A company making high profits must necessarily have a net cash inflow from operating activities.

3   Profits and losses on disposals of fixed assets appear as items under cash flows from investing activities in the cash flow statement or a note to it.

A   Item 1 only
B   Items 2 and 3
C   None of the items   **(1 mark)**

7   Panther owns her own business selling Gladiator dolls to department stores. At 30 June 20X2 she had the following balances in her books:

	£
Trade debtors	31,450
Allowance for debtors (General)	(450)
(as at 1 July 20X1)	
	31,000

A balance of £1,000 due from Selfrodges Ltd is considered irrecoverable and is to be written off. Horrids Ltd was in financial difficulty and Panther wished to provide for 60% of their balance of £800. She also decided to make a general provision of 10% on her remaining trade debtors. What was the allowance for debtors in her balance sheet at 30 June 20X2?

A   £3,477
B   £3,765
C   £3,445
D   £3,545   **(2 marks)**

8   Curtis and Sillett are in partnership, sharing profits in the ratio 3:2 and compiling their accounts to 30 June each year.

On 1 January 20X2, Mcallister joined the partnership, and from that the date the profit sharing ratio became Curtis 50%, Sillett 25% and Mcallister 25%, after providing for salaries for Sillet and Mcallister of £20,000 and £12,000 pa respectively.

The partnership profit for the year ended 30 June 20X2 was £480,000, accruing evenly over the year.

What are the partners' total profit shares for the year ended June 20X2?

	Curtis	Sillett	Mcallister
A	256,000	162,000	62,000
B	248,000	168,000	64,000
C	264,000	166,000	66,000
D	264,000	156,000	60,000

                                                                                                              (2 marks)

9   Which of the following items could appear on the credit side of a sales ledger control account?

1   cash received from customers
2   irrecoverable debts written off
3   increase in the allowance for debtors
4   discounts allowed
5   sales
6   credits for goods returned by customers
7   cash refunds to customers

A   1, 2, 4, and 6
B   1, 2, 4 and 7
C   3, 4, 5 and 6   **(1 mark)**

---

10   A business has compiled the following information for the year ended 31 October 20X2:

	£
Opening stocks	386,200
Purchases	989,000
Closing stocks	422,700

The gross profit percentage of sales is 40%

What is the sales figure for the year?

A   £1,333,500
B   £1,587,500
C   £2,381,250
D   The sales figure is impossible to calculate from this information.   **(2 marks)**

---

11   On 30 September 20X1 part of the stock of a company was completely destroyed by fire.

The following information is available:

–   Stock at 1 September 20X1 at cost £49,800
–   Purchases for September 20X1 £88,600
–   Sales for September 20X1 £130,000
–   Stock at 30 September 20X1 – undamaged items £32,000
–   Standard gross profit percentage on sales 30%

Based on this information, what is the cost of the stock destroyed?

A   £17,800
B   £47,400
C   £15,400
D   £6,400   **(2 marks)**

---

12   Catt sells goods at a margin of 50%. During the year to 31 March 20X3 the business made purchases totalling £134,025 and sales totalling £240,000. Stocks in hand at 31 March 20X3, valued at cost, was £11,385 higher than the corresponding figure at 1 April 20X2. Catt had drawn out goods costing

A   £2,640
B   £14,590
C   £25,410
D   £37,360   **(2 marks)**

---

13   At 1 July 20X0 the share capital and share premium account of a company were as follows:

	£
Share capital – 300,000 ordinary shares of 25p each	75,000
Share premium account	200,000

During the year ended 30 June 20X1 the following events took place:

1   On 1 January 20X1 the company made a rights issue of one share for every five held, at £1.20 per share.
2   On 1 April 20X1 the company made a bonus (capitalisation) issue of one share for every three in issue at that time, using the share premium account to do so.

What are the correct balances on the company's share capital and share premium accounts at 30 June 20X1?

	Share capital	Share premium account
A	£460,000	£287,000
B	£480,000	£137,000
C	£120,000	£137,000
D	£120,000	£227,000

(2 marks)

14   A cash flow statement prepared in accordance with FRS 1 *Cash flow statements* opens with the calculation of cash flows from operating activities from the net profit before taxation.

Which of the following lists of items consists only of items that would be ADDED to net profit before taxation in that calculation?

A   Decrease in stocks, depreciation, profit on sale of fixed assets.
B   Increase in trade creditors, decrease in trade debtors, profit on sale of fixed assets.
C   Loss on sale of fixed assets, depreciation, increase in trade debtors.
D   Decrease in trade debtors, increase in trade creditors, loss on sale of fixed assets.

(2 marks)

15   The issued share capital of Maelstrom Ltd is as follows:

Ordinary shares of 10p each	1,000,000
8% preference shares of 50p each	500,000

In the year ended 31 October 20X2, the company has paid the preference dividend for the year and an interim dividend of 2p per share on the ordinary shares. A final ordinary dividend of 3p per share is declared on 30 October 20X2.

What is the total amount of dividends relating to the year ended 31 October 20X2?

A   £580,000
B   £90,000
C   £130,000
D   £540,000

(2 marks)

16   When a company makes a rights issue of equity shares which of the following effects will the issue have?

(1)   Working capital is increased.
(2)   Gearing ratio is increased.
(3)   Share premium account is reduced.
(4)   Investments are increased.

A   1 only
B   1 and 2
C   3 only
D   1 and 4

(2 marks)

17   The following information relates to Eva Ltd's VAT for the month of March 20X3:

	£
Sales (including VAT)	109,250
Purchases (net of VAT)	64,000

VAT is charged at a flat rate of 15%. Eva Ltd's VAT account showed an opening credit balance of £4,540 at the beginning of the month and a closing debit balance of £2,720 at the end of the month.

What was the total VAT paid to regulatory authorities during the month of March 20X3?

A   £6,470.00
B   £11,910.00
C   £14,047.50
D   £13,162.17   **(2 marks)**

18   Which of the following may appear as current liabilities in a company's balance sheet?

(1)   Minority interest
(2)   Loan due for repayment within 1 year
(3)   Corporation tax payable
(4)   Preference dividends payable

A   1,2 and 3
B   1,2 and 4
C   1,3 and 4
D   2,3 and 4   **(2 marks)**

19   Which of the following errors would cause a trial balance imbalance?

(i)   The discounts received column of the cash payments book was overcast.
(ii)   Cash paid for the purchase of office furniture was debited to the general expenses account
(iii)   Returns inwards were included on the credit side of the trial balance

A   (i) only
B   (i) and (ii)
C   (iii) only   **(1 mark)**

20   On 1 September 2006, a business had stock of £380,000. During the month, sales totaled £650,000 and purchases £480,000. On 30 September 2006 a fire destroyed some of the stock. The undamaged goods in stock were valued at £220,000. The business operates with a standard gross profit margin of 30%.

Based on this information, what is the cost of the stock destroyed in the fire?

A   £185,000
B   £140,000
C   £405,000
D   £360,000   **(2 marks)**

21   A company had the following transactions:

1   Goods in stock that had cost £1,000 were sold for £1,500 cash.
2   A credit customer whose £500 debt had been written off paid the amount in full.
3   The company paid credit suppliers £1,000

What will be the combined effect of these transactions on the company's total working capital (current assets less current liabilities)?

A   Increase of £1,000
B   Working capital remains unchanged
C   Increase of £2,000   **(1 mark)**

22   Which of the following should appear as items in a company's statement of movements in reserves?

1   Profit for the financial year
2   Income from investments
3   Gain on revaluation of fixed assets
4   Dividends paid

A   1, 3 and 4
B   1 and 4 only
C   2 and 3 only
D   1, 2 and 3   **(2 marks)**

23   The following information is available about a company's dividends:

                                             £

2005
Sept.   Final dividend for the year ended
            30 June 2005 paid (declared August 2005)   100,000

2006
March   Interim dividend for the year ended
            30 June 2006 paid   40,000

Sept.   Final dividend for the year ended
            30 June 2006 paid (declared August 2006)   20,000

What figures, if any, should be disclosed in the company's profit and loss account for the year ended 30 June 2006 and its balance sheet as at that date?

	Profit and loss account for the period	Balance sheet liability
A	£160,000 deduction	£120,000
B	£140,000 deduction	nil
C	nil	£120,000
D	nil	nil

                                                              (2 marks)

24   A and B are in partnership, sharing profits in the ratio 3:2 and preparing their accounts to 30 June each year. On 1 January 2006, C joined the partnership and the profit sharing ratio became A 40%, B 30%, and C 30%.

Profits for the year ended 30 June 2006 were:

                                            £

6 months ended 31 December 2005   300,000
6 months ended 30 June 2006   450,000

An irrecoverable debt of £50,000 was written off in the six months to 30 June in computing the £450,000 profit. It was agreed that this expense should be borne by A and B only, in their original profit-sharing ratios.

What is A's total profit share for the year ended 30 June 2006?

        £
A   330,000
B   310,000
C   340,000
D   350,000   **(2 marks)**

25   At 1 July 2005 a company's allowance for debtors was £48,000.

At 30 June 2006, trade debtors amounted to £838,000. It was decided to write off £72,000 of these debts and adjust the allowance for debtors to £60,000.

What are the final amounts for inclusion in the company's balance sheet at 30 June 2006?

	Trade debtors £	Allowance for debtors £	Net balance £
A	838,000	60,000	778,000
B	766,000	60,000	706,000
C	766,000	108,000	658,000
D	838,000	108,000	730,000

                                                              (2 marks)

26   Which of the following statements about stock valuation for balance sheet purposes are correct?

1   According to SSAP 9 *Stocks and Long-Term Contracts,* average cost and FIFO (first in and first out) are both acceptable methods of arriving at the cost of stocks.

2   Stocks of finished goods may be valued at labour and materials cost only, without including overheads.

3   Stocks should be valued at the lowest of cost, net realisable value and replacement cost.

4   It may be acceptable for stocks to be valued at selling price less estimated profit margin.

A   1 and 3
B   2 and 3
C   1 and 4
D   2 and 4   (1 mark)

27   A business received a delivery of goods on 29 June 2006, which was included in stock at 30 June 2006.

The invoice for the goods was recorded in July 2006.

What effect will this have on the business?

1   Profit for the year ended 30 June 2006 will be overstated.
2   Stock at 30 June 2006 will be understated.
3   Profit for the year ending 30 June 2007 will be overstated.
4   Stock at 30 June 2006 will be overstated.

A   1 and 2
B   2 and 3
C   1 only
D   1 and 4   (2 marks)

28   Which of the following statements are correct?

1   A company's authorised share capital must be included in its published balance sheet as part of shareholders' funds.

2   If a company makes a bonus issue of ordinary shares, the total shareholders' interest (share capital plus reserves) remains unchanged.

3   A company's statement of movements in reserves must include the proceeds of any share issue during the period.

4   A company must disclose its significant accounting policies by note to its financial statements.

A   1 and 2 only
B   1 and 3 only
C   3 and 4 only
D   2, 3 and 4   (2 marks)

29   Which, if any, of the following statements about intangible assets are correct?

1   Deferred development expenditure must be amortised over a period not exceeding five years.

2   If the conditions specified in FRS 10 are met, development expenditure may be capitalised, if the directors decide to do so.

3   Trade investments must appear in a company's balance sheet under the heading of intangible assets.

A   1 only
B   2 only
C   2 and 3
D   None of the statements is correct   (2 marks)

30   Which of the following characteristics of financial information contribute to reliability, according to the ASB's *Statement of Principles*?

1   Completeness
2   Prudence
3   Neutrality
4   Faithful representation

A   All four items
B   1, 2 and 3 only
C   1, 2 and 4 only
D   2, 3 and 4 only   **(2 marks)**

31   Details of a company's insurance policy are shown below:

Premium for year ended 31 March 2006 paid April 2005   £10,800
Premium for year ending 31 March 2007 paid April 2006   £12,000

What figures should be included in the company's financial statements for the year ended 30 June 2006?

	Profit and Loss account £	Balance sheet £
A	11,100	9,000 prepayment (Dr)
B	11,700	9,000 prepayment (Dr)
C	11,100	9,000 accrual (Cr)
D	11,700	9,000 accrual (Cr)

                                                                                                          (2 marks)

32   Which of the following statements about bank reconciliations are correct?

1   In preparing a bank reconciliation, unpresented cheques must be deducted from a balance of cash at bank shown in the bank statement.

2   A cheque from a customer paid into the bank but dishonored must be corrected by making a debit entry in the cash book.

3   An error by the bank must be corrected by an entry in the cash book.

4   An overdraft is a debit balance in the bank statement.

A   1 and 3
B   2 and 3
C   1 and 4
D   2 and 4   **(2 marks)**

33   At 30 June 2005 the capital and reserves of Meredith, a limited company, were:

	£m
Share capital	
Ordinary shares of £1 each	100
Share premium account	80

During the year ended 30 June 2006, the following transactions took place:

1 September 2005 A bonus issue of one ordinary share for every two held, using the share premium account.

1 January 2006 A fully subscribed rights issue of two ordinary shares for every five held at that date, at

£1.50 per share.

What would the balances on each account be at 30 June 2006?

	Share capital £m	Share premium account £m
A	210	110
B	210	60
C	240	30
D	240	80

(2 marks)

34 The following items have to be considered in finalising the financial statements of Q, a limited company:

1 The company gives warranties on its products. The company's statistics show that about 5% of sales give rise to a warranty claim.

2 The company has guaranteed the overdraft of another company. The likelihood of a liability arising under the guarantee is assessed as possible.

What is the correct action to be taken in the financial statements for these items?

	Create a provision	Disclose by note only	No action
A	1	2	
B		1	2
C	1.2		

(1 mark)

35 Which of the following errors would cause a trial balance not to balance?

1 An error in the addition in the cash book.

2 Failure to record a transaction at all.

3 Cost of a motor vehicle debited to motor expenses account. The cash entry was correctly made.

4 Goods taken by the proprietor of a business recorded by debiting purchases and crediting drawings account.

A 1 only
B 1 and 2 only
C 3 and 4 only
D All four items

(2 marks)

36 How should interest charged on partners' drawings be dealt with in partnership financial statements?

A Credited as income in the profit and loss account
B Deducted from profit in allocating the profit among the partners
C Added to profit in allocating the profit among the partners
D Debited as an expense in the profit and loss account.

(2 marks)

37 All the sales made by a retailer are for cash, and her sale prices are fixed by doubling cost. Details recorded of her transactions for September 2006 are as follows:

		£
1 Sept.	Stocks	40,000
30 Sept.	Purchases for month	60,000
	Cash banked for sales for month	95,000
	Stocks	50,000

Which two of the following conclusions could separately be drawn from this information?

1 £5,000 cash has been stolen from the sales revenue prior to banking
2 Goods costing £5,000 have been stolen
3 Goods costing £2,500 have been stolen
4 Some goods costing £2,500 had been sold at cost price

A	1 and 2
B	1 and 3
C	2 and 4
D	3 and 4

(2 marks)

38 A company owns a number of properties which are rented to tenants. The following information is available for the year ended 30 June 2006:

	Rent in advance £	Rent in arrears £
30 June 2005	134,600	4,800
30 June 2006	144,400	8,700

Cash received from tenants in the year ended 30 June 2006 was £834,600.

All rent in arrears was subsequently received.

What figure should appear in the company's profit and loss account for rent receivable in the year ended 30 June 2006?

A	£840,500
B	£1,100,100
C	£569,100
D	£828,700

(2 marks)

39 In October 2006 Utland sold some goods on sale or return terms for £2,500. Their cost to Utland was £1,500. The transaction has been treated as a credit sale in Utland's financial statements for the year ended 31 October 2006. In November 2006 the customer accepted half of the goods and returned the other half in good condition.

What adjustments, if any, should be made to the financial statements?

A	Sales and debtors should be reduced by £2,500, and closing stock increased by £1,500.
B	Sales and debtors should be reduced by £1,250, and closing stock increased by £750
C	Sales and debtors should be reduced by £2,500, with no adjustment to closing stock
D	No adjustment is necessary

(2 marks)

40 The purchase ledger control account below contains a number of errors:

Purchase ledger control account

	£		£
Opening balance (amounts owed to suppliers)	318,600	Purchases	1,268,600
Cash paid to suppliers	1,364,300	Contras against debt balances in sales ledger	48,000
Purchases returns	41,200	Discounts received	8,200
Refunds received from suppliers	2,700	Closing balance	402,000
	1,726,800		1,726,800

All items relate to credit purchases.

What should the closing balance be when all the errors are corrected?

A	£128,200
B	£509,000
C	£224,200
D	£144,600

(2 marks)

41   Which of the following is the correct format for the accounting equation?

A   Assets + Liabilities = Capital
B   Assets + Capital = Liabilities
C   Assets − Liabilities = Capital   (1 mark)

42   Which of the following transactions is a capital transaction?

A   Depreciation of plant and equipment
B   Expenditure on rent
C   Payment of interest on loan stock
D   Buying shares as an investment   (2 marks)

43   Which of the following transactions is revenue expenditure?

A   Expenditure resulting in improvements to property
B   Expenditure on heat and light
C   Purchasing fixed assets
D   Repaying a bank overdraft   (2 marks)

44   A business operates an imprest system for petty cash. The imprest amount is £400.

At the end of the month, £30 has been received for private phone calls and there are vouchers for
expenditure of £205. There is an IOU for £25. What is the physical amount of cash left in petty cash prior to
reimbursement?

A   £400
B   £200
C   £225
D   £170   (2 marks)

45   Which of the following would be recorded in the sales daybook?

A   Discounts allowed
B   Sales invoices
C   Credit notes received
D   Trade discounts   (2 marks)

46   Which of the following statements is true?

A   A debit records an increase in liabilities
B   A debit records a decrease in assets
C   A credit records an increase in liabilities   (1 mark)

47   How is the total of the purchases daybook posted to the nominal ledger?

A   Debit purchases, Credit cash
B   Debit creditors control, Credit purchases
C   Debit cash, Credit purchases
D   Debit purchases, Credit creditors control   **(2 marks)**

48   Why do we prepare a trial balance?

A   To test the accuracy of the double entry bookkeeping records
B   To prepare management accounts
C   To prepare financial accounts
D   To clear the suspense account   (2 marks)

49   What are the journal entries for an accrual of rent expenses of £500?

    A   Debit prepayments £500, credit rent £500

    B   Debit accrual £500, credit rent £500

    C   Debit rent £500, credit accruals £500

    D   Debit rent £500, credit prepayments £500   (2 marks)

50   What is goodwill?

    A   A tangible fixed asset

    B   An intangible fixed asset

    C   The revaluation reserve   (1 mark)

Mock Exam 1
Answers

DO NOT TURN THIS PAGE UNTIL YOU HAVE
COMPLETED THE MOCK EXAM

1 A

FIXED ASSETS (NBV)

	£		£
b/d	155	Depreciation charge in year	25
Purchases of fixed assets	10	∴ NBV of sale	15
		c/d	125
	165		165

So, NBV   15
     Proceeds (7)
     Loss   8

2 B ££200 debit which should have been credited – correction will bring trial balance into agreement

3 C

4 A

	£
∴ NA b/d	67,526
Profit	41,320
Drawings	(24,000)
Revaluation	25,000
NA c/d	109,846

5 D £73,680 + 102,480 – 87,240 = 58,440 overdrawn

6 C 1, 2 and 3 are all incorrect.

7 C

Trade debtors

	£		£
B/d	31,450	Irrecoverable debt	1,000
		c/d	30,450
	31,450		31,450

Allowance for debtors

	£		£
		b/d	450
		P&L	2,995
c/d (W)	3,445		
	3,445		3,445

	£
Net trade debtors	30,450
Less: Horrids	(800)
	29,650
Allowance @ 10%	2,965

	£
General allowance	2,965
Specific allowance = 800 × 60%	480
	3,445

8 A

	£	£
Period to 31/12/X1		
Profit (1/2 × 48,000)		240,000
Allocated:		
Curtis (3/5)	144,000	
Sillett (2/5)	96,000	
		240,000
Period to 30/6/X2		
Profit (1/2 × 480,000)		240,000
Salaries ((20,000 + 12,000) × ½)		(16,000)
		224,000

	£	£
Allocated:		
Curtis (50%)	112,000	
Sillett (25%)	56,000	
Mcallister (25%)	56,000	
		224,000

	Curtis £	Sillett £	Mcallister £	Total £
Salary	–	10,000	6,000	16,000
Profit shares – to 31/12/X1	144,000	96,000	–	240,000
– to 30/6/X2	112,000	56,000	56,000	224,000
	256,000	162,000	62,000	480,000

9　A

10　B　　£952,500 × 100/60 = £1,587,500

11　C

	£
Theoretical gross profit (£130,000 × 30%)	39,000
Actual gross profit (£130,000 – £49,800 – £88,600 + £32,000)	23,600
Shortfall – missing stock	15,400

12　A

	£	£
Sales		240,000
Purchases	134,025	
∴ Drawings	(2,640)	
Stock adjustment	(11,385)	
Cost of sales (50% × 240,000)		120,000
		120,000

13　D

	£
Share capital 75,000 + 15,000 + 30,000 =	120,000
Share premium 200,000 + 57,000 – 30,000 =	227,000
(Remember shares are 25p)	

14　D

15　D　　5p × 10,000,000 + 8% × £500,000

16　A

17　B

VAT CONTROL ACCOUNT

	£		£
		b/d	4,540
Purchases (£64,000 × 15%)	9,600	Sales (£109,250 × 15%/115%)	14,250
∴ Cash	11,910	c/d	2,720
	21,510		21,510

18　D

19　C

20 **A**

	£	£
Sales		650,000
Opening stock	380,000	
Purchases	480,000	
	860,000	
Closing stock(bal. fig.)	405,000	
Cost of sales (650,000 – 195,000)		455,000
Gross profit (30% × 650,000)		195,000
Closing stock should be		405,000
Undamaged goods		(220,000)
Goods lost in fire		185,000

21 **A**

	£
(1) Increase	500
(2) Increase	500
(3) No effect (see below)	–
Total increase	1,000

Item (3) has no effect because assets (bank) will decrease by £1,000 and liabilities (creditors) will also decrease by £1,000.

22 **A** Income from investments appears in the profit and loss account.

23 **D** The dividends actually paid will go through the statement of movements in reserves. The final proposed dividend of £120,000 is disclosed in the notes to the balance sheet.

24 **D**

6 months to 31 December 2005:	£
Profits	300,000
Profit share:	
A (3/5)	180,000
B (2/5)	120,000
	300,000
6 months to 30 June 2006:	
Profits	450,000
Irrecoverable debts	50,000
	500,000
Profit share:	
A (40%)	200,000
B (30%)	150,000
C (30%)	150,000
	500,000

A's total share = 180,000 + 200,000 – 30,000 (3/5 × 50,000)

= 350,000

25 **B** Trade debtors = £838,000 – £72,000

= £766,000

Allowance for debtors is increased by £12,000 to £60,000.

26 **C**

27 **C** The effect is to understate purchases for the year to 30 June 2006 and so to overstate profit for that year.

28 **D**

29 **B**

30 A

31 A   Profit and loss account = $\frac{9}{12} \times £10,800 + \frac{3}{12} \times £12,000 = £11,100$

Balance sheet = prepayment of $\frac{9}{12} \times £12,000$

$= £9,000$

32 C

33 B

SHARE CAPITAL

	£m		£m
		Bal b/f	100
		Share premium (bonus)	50
Bal c/f	210	Bank (rights)	60
	210		210

SHARE PREMIUM

	£m		£m
Share capital (bonus)	50	Bal b/f	80
Bal c/f	60	Bank (rights)	30
	110		110

34 A

35 A

36 C

37 B   Sales should be (40,000 + 60,000 − 50,000) × 2 = £100,000. Therefore either £5,000 cash has been stolen or goods costing £2,500 have been stolen.

38 D

RENT

	£		£
Bal b/f (rent in arrears)	4,800	Bal b/f (rent in advance)	134,600
Profit and loss account (bal. fig.)	828,700	Bank	834,600
Bal c/f (rent in advance)	144,400	Bal c/f (rent in arrears)	8,700
	977,900		977,900

39 A

40 A

PURCHASE LEDGER CONTROL ACCOUNT

	£		£
Cash paid to suppliers	1,364,300	Opening balance	318,600
Discounts received	8,200	Purchases	1,268,600
Purchases returns	41,200	Refunds received from suppliers	2,700
Contras	48,000		
Closing balance	128,200		
	1,589,900		1,589,900

41 C   The accounting equation is Assets = Capital + Liabilities. Rearranged, this becomes Assets − Liabilities = Capital.

42 D   A, B and C all income items reflected in the profit and loss account. In contrast D is reflected in the balance sheet.

43 B   Items A, C and D are all capital items, reflected in the balance sheet.

44	B	Amount of cash still held = 400 + 30 − 205 − 25 = £200.
45	B	Discounts allowed are recorded in the cash book. Credit notes received are to do with returned purchases (not sales). Trade discounts are not recorded, as they are deducted on the sales invoices and only the net sale is recorded.
46	C	A debit records an increase in assets or a decrease in liabilities. A credit records an increase in liabilities and/or capital. Therefore only C is true.
47	D	Remember that only credit purchases are listed in the purchases daybook.
48	A	Although we may use a trial balance as a step in preparing management or financial accounts, the main reason is A.
49	C	We need to increase the rent expenses (debit) and set up a liability to pay this amount (credit accruals).
50	B	Goodwill is an intangible asset and represents the excess of the purchase price of a business over the fair value of its net assets.

ACCA Fundamentals Level

Paper F3 (UK)
Financial Accounting

Mock Examination 2
(Computer-based exam)

Question Paper	
Time allowed	2 hours
ALL FIFTY questions are compulsory and MUST be attempted	

DO NOT OPEN THIS PAPER UNTIL YOU ARE READY TO START UNDER EXAMINATION CONDITIONS

30/6/01

400
720
900
840
acc c/f 560

3620

300
400
7
3120

30/12/00   Profit 7200

200
1300
1500
2100
7 2000

7000

680

Answer ALL fifty questions.

1   The Government issues Financial Reporting Standards.

	True
	False

(1 mark)

2   The provision of depreciation is itself an accounting concept.

	True
	False

(1 mark)

3   When preparing financial statements in periods of inflation, directors must reduce asset values.

	True
	False

(1 mark)

4   The following information relates to a bank reconciliation.

(i)   The bank balance in the cashbook before taking the items below into account was £8,970 overdrawn.

(ii)   Bank charges of £550 on the bank statement have not been entered in the cashbook.

(iii)   The bank has credited the account in error with £425 which belongs to another customer.

(iv)   Cheque payments totalling £3,275 have been entered in the cashbook but have not been presented for payment.

(v)   Cheques totalling £5,380 have been correctly entered on the debit side of the cashbook but have not been paid in at the bank.

What was the balance as shown by the bank statement *before* taking the above items into account?

£ [   ] overdrawn.   (2 marks)

5   W Ltd bought a new printing machine from abroad. The cost of the machine was £80,000. The installation costs were £5,000 and the employees received specific training on how to use this particular machine, at a cost of £2,000. Before using the machine to print customers' orders, a test was undertaken and the paper and ink cost £1,000.

What should be the cost of the machine in the company's balance sheet?

£ [   ]   (2 marks)

6   The electricity account for the year ended 30 June 20X1 was as follows.

	£
Opening balance for electricity accrued at 1 July 20X0	300
Payments made during the year	
1 August 20X0 for three months to 31 July 20X0	600
1 November 20X0 for three months to 31 October 20X0	720
1 February 20X1 for three months to 31 January 20X1	900
30 June 20X1 for three months to 30 April 20X1	840

Calculate the appropriate entry for electricity in the balance sheet £ [   ] and the profit and loss account as a [   ].   (2 marks)

7   The year end of M Plc is 30 November 20X0. The company pays for its gas by a standing order of £600 per month. On 1 December 20W9, the statement from the gas supplier showed that M Plc had overpaid by £200. M Plc received gas bills for the four quarters commencing on 1 December 20W9 and ending on 30 November 20X0 for £1,300, £1,400, £2,100 and £2,000 respectively.

Calculate the correct charge for gas in M Plc's profit and loss account for the year ended 30 November 20X0.

£ [   ]   (2 marks)

8   S Ltd sell three products - Basic, Super and Luxury. The following information was available at the year end.

	Basic £ per unit	Super £ per unit	Luxury £ per unit
Original cost	6	9	18
Estimated selling price	9	12	15
Selling and distribution costs	1	4	5
	units	units	units
Units of stock	200	250	150

The value of stock at the year end should be £ [   ]   **(2 marks)**

---

9   A car was purchased by a newsagent business in May 20W7 for:

	£
Cost	10,000
Vehicle tax	150
Total	10,150

The business adopts a date of 31 December as its year end.

The car was traded in for a replacement vehicle in August 20X0 at an agreed value of £5,000.

It has been depreciated at 25% per annum on the reducing-balance method, charging a full year's depreciation in the year of purchase and none in the year of sale.

What was the profit or loss on disposal of the vehicle during the year ended December 20X0?
£[   ] profit/loss (delete as appropriate).   **(2 marks)**

---

10   A summary of the balance sheet of M Ltd at 31 March 20X0 was as follows

	£000
Total assets less current liabilities	120
Ordinary share capital	40
Share premium account	10
Revenue reserve	10
5% debentures 20Y0	?

What is the amount of the debentures? [   ]   **(2 marks)**

---

11   The annual sales of a company are £235,000 including VAT at 17.5%. Half of the sales are on credit terms; half are cash sales. The debtors in the balance sheet are £23,500.

What is the output tax? [   ]   **(2 marks)**

---

12   Beta purchased some plant and equipment on 1 July 20X1 for £40,000. The estimated scrap value of the plant in ten years' time is estimated to be £4,000. Beta's policy is to charge depreciation on the straight line basis, with a proportionate charge in the period of acquisition.

The depreciation charge on the plant in Beta's accounting period of twelve months to 30 September 20X1 should be £ [   ]   **(2 marks)**

---

13   An stock record card shows the following details.

February	1	50 units in stock at a cost of £40 per unit
	7	100 units purchased at a cost of £45 per unit
	14	80 units sold
	21	50 units purchased at a cost of £50 per unit
	28	60 units sold

What is the value of stock at 28 February using the FIFO method? £ [   ]   **(2 marks)**

14 A particular source of finance has the following characteristics: a fixed return, a fixed repayment date, it is secured and the return is classified as an expense.

The source of finance is a preference share.

	True
	False

(1 mark)

15 Which of the following statements gives the best definition of the objective of accounting?

- [ ] A   To provide useful information to users
- [ ] B   To record, categorise and summarise financial transactions
- [ ] C   To calculate the taxation due to the government
- [ ] D   To calculate the amount of dividend to pay to shareholders

(2 marks)

16 During the year ended 31 December 20X1, Alpha Rescue had the following transactions on the sales ledger.

	£
Debtors at 1 January 20X1	100,000
Debtors at 31 December 20X1	107,250
Goods returned	12,750
Amounts paid into the bank from debtors	225,000
Discount received	75,000
Discounts allowed	5,000

Sales for the year were £ [   ]

(2 marks)

17 The net book value of a company's fixed assets was £200,000 at 1 August 20X0. During the year ended 31 July 20X1, the company sold fixed assets for £25,000 on which it made a loss of £5,000. The depreciation charge of the year was £20,000. What was the net book value of fixed assets at 31 July 20X1?

£ [   ]

(2 marks)

18 The draft balance sheet of B Ltd at 31 March 20X0 is set out below.

	£	£
Fixed assets		450
Current assets		
Stock	65	
Debtors	110	
Prepayments	30	
		205
		655
Current liabilities		
Creditors	30	
Bank overdraft (Note 1)	50	
		(80)
Non current liability		
Loan		
		500
Ordinary share capital		400
Revenue reserve		100
		500

Note 1: The bank overdraft first occurred on 30 September 20W9.

What is the amount outstanding on the loan? £ [   ]

(2 marks)

19   It is important to produce a trial balance prior to preparing the final accounts because it shows that the ledger accounts contain debit and credit entries of an [   ] value. *Complete the missing word.*
(1 mark)

20   A computerised accounts package would be *most* useful in maintaining a register of fixed assets.

[   ]   True

[   ]   False   **(1 mark)**

21   An error of original entry would occur if the purchase of goods for resale was debited and credited to the correct accounts using the correct/incorrect *(delete as appropriate)* amount in both cases.   **(1 mark)**

22   An asset was purchased for £100,000 exactly two years ago. The business uses depreciation of 20% reducing balance. Therefore the net book value now is £ [   ]   **(2 marks)**

23   Your organisation has received a statement of account from one of its suppliers, showing an outstanding balance due to them of £1,350. On comparison with your ledger account, the following is determined:

- Your ledger account shows a credit balance of £260
- The supplier has disallowed a cash discount of £80 due to late payment of an invoice
- The supplier has not yet allowed for goods returned at the end of the period of £270
- Cash in transit of £830 has not been received by the supplier

Following consideration of these items, the unreconciled difference between the two records is
£ [   ]   **(2 marks)**

24   A Ltd is preparing its cash flow statement for the year ended 31 December 20X2. Relevant extracts from the accounts are as follows.
Profit and loss account

Depreciation	15,000
Profit on sale of fixed assets	40,000

Balance sheet	20X2	20X1
Plant and machinery-cost	185,000	250,000
Plant and machinery-depreciation	45,000	50,000

Plant and machinery additions during the year were £35,000. The cash flow arising from the sale of fixed assets is £ [   ]   **(2 marks)**

25   Your organisation's trial balance at 31 October 20X9 is out of agreement, with the debit side totalling £500 less than the credit side. During November, the following errors are discovered:

- The sales journal for October had been undercast by £150
- Rent received of £240 had been credited to the rent payable account
- The allowance for debtors, which decreased by £420, had been recorded in the allowance for debtors account as an increase

Following the correction of these errors, the balance on the suspense account would be £ [   ]
(delete as appropriate).   **(2 marks)**

The following scenario relates to questions 26 to 28

P & Co maintain a sales ledger control account within the nominal ledger. At 30 November 20X0, the total of the list of individual balances extracted from the sales ledger was £15,800, which did not agree with the balance on the sales ledger control account. An examination of the books revealed the following information, which can be used to reconcile the sales ledger and the sales ledger control account.

(i)   The credit balance of £420 in Ahmed's purchase ledger account had been set off against his account in the sales ledger, but no entries had been made in the sales and purchase ledger control accounts.

(ii)   The personal account of Mahmood was undercast by £90.

(iii)   Yasmin's balance of (debit) £780 had been omitted from the list of balances.

(iv)   Thomas' personal account balance of £240 had been removed from the sales ledger as an irrecoverable debt, but no entry had been made in the sales ledger control account.

(v)   The January total of £8,900 in the sales daybook had been posted as £9,800.

(vi)   A credit note to Charles for £1,000, plus VAT of £300, had been posted to the sales ledger control account as £1,300 and to Charles' personal account as £1,000.

(vii)   The total on the credit side of Edward's personal account had been overcast by £125.

---

26   Which of these items need to be corrected by journal entries?

       ☐

       ☐

       ☐   **(2 marks)**

---

27   Calculate the revised total of the balances in the sales ledger after the errors have been corrected.

       £ ☐

---

28   Assuming that the closing balance on the sales ledger control account should be £16,000, calculate the opening balance before the errors were corrected. £ ☐   **(2 marks)**

---

29   Jay Ltd values stocks on the first in first out (FIFO) basis. During October 20X9, these are the following details regarding stocks of product A

1 October	Balance in stock	120 items valued at £8 each
3 October	Purchases	180 items at £9 each
4 October	Sales	150 items at £12 each
8 October	Sales	80 items at £15 each
18 October	Purchases	300 items at £10 each
22 October	Sales	100 items at £15 each

       (a)   Calculate the closing balance on the stock account. £ ☐   **(2 marks)**

       (b)   Calculate the closing balance using the AVCO (weighted average cost) method. £ ☐

                                                                                           (2 marks)

The following scenario applies to questions 30 to 33

MMM Ltd is a recently-formed limited company, which provides training and educational services. The company was formed with an authorised share capital of 1,000,000 £1 shares. The three shareholders, who are also directors, each purchased 120,000 shares at £1.40 per share. It is expected that the business will grow rapidly during the first two years, and that funds for that expansion will be sought by issuing shares to family members and obtaining bank finance.

During the first year of trading, a net profit (before tax) of £48,800 was made, after deducting salaries to the three directors, of £60,000 in total. Corporation tax of £6,500 was provided for the year. As well as the salaries, the three directors declared dividends for themselves of 5p per share. They also decided to transfer £5,000 into general reserves.

During the second year of trading, net profit (before tax) was £55,000. Family members purchased a further 30,000 shares at £1.50 per share, at the start of the year. Salaries were as in the first year. Interim dividends of 3p per share were paid. Corporation tax of £8,000 was provided for the year, and a further £5,000 transferred into general reserves. A final dividend of 5p per share was proposed before the year end.

---

30   Calculate the retained profits for year 1 £ ☐   **(2 marks)**

---

31   Calculate the retained profits for year 2 £ [   ]   **(2 marks)**

32   Calculate the equity (capital and reserves) at the end of year 1 £ [   ]   **(2 marks)**

33   Calculate the equity (capital and reserves) at the end of year 2 £ [   ]   **(2 marks)**

34   The closing stock of Epsilon amounted to £284,000 at 30 September 20X1, the balance sheet date. This total includes two stock lines about which the stock taker is uncertain.

    1   500 items which had cost £15 each and which were included at £7,500. These items were found to have been defective at the balance sheet date. Remedial work after the balance sheet date cost £1,800 and they were then sold for £20 each. Selling expenses were £400.

    2   100 items which had cost £10 each. After the balance sheet date they were sold for £8 each, with selling expenses of £150.

    The figure which should appear in Epsilon's balance sheet for stock is £ [   ]

                                                                  (2 marks)

35   Which of these statements about research and development expenditure are correct?

    1   If certain conditions are satisfied, research and development expenditure must be capitalised.

    2   One of the conditions to be satisfied if development expenditure is to be capitalised is that the technical feasibility of the project is reasonably assured.

    3   If capitalised, development expenditure must be amortised over a period not exceeding five years.

    4   The amount of capitalised development expenditure for each project should be reviewed each year. If circumstances no longer justify the capitalisation, the balance should be written off over a period not exceeding five years.

    5   Development expenditure may only be capitalised if it can be shown that adequate resources will be available to finance the completion of the project.

    Tick the box(es)

    1   [   ]

    2   [   ]

    3   [   ]

    4   [   ]

    5   [   ]   **(2 marks)**

36   FRS 21 *Events after the balance sheet date* defines the treatment to be given to events arising after the balance sheet date but before the financial statements are approved by the Board of Directors.

    Consider each of the following two post balance sheet events.

    You may assume that all the amounts are material but that none is large enough to jeopardise the going concern status of the company.

    (a)   The company makes an issue of 100,000 shares which raises £180,000 shortly after the balance sheet date. Is this an adjusting event?

            [   ] Yes

            [   ] No   **(2 marks)**

    (b)   A legal action brought against the company for breach of contract is decided shortly after the balance sheet date, and as a result the company will have to pay costs and damages totalling £50,000. No provision has currently been made for this event. The breach of contract occurred before the balance sheet date. Is this an adjusting event?

☐ Yes

☐ No

(2 marks)

37 At 30 September 20X0 a company has debtors totalling £350,000 and an allowance for debtors of £22,000 brought forward from the previous year.

It has been decided to write off debtors totalling £27,500 and adjust the allowance for debtors to 7% of remaining debtors.

The total charge for irrecoverable debts and debtors allowance appearing in the company's profit and loss account for the year ended 30 September 20X0 will be £ ⬚ **(2 marks)**

38 A company has the following capital structure:

	£
Ordinary share capital	
200,000 shares of 25p	50,000
Share premium account	75,000

It makes a 1 for 5 rights issue at £1.25, which is fully subscribed.

The balance on the share premium account following the rights issue is:£ ⬚ **(2 marks)**

39 Capital Ltd has an adjusted net profit for the year of £125,750. During the year trade debtors have declined by £32,000, trade creditors have increased by £14,000, and stock has increased by £11,000.

The net cash flow from operating activities is £ ⬚ **(2 marks)**

The following scenario relates to questions 40 to 42

Daedalus had a bonus issue of 1 share for 2 on 30 June 20X9. On 1 September 20X9 the company then had a rights issue of 1 for 5 at a cost of £1.50. Balance sheet extract for the company at 31 December 20X8 was:

	Daedalus
	£
Ordinary shares (£1)	700,000
Reserves (revenue)	530,000

40 The balance on revenue reserves at 31 December 20X9 was £ ⬚ **(2 marks)**

41 The total ordinary share capital at 31 December 20X9 was £ ⬚ **(2 marks)**

42 The balance on the share premium account at 31 December 20X9 was £ ⬚ **(2 marks)**

The following scenario relates to questions 43 to 45

Dennis, Jim and Arthur are in business together sharing profits in the ratio 3:3:4 after providing for salaries for Dennis and Jim of £10,000 and £12,000 respectively. They each receive interest of 8% per annum on their capital balances and pay interest of 10% on their drawings. The profit for the year is £127,000 before providing for salaries or interest and the partners' capital balances and drawings are as follows:

	Capital balance	Drawings
	£	£
Dennis	50,000	23,000
Jim	45,000	19,000
Arthur	66,000	24,000

43   Dennis' total profit share is £ [   ]   **(2 marks)**

44   Jim's total profit share is   £ [   ]   **(2 marks)**

45   Arthur's total profit share is £ [   ]   **(2 marks)**

46   The balance on Janet's cash book is £27 overdrawn. Her bank statement shows that she is £625 in credit. When Janet does a reconciliation she finds that there are unpresented cheques of £327 and unposted direct debits of £200. However, one of her customers has paid £525 directly into her bank account, so her cash book now has a debit balance, which is £ [   ]   **(2 marks)**

47   Alexander's net assets have increased by £127,000 over the year. He took drawings of £47,000 and paid in the proceeds of an insurance policy amounting to £25,000. His net profit for the year was
      £ [   ]   **(2 marks)**

48   Curtis sells clothes for cash from a market stall, at 80% mark-up on cost. His opening stock is valued at £27,500 and his closing stock is valued at £15,000. His purchases during the year were £136,000. Curtis can account for cash receipts of £245,000 but thinks some may be missing. The amount of missing cash is
      £ [   ]   **(2 marks)**

49   Exe Ltd., which has a year end of 31 December, purchased a machine on 28 February 20X1 for £35,000. It was depreciated at 40% per annum on the reducing balance basis with a full year's charge in the year of acquisition and no charge in the year of disposal. On 30 June 20X4 Exe Ltd part-exchanged this machine for a more advanced model. They paid £30,000 and realised a profit on disposal of £2440.

      The price of the new machine was £ [   ]   **(2 marks)**

50   A company has a net profit percentage of 11%, if its sales are £150,000, the cost of sales are
      £ [   ]   **(1 mark)**

Mock Exam 2
(Computer-based exam)
Answers

DO NOT TURN THIS PAGE UNTIL YOU HAVE
COMPLETED THE MOCK EXAM

1 ✓ False. The Accounting Standards Board issues SSAPs and FRSs.

2 ✓ False. Depreciation is an example of the accruals concept.

3 ✓ False. Directors need make no adjustments.

4 £11,200 overdrawn.

Cash book	£	Bank statement	£
Balance	(8,970)	Balance b/f (bal fig)	(11,200)
Bank charges	(550)	Credit in error	(425)
		Unpresented cheques	(3,275)
		Outstanding deposits	5,380
	(9,520)		(9,520)

5 £88,000

	£
Cost of machine	80,000
Installation	5,000
Training	2,000
Testing	1,000
	88,000

6 Balance sheet £560, Profit and loss account £3,320.

ELECTRICITY ACCOUNT

		£			£
			Balance b/fwd		300
20X9:					
1 August	Paid bank	600			
1 November	Paid bank	720			
20Y0:					
1 February	Paid bank	900			
30 June	Paid bank	840			
30 June	Accrual c/d £840 x ²/₃	560	Profit and loss account		3,320
		3,620			3,620

7 £6,800

GAS SUPPLIER ACCOUNT

	£			£
Balance b/fwd	200			
Bank £600 x 12	7,200	28 February	invoice	1,300
		31 May	invoice	1,400
		31 August	invoice	2,100
		30 November	invoice	2,000
		30 November	bal. c/d	600
	7,400			7,400

GAS ACCOUNT

		£			£
28 February	invoice	1,300			
31 May	invoice	1,400			
31 August	invoice	2,100			
30 November	invoice	2,000	30 November	Profit and loss account	6,800
		6,800			6,800

8   £4,700

	Cost	Net realisable value	Lower of cost & NRV	Units	Value
	£	£	£		£
Basic	6	8	6	200	1,200
Super	9	8	8	250	2,000
Luxury	18	10	10	150	1,500
					4,700

9   £781 profit

	£
Cost	10,000
20W7 Depreciation	2,500
	7,500
20W8 Depreciation	1,875
	5,625
20W9 Depreciation	1,406
	4,219
20X0 Part exchange	5,000
Profit	781

10   £60,000

Capital = Assets – Liabilities

60 = 120 – debentures

so debentures = 60

11   £35,000

$$\text{Output Tax} = \frac{235,000}{117.5} \times 17.5$$

12   £900. $£36,000 \times 10\% \times {}^{3}/_{12}$

13   £2,950 (10 units @ £45 + 50 units @ £50)

14   ☑ False. It is a loan note because it is secured.

15   ☑ A

16   £250,000

SALES LEDGER CONTROL ACCOUNT

	£		£
Bal b/f	100,000	Bank	225,000
Sales (balancing figure)	250,000	Discounts allowed	5,000
		Returns	12,750
		Bal c/f	107,250
	350,000		350,000

Discounts received refer to purchases and go in the purchase ledger control account.

17   £150,000

	£
Net book value at 1st August 20X9	200,000
Less depreciation	(20,000)
	25,000
Proceeds	5,000
Loss	(30,000)
Therefore net book value	150,000

18   £75

$$655 - 500 - 80 = 75$$

19   Equal

20   ☑   False. It would be most useful in maintaining the ledger accounts.

21   Incorrect

22   £64,000

	£
Cost	100,000
Depreciation – year 1	20,000
	80,000
Depreciation – year 2	16,000
NBV	64,000

Alternatively, the answer is £100,000 × 0.8 × 0.8 = £64,000.

23   £90

		£
	Ledger balance	260
	Add back: disallowed discount	80
	returns goods	270
	cash in transit	830
	Total balance	1,440
	As stated by the supplier	1,350
	Unreconciled difference	90

24   £120,000

	£
Sale proceeds (balancing figure)	120,000
NBV (see below)	80,000
Profit on sale	40,000
NBV at 31 December 20X1 (250,000 – 50,000)	200,000
Additions	35,000
	235,000
NBV of disposals (balancing figure)	(80,000)
Depreciation	(15,000)
NBV at 31 December 20X2 (185,000 – 45,000)	140,000

25   £190 credit

Opening balance on suspense account	500
Undercast sales figure	150
Misposted debtors allowance (420 x 2)	(840)
Balance on the suspense account	(190)

26   (i), (iv) and (v)

JOURNAL ENTRIES

		£ DR	£ CR
Error (i)	Purchase ledger control	420	
	Sales ledger control		420
Error (iv)	Irrecoverable debts	240	
	Sales ledger control		240
Error (v)	Sales	900	
	Sales ledger control		900

27 £16,495

BALANCES EXTRACTED FROM THE SALES LEDGER

		+ £	− £	£
Total before corrections for errors				15,800
Error (ii)	Mahmood	90		
Error (iii)	Yasmin	780		
Error (vi)	Charles		300	
Error (vii)	Edward	125		
		995	300	695
				16,495

28 £17,560

SALES LEDGER CONTROL ACCOUNT

	£			£
∴ Balance b/f	17,560	Error (i)	Ahmed	420
		Error (iv)	Thomas	240
		Error (v)	Sales daybook total	900
				1,560
		Balance c/f		16,000
	17,560			17,560

29 (a) £2,700

Date		No. of items	Unit price £	Value £
1.10.X9	Balance	120	8	960
3.10.X9	Purchases	180	9	1,620
	Balance	300	8.60	2,580
4.10.X9	Sales	(120)	8	(960)
	Sales	(30)	9	(270)
	Balance	150	9	1,350
8.10.X9	Sales	(80)	9	(720)
	Balance	70	9	630
18.10.X9	Purchases	300	10	3,000
	Balance	370	9.81	3,630
22.10.X9	Sales	(70)	9	(630)
	Sales	(30)	10	(300)
	Balance	270	10	2,700

(b) £2,628

Date		No. of items	Unit price £	Value £
1.10.X9	Balance	120	8	960
3.10.X9	Purchases	180	9	1,620
	Balance	300	8.60	2,580
4.10.X9	Sales	(150)	8.60	(1,290)
	Balance	150	8.60	1,290
8.10.X9	Sales	(80)	8.60	(688)
	Balance	70	8.60	602
18.10.X9	Purchases	300	10	3,000
	Balance	370	9.74	3,602
22.10.X9	Sales	(100)	9.74	(974)
	Balance	270	9.73	2,628

30   £19,300
and
31   £10,800

Retained profits

	Year 1 £	Year 2 £
Profit before taxation	48,800	55,000
Taxation	(6,500)	(8,000)
Profit for the period	42,300	47,000
Interim dividend	–	(11,700)
Final dividend	(18,000)	(19,500)
Transfer to general reserves	(5,000)	(5,000)
Retained profit for the year	19,300	10,800

32   £528,300
and
33   £589,100

Capital and reserve

	Year 1 £	Year 2 £
Share capital £1 ordinary shares	360,000	390,000
Share premium account	144,000	159,000
Retained profits	19,300	30,100
General reserves	5,000	10,000
	528,300	589,100

34

		£	
		284,000	
£283,650	Item 1	–	No change as NRV exceeds cost
	Item 2	(350)	Reduce to NRV (1,000 – 650)
		283,650	

35   2 ✓   5 ✓   Statements 1, 3 and 4 are incorrect.

36   (a) ✓ No. This is a **non-adjusting event**. An appropriate note might be as follows.

'On 7 January 20X7 the company issued 100,000 £1 ordinary shares at a premium of 80p per share. The purpose of the share issue was to raise money to expand the fixed asset base.'

(b) ☑ Yes. This is an **adjusting event** as it provides evidence of conditions existing at the balance sheet date. The appropriate treatment would be to reduce profit by £50,000 and to increase creditors due within one year by the same amount.

37 £28,075

	£
Debtors total	350,000
less write-off	(27,500)
	322,500
x 7%	22,575
deduct opening balance	(22,000)
Additional allowance	575
Add write off	27,500
Total charge	28,075

38 £115,000

1 for 5 issue means 40,000 shares issued at premium of £1.

Balance on share premium account becomes £75,000 + £40,000 = £115,000

39 £160,750

	£
Adjusted net profit	125,750
Decrease in debtors	32,000
Increase in creditors	14,000
Increase in stock	(11,000)
Net cash flow from operating activities	160,750

40 £180,000

$$\text{Bonus issue of 1 for 2} = \frac{700,000}{2}$$

$$= 350,000$$

Balance on revenue reserves = £530,000 - £350,000

$$= £180,000$$

41 £1,260,000

	£
Ordinary shares at 1 January 20X9	700,000
Bonus issue (1 for 2)	350,000
	1,050,000
Rights issue (1 for 5)	210,000
	1,260,000

42 £105,000

Rights issue (as above) = 210,000 shares

Proceeds = 210,000 × £1.50

$$= £315,000$$

Allocated as follows:

	£
Share capital	210,000
Share premium	105,000
	315,000

43 £41,316 see below

44 £43,316 see below

45 £42,368 see below

	Dennis	Jim	Arthur	Total
	£	£	£	£
Salaries	10,000	12,000		22,000
Interest on capital	4,000	3,600	5,280	12,880
Interest on drawings	(2,300)	(1,900)	(2,400)	(6,600)
Profit share	29,616	29,616	39,488	98,720
	41,316	43,316	42,368	127,000

46 £298

	Cash book	Bank statement
	£	£
	(27)	625
Unpresented cheques		(327)
Direct debits	(200)	
Receipt	525	
	298	298

47 £149,000

	£
Increase in net assets	127,000
Add drawings	47,000
Deduct capital paid in	(25,000)
Net profit	149,000

48 £22,300

	£
Opening stock	27,500
Purchases	136,000
Closing stock	(15,000)
Cost of sales	148,500
Theoretical sales (148,500 x 180%)	267,300
Cash accounted for	(245,000)
Missing cash	22,300

49 £40,000

The machine has had 3 years depreciation at 40% reducing balance.

	£
NBV is therefore (£35,000 x 60% x 60% x 60%) =	7,560
Add profit on disposal	2,440
Part-exchange allowance	10,000
Payment	30,000
Price of new machine	40,000

50 £133,500

	£
Sales (100%)	150,000
Cost of sales (89%)	133,500
Net profit (11%)	16,500

ACCA

Paper F3 (UK)

Financial Accounting

Mock Examination 3

Pilot paper

Question Paper	
Time allowed	**2 hours**
ALL 50 questions are compulsory and MUST be attempted	

DO NOT OPEN THIS PAPER UNTIL YOU ARE READY TO START UNDER EXAMINATION CONDITIONS

If you are sitting your exam on the computer, you can attempt the Pilot Paper as a computer-based exam on ACCA's website:

http://62.254.188.145/main.html

ALL 50 questions are compulsory and **MUST** be attempted

Please use the Candidate Registration Sheet provided to indicate your chosen answer to each multiple choice question.

1   Should details of material adjusting or material non-adjusting events after the balance sheet date be disclosed in the notes to financial statements according to **FRS 21** *Events After the Balance Sheet Date?*

   A   Adjusting events

   B   Non-Adjusting events

(1 mark)

2   At 30 June 2005 a company's allowance for debtors was £39,000. At 30 June 2006 trade debtors totalled £517,000. It was decided to write off debts totalling £37,000 and to adjust the allowance for debtors to the equivalent of 5 per cent of the trade debtors based on past events.

   What figure should appear in the profit and loss account for the year ended 30 June 2006 for these items?

   A   £61,000

   B   £22,000

   C   £24,000

   D   £23,850

(2 marks)

3   In times of rising prices, what effect does the use of the historical cost concept have on a company's asset values and profit?

   A   Asset values and profit both understated

   B   Asset values and profit both overstated

   C   Asset values understated and profit overstated

   D   Asset values overstated and profit understated.

(2 marks)

4   The ASB's *Statement of principles for financial reporting* gives qualitative characteristics that make financial information reliable.

   Which of the following are examples of those qualitative characteristics?

   A   Faithful representation, neutrality and prudence

   B   Neutrality, comparability and true and fair view

   C   Prudence, comparability and accruals

   D   Neutrality, accruals and going concern

(2 marks)

5   The following bank reconciliation statement has been prepared by a trainee accountant:

	£
Overdraft per bank statement	3,860
less: Outstanding cheques	9,160
	5,300
add: Deposits credited after date	16,690
Cash at bank as calculated above	21,990

What should be the correct balance per the cash book?

A   £21,990 balance at bank as stated

B   £3,670 balance at bank

C   £11,390 balance at bank

D   £3,670 overdrawn.

(2 marks)

6   **Which of the following calculates a trader's net profit for a period?**

A   Closing net assets + drawings – capital introduced – opening net assets

B   Closing net assets – drawings + capital introduced – opening net assets

C   Closing net assets – drawings – capital introduced – opening net assets

D   Closing net assets + drawings + capital introduced – opening net assets.

(2 marks)

7   A sole trader took some goods costing £800 from stock for his own use. The normal selling price of the goods is £1,600.

Which of the following journal entries would correctly record this?

		Dr £	Cr £
A	Drawings account	800	
	Stock account		800
B	Drawings account	800	
	Purchases account		800
C	Sales account	1,600	
	Drawings account		1,600

(1 mark)

8   The debit side of a company's trial balance totals £800 more than the credit side.

Which one of the following errors would fully account for the difference?

A   £400 paid for plant maintenance has been correctly entered in the cash book and credited to the plant asset account.

B   Discount received £400 has been debited to discount allowed account

C   A receipt of £800 for commission receivable has been omitted from the records

D   The petty cash balance of £800 has been omitted from the trial balance.

(2 marks)

9   A company's profit and loss account for the year ended 31 December 2005 showed a net profit of £83,600. It was later found that £18,000 paid for the purchase of a motor van had been debited to the motor expenses account. It is the company's policy to depreciate motor vans at 25 per cent per year on the straight line basis, with a full year's charge in the year of acquisition.

What would the net profit be after adjusting for this error?

A   £106,100

B   £70,100

C   £97,100

D   £101,600

(2 marks)

10 **Should dividends paid appear on the face of a company's profit and loss account?**

A   Yes

B   No

(1 mark)

11 The following control account has been prepared by a trainee accountant:

Debtors ledger control account

	£		£
Opening balance	308,600	Cash received from credit customers	147,200
Credit sales	154,200	Discounts allowed to credit customers	1,400
Cash sales	88,100	Interest charged on overdue accounts	2,400
Contras against credit balances in creditors ledger	4,600	Bad debts written off	4,900
		Allowance for debtors	2,800
		Closing balance	396,800
	555,500		555,500

What should the closing balance be when all the errors made in preparing the debtors ledger control account have been corrected?

A   £395,200

B   £304,300

C   £309,500

D   £307,100

(2 marks)

12 At 31 December 2004 Q, a limited liability company, owned a building that cost £800,000 on 1 January 1995. It was being depreciated at two per cent per year.

On 1 January 2005 a revaluation to £1,000,000 was recognised. At this date the building had a remaining useful life of 40 years.

What is the depreciation charge for the yeae ended 31 December 2005 and the revaluation reserve balance as at 1 January 2005?

	Depreciation charge for year ended 31 December 2005 £	Revaluation reserve as at 1 January 2005 £
A	25,000	200,000
B	25,000	360,000
C	20,000	200,000
D	20,000	360,000

(2 marks)

13 P and Q are in partnership, sharing profits equally.

On 30 June 2005, R joined the partnership and it was agreed that from that date all three partners should share equally in the profit.

In the year ended 31 December 2005 the profit amounted to £300,000, accruing evenly over the year, after charging a bad debt of £30,000 which it was agreed should be borne equally by P and Q only.

What should P's total profit share be for the year ended 31 December 2005?

A   £ 95,000

B   £122,500

C   £125,000

D   £110,000

(2 marks)

14 A company has made a material change to an accounting policy in preparing its current financial statements.

Which of the following disclosures are required by FRS 18 *Accounting policies* in the financial statements?

1   The reasons for the change.
2   The amount of the adjustment in the current period and in comparative information for prior periods.
3   An estimate of the effect of the change on the next five accounting periods.

A   1 and 2 only

B   1 and 3 only

C   2 and 3 only

D   1, 2 and 3

(2 marks)

15 According to SSAP 9 *Stocks and long-term contracts*, which of the following costs should be included in valuing the stock of a manufacturing company?

(1) Carriage inwards

(2) Carriage outwards

(3) Depreciation of factory plant

(4) General administrative overheads

A All four items

B 1, 2 and 4 only

C 2 and 3 only

D 1 and 3 only

(2 marks)

16 Part of a company's cash flow statement is shown below:

	£'000
Operating profit	8,640
Depreciation charges	(2,160)
Increase in stock	(330)
Increase in trade creditors	440

The following criticisms of the extract have been made:

(1) Depreciation charges should have been added, not deducted.

(2) Increase in stock should have been added, not deducted.

(3) Increase in trade creditors should have been deducted, not added.

Which of the criticisms are valid?

A 2 and 3 only

B 1 only

C 1 and 3 only

D 2 only

(2 marks)

17 Which of the following explains the imprest system of operating petty cash?

A Weekly expenditure cannot exceed a set amount.

B The exact amount of expenditure is reimbursed at intervals to maintain a fixed float.

C All expenditure out of the petty cash must be properly authorised.

D Regular equal amounts of cash are transferred into petty cash at intervals.

(2 marks)

18 **Which of the following are differences between sole traders and limited liability companies?**

    (1) A sole traders' financial statements are private; a company's financial statements are sent to shareholders and may be publicly filed

    (2) Only companies have capital invested into the business

    (3) A sole trader is fully and personally liable for any losses that the business might make; a company's shareholders are not personally liable for any losses that the company might make.

    A   1 and 2 only

    B   2 and 3 only

    C   1 and 3 only

    D   1, 2 and 3

                                                               (2 marks)

19 **Which of the following documents should accompany a payment made to a supplier?**

    A   Supplier statement

    B   Remittance advice

    C   Purchase invoice

                                                                 (1 mark)

20 Goodwill should **never** be shown on the balance sheet of a partnership.

    Is this statement true or false?

    A   False

    B   True

                                                                 (1 mark)

21 **Which of the following journal entries are correct, according to their narratives?**

		Dr £	CR £
1	Suspense account	18,000	
	Rent received account		18,000
	Correction of error in posting £24,000 cash received for rent to the rent received account as £42,000		
2	Share premium account	400,000	
	Share capital account		400,000
	1 for 3 bonus issue on share capital of 1,200,000 50p shares		
3	Trade investment in X	750,000	
	Share capital account		250,000
	Share premium account		500,000
	500,000 50p shares issued at £1.50 per share in exchange for shares in X		

    A   1 and 2

    B   2 and 3

    C   1 only

    D   3 only

                                                                 (2 marks)

22 The plant and machinery account (at cost) of a business for the year ended 31 December 2005 was as follows:

Plant and machinery – cost

2005	£	2005	£
1 Jan Balance	240,000	31 March Transfer disposal account	60,000
30 June Cash – purchase of plant	160,000	31 Dec Balance	340,000
	400,000		400,000

The company's policy is to charge depreciation at 20% per year on the straight line basis, with proportionate depreciation in the years of purchase and disposal.

What should be the depreciation charge for the year ended 31 December 2005?

A   £68,000

B   £64,000

C   £61,000

D   £55,000

(2 marks)

23 **Which of the following should appear in a company's statement of total recognised gains and losses?**

1   Profit for the financial year
2   Amortisation of capitalised development costs
3   Surplus on revaluation of fixed assets

A   All three items

B   2 and 3 only

C   1 and 3 only

D   1 and 2 only

(2 marks)

24 **Which of the following statements are correct?**

(1)   Capitalised development expenditure must be amortised over a period not exceeding five years.

(2)   Capitalised development costs are shown in the balance sheet under the heading of Fixed Assets

(3)   If certain criteria are met, research expenditure must be recognised as an intangible asset.

A   2 only

B   2 and 3

C   1 only

D   1 and 3

(2 marks)

25 A fire on 30 September destroyed some of a company's stock and its stock records.

The following information is available:

	£
Stock 1 September	318,000
Sales for September	612,000
Purchases for September	412,000
Stock in good condition at 30 September	214,000

Standard gross profit percentage on sales is 25%

Based on this information, what is the value of the stock lost?

A   £96,000

B   £271,000

C   £26,400

D   £57,000

(2 marks)

26 At 31 December 2004 a company's capital structure was as follows:

	£
Ordinary share capital	
(500,000 shares of 25p each)	125,000
Share premium account	100,000

In the year ended 31 December 2005 the company made a rights issue of 1 share for every 2 held at £1 per share and this was taken up in full. Later in the year the company made a bonus issue of 1 share for every 5 held, using the share premium account for the purpose.

What was the company's capital structure at 31 December 2005?

	Ordinary share capital £	Share premium account £
A	450,000	25,000
B	225,000	250,000
C	225,000	325,000
D	212,500	262,500

(2 marks)

27 The stock value for the financial statements of Q for the year ended 31 May 2006 was based on a stock count on 4 June 2006, which gave a total stock value of £836,200.

Between 31 May and 4 June 2006, the following transactions took place:

	£
Purchases of goods	8,600
Sales of goods (profit margin 30% on sales)	14,000
Goods returned by Q to supplier	700

What adjusted figure should be included in the financial statements for stock at 31 May 2006?

A   £838,100

B   £853,900

C   £818,500

D   £834,300

(2 marks)

28 In preparing a company's bank reconciliation statement at March 2006, the following items are causing the difference between the cash book balance and the bank statement balance:

(1) Bank charges £380

(2) Error by bank £1,000 (cheque incorrectly debited to the account)

(3) Lodgements not credited £4,580

(4) Outstanding cheques £1,475

(5) Direct debit £350

(6) Cheque paid in by the company and dishonoured £400.

Which of these items will require an entry in the cash book?

A   2, 4 and 6

B   1, 5 and 6

C   3, 4 and 5

D   1, 2 and 3

(2 marks)

29 At 31 December 2005 the following require inclusion in a company's financial statements:

(1) On 1 January 2005 the company made a loan of £12,000 to an employee, repayable on 1 January 2006, charging interest at 2 per cent per year. On the due date she repaid the loan and paid the whole of the interest due on the loan to that date.

(2) The company has paid insurance £9,000 in 2005, covering the year ending 31 August 2006.

(3) In January 2006 the company received rent from a tenant £4,000 covering the six months to 31 December 2005.

For these items, what total figures should be included in the company's balance sheet at 31 December 2005?

	Current assets £	Current liabilities £
A	10,000	12,240
B	22,240	nil
C	10,240	nil
D	16,240	6,000

(2 marks)

30 **How should a contingent liability be included in a company's financial statements if the likelihood of a transfer of economic benefits to settle it is remote?**

A   Disclosed by note with no provision being made

B   No disclosure or provision is required

(1 mark)

Which of the following material events after the balance sheet date and before the financial statements are approved are adjusting events?

(1) A valuation of property providing evidence of impairment in value at the balance sheet date.

(2) Sale of stock held at the balance sheet date for less than cost.

(3) Discovery of fraud or error affecting the financial statements.

(4) The insolvency of a customer with a debt owing at the balance sheet date which is still outstanding.

A   1, 2, 3 and 4

B   1, 2 and 4 only

C   3 and 4 only

D   1, 2 and 3 only.

(2 marks)

32 Alpha received a statement of account from a supplier Beta, showing a balance to be paid of £8,950. Alpha's purchase ledger account for Beta shows a balance due to Beta of £4,140.

Investigation reveals the following:

(1) Cash paid to Beta £4,080 has not been allowed for by Beta
(2) Alpha's ledger account has not been adjusted for £40 of cash discount disallowed by Beta.

What discrepancy remains between Alpha's and Beta's records after allowing for these items?

A   £690

B   £770

C   £9,850

D   £9,930

(2 marks)

33 The business entity concept requires that a business is treated as being separate from its owners.

Is this statement true or false?

A   True

B   False

(1 mark)

34 Theta prepares its financial statements for the year to 30 April each year. The company pays rent for its premises quarterly in advance on 1 January, 1 April, 1 July and 1 October each year. The annual rent was £84,000 per year until 30 June 2005. It was increased from that date to £96,000 per year.

What rent expense and end of year prepayment should be included in the financial statements for the year ended 30 April 2006?

	Expense	Prepayment
A	£93,000	£8,000
B	£93,000	£16,000
C	£94,000	£8,000
D	£94,000	£16,000

(2 marks)

35 Which of the following items could appear in a company's cash flow statement?

   (1) Surplus on revaluation of fixed assets

   (2) Proceeds of issue of shares

   (3) Proposed dividend

   (4) Dividends received

   A   1 and 2

   B   3 and 4

   C   1 and 3

   D   2 and 4

                                                                                    (2 marks)

36 What is the role of the Financial Reporting Review Panel?

   A   To create a set of accounting standards

   B   To ensure public and large private companies comply with relevant reporting requirements

                                                                                    (1 mark)

37 Q's trial balance failed to agree and a suspense account was opened for the difference.
    Q does not keep debtors and creditors control accounts. The following errors were found in Q's accounting records:

   (1) In recording an issue of shares at par, cash received of £333,000 was credited to the ordinary share capital
        account as £330,000

   (2) Cash £2,800 paid for plant repairs was correctly accounted for in the cash book but was credited to the plant asset
        account

   (3) The petty cash book balance £500 had been omitted from the trial balance

   (4) A cheque for £78,400 paid for the purchase of a motor car was debited to the motor vehicles account as
        £87,400.

   Which of the errors will require an entry to the suspense account to correct them?

   A   1, 2 and 4 only

   B   1, 2, 3 and 4

   C   1 and 4 only

   D   2 and 3 only

                                                                                    (2 marks)

38 Mountain sells goods on credit to Hill. Hill receives a 10% trade discount from Mountain and a further 5% settlement
    discount if goods are paid for within 14 days. Hill bought goods with a list price of £200,000 from Mountain. VAT is
    at 17.5%.

   What amount should be included in Mountain's sales ledger for this transaction?

   A   £235,000

   B   £211,500

   C   £200,925

   D   £209,925

                                                                                    (2 marks)

39 A computerised accounting system operates using the principle of double entry accounting.

Is this statement true or false?

A   False

B   True

(1 mark)

40 A company receives rent from a large number of properties. The total received in the year ended 30 April 2006 was £481,200.

The following were the amounts of rent in advance and in arrears at 30 April 2005 and 2006:

	30 April 2005	30 April 2006
	£	£
Rent received in advance	28,700	31,200
Rent in arrears (all subsequently received)	21,200	18,400

What amount of rental income should appear in the company's profit and loss account for the year ended 30 April 2006?

A   £486,500

B   £460,900

C   £501,500

D   £475,900

(2 marks)

41 Annie is a sole trader who does not keep full accounting records. The following details relate to her transactions with credit customers and suppliers for the year ended 30 June 2006:

	£
Trade debtors, 1 July 2005	130,000
Trade creditors, 1 July 2005	60,000
Cash received from customers	686,400
Cash paid to suppliers	302,800
Discounts allowed	1,400
Discounts received	2,960
Contra between purchase and sales ledgers	2,000
Trade debtors, 30 June 2006	181,000
Trade creditors, 30 June 2006	84,000

What figure should appear in Annie's profit and loss account for the year ended 30 June 2006 for purchases?

A   £331,760

B   £740,800

C   £283,760

D   £330,200

(2 marks)

42 The bookkeeper of Field made the following mistakes:

Discounts allowed £3,840 was credited to the discounts received account

Discounts received £2,960 was debited to the discounts allowed account

Which journal entry will correct the errors?

		DR	CR
A	Discounts allowed	£7,680	
	Discounts received		£5,920
	Suspense account		£1,760
B	Discounts allowed	£880	
	Discounts received	£880	
	Suspense account		£1,760
C	Discounts allowed	£6,800	
	Discounts received		£6,800
D	Discounts allowed	£3,840	
	Discounts received		£2,960
	Suspense account		£880

(2 marks)

43 Which of the following statements are correct?

(1) Materiality means that only items having a physical existence may be recognised as assets.

(2) The substance over form convention means that the legal form of a transaction must always be shown in financial statements even if this differs from the commercial effect.

(3) The money measurement concept is that only items capable of being measured in monetary terms can be recognised in financial statements.

A 2 only

B 1, 2 and 3

C 1 only

D 3 only

(2 marks)

44 The total of the list of balances in Valley's purchase ledger was £438,900 at 30 June 2006. This balance did not agree with Valley's purchase ledger control account balance. The following errors were discovered:

1 A contra entry of £980 was recorded in the purchase ledger control account, but not in the purchase ledger.
2 The total of the purchase returns daybook was undercast by £1,000.
3 An invoice for £4,344 was posted to the supplier's account as £4,434.

What amount should Valley report in its balance sheet as trade creditors at 30 June 2006?

A £436,830

B £438,010

C £439,790

D £437,830

(2 marks)

Which of the following statements are correct?

(1) A cash flow statement prepared using the direct method produces a different figure for operating cash flow from that produced if the indirect method is used.

(2) Rights issues of shares do not feature in cash flow statements.

(3) A surplus on revaluation of a fixed asset will not appear as an item in a cash flow statement

(4) A profit on the sale of a fixed asset will appear as an item under Capital Expenditure in a cash flow statement.

A   1 and 4

B   2 and 3

C   3 only

D   2 and 4

(2 marks)

---

46   Gareth, a VAT registered trader purchased a computer for use in his business. The invoice for the computer showed the following costs related to the purchase:

	£
Computer	890
Additional memory	95
Delivery	10
Installation	20
Maintenance (1 year)	25
	1,040
VAT (17.5%)	182
Total	1,222

How much should Gareth capitalise as a fixed asset in relation to the purchase?

A   £1,222

B   £1,040

C   £890

D   £1,015

(2 marks)

---

47   A and B are in partnership sharing profits and losses in the ratio 3:2 respectively. Profit for the year was £86,500. The partners' capital and current account balances at the beginning of the year were as follows:

	A	B
	£	£
Current accounts	5,750CR	1,200CR
Capital accounts	10,000CR	8,000CR

A's drawings during the year were £4,300, and B's were £2,430.

What should A's current account balance be at the end of the year?

A   £57,650

B   £51,900

C   £61,950

D   £53,350

(2 marks)

48 What is the correct double entry to record the depreciation charge for a period?

   A   DR Depreciation expense
            CR Accumulated depreciation

   B   DR Accumulated depreciation
            CR Depreciation expense

(1 mark)

49 A company values its stock using the first in, first out (FIFO) method. At 1 May 2005 the company had 700 engines in stock, valued at £190 each.

During the year ended 30 April 2006 the following transactions took place:

2005

| 1 July | Purchased | 500 engines | at £220 each |
| 1 November | Sold | 400 engines | for £160,000 |

2006

| 1 February | Purchased | 300 engines | at £230 each |
| 15 April | Sold | 250 engines | for £125,000 |

What is the value of the company's closing stock of engines at 30 April 2006?

   A   £188,500

   B   £195,500

   C   £166,000

   D   £106,000

(2 marks)

50 A company's motor vehicles at cost account at 30 June 2006 is as follows:

Motor vehicles – cost

	£		£
Balance b/f	35,800	Disposal	12,000
Additions	12,950	Balance c/f	36,750
	48,750		48,750

What opening balance should be included in the following period's trial balance for motor vehicles – cost at 1 July 2006?

   A   £36,750 DR

   B   £48,750 DR

   C   £36,750 CR

   D   £48,750 CR

(2 marks)

ACCA examiner's answers:
Pilot paper

1	B	
2	B	37,000 + ((517,000 – 37,000)*5%) –39,000) = 22,000
3	C	
4	A	
5	B	-3,860 – 9,160 + 16,690 = 3,670
6	A	
7	B	
8	B	
9	C	83,600 +18,000 – (18,000*25%) = 97,100
10	B	
11	D	

Debtors ledger control account

	£		£
Opening balance	308,600	Contras	4,600
Credit sales	154,200	Cash received	147,200
Interest charged	2,400	Discounts allowed	1,400
		Bad debts	4,900
		Closing balance	307,100
	465,200		465,200

12	B	1,000,000/40years = 25,000; 1,000,000 – (800,000 – (800,000*2%*10years)) = 360,000
13	B	((300,000 + 30,000) / 2 * ½) + (300,000 + 30,000) / 2 * 1/3) – (30,000 * ½) = 122,500
14	A	
15	D	
16	B	
17	B	
18	C	
19	B	
20	A	(BPP LM: **Purchased** goodwill will be shown on the face of the B/S)
21	D	
22	D	(240,000*20%) + (6/12*160,000*20%) – (9/12*60,000*20%) = 55,000
23	C	
24	A	
25	D	(318,000 + 412,000 – 214,000) – (612,000*75%) = 57,000
26	B	125,000 + (500,000*1/2*25p) + (750,000*1/5*25p) = 225,000; 100,000 + (500,000*1/2*75p) – (750,000*1/5*25p) = 250,000
27	A	836,200 – 8,600 + (14,000*70%) + 700 = 838,100
28	B	
29	B	12,000 + (12,000*2%) + (9,000*8/12) + 4,000 = 22,240
30	B	
31	A	
32	A	(8,950 – 4,080) – (4,140 + 40) = 690
33	A	
34	D	(84,000*2/12) + (96,000*10/12) = 94,000; 96,000*2/12 = 16,000
35	D	
36	B	
37	B	
38	D	

List Price	200,000
Trade discount	(20,000)
	180,000
VAT (17.5%*95%*180,000)	29,925
	209,925

39	B	
40	D	

Rent receivable

	£		£
O/Balance	21,200	O/Balance	28,700
Profit and Loss	475,900	Disposal	481,200
C/Balance	31,200	C/Balance	18,400
	528,300		528,300

(BBP LM: 'Disposal' is incorrect, it should be 'cash received')

41 A

Purchase ledger

	£		£
Cash paid	302,800	O/balance	60,000
Discounts received	2,960	Purchases	331,760
Contra	2,000		
C/balance	84,000		
	391,760		391,760

42 B

43 D

44 D $438,900 - 980 - 90 = 437,830$

45 C

46 D $890 + 95 + 10 + 20 = 1,015$

47 D $5,750 + (86,500 * 3/5) - 4,300 = 53,350$

48 A

49 A $(300@230) + (500@220) + (50@190) = 188,500$

50 A

Review Form & Free Prize Draw – Paper F3 Financial Accounting (UK) (1/09)

All original review forms from the entire BPP range, completed with genuine comments, will be entered into one of two draws on 31 July 2009 and 31 January 2010. The names on the first four forms picked out on each occasion will be sent a cheque for £50.

Name: _____   Address: _____

_____

_____

How have you used this Kit?
(Tick one box only)

☐ Home study (book only)

☐ On a course: college _____

☐ With 'correspondence' package

☐ Other _____

Why did you decide to purchase this Kit?
(Tick one box only)

☐ Have used the complementary Study text

☐ Have used other BPP products in the past

☐ Recommendation by friend/colleague

☐ Recommendation by a lecturer at college

☐ Saw advertising

☐ Other _____

During the past six months do you recall seeing/receiving any of the following?
(Tick as many boxes as are relevant)

☐ Our advertisement in *Student Accountant*

☐ Our advertisement in *Pass*

☐ Our advertisement in *PQ*

☐ Our brochure with a letter through the post

☐ Our website www.bpp.com

Which (if any) aspects of our advertising do you find useful?
(Tick as many boxes as are relevant)

☐ Prices and publication dates of new editions

☐ Information on product content

☐ Facility to order books off-the-page

☐ None of the above

Which BPP products have you used?

Text	☐	Success CD	☐	Learn Online	☐
Kit	☑	i-Learn	☐	Home Study Package	☐
Passcard	☐	i-Pass	☐	Home Study PLUS	☐

Your ratings, comments and suggestions would be appreciated on the following areas.

	Very useful	Useful	Not useful
Passing ACCA exams	☐	☐	☐
Passing F3	☐	☐	☐
Questions	☐	☐	☐
Mock exam answers	☐	☐	☐

Overall opinion of this Kit   *Excellent* ☐   *Good* ☐   *Adequate* ☐   *Poor* ☐

Do you intend to continue using BPP products?   *Yes* ☐   *No* ☐

The BPP author of this edition can be e-mailed at: janiceross@bpp.com

Please return this form to: Lesley Buick, ACCA Publishing Manager, BPP Learning Media Ltd, FREEPOST, London, W12 8BR

Review Form & Free Prize Draw (continued)

TELL US WHAT YOU THINK

Please note any further comments and suggestions/errors below.

Free Prize Draw Rules

1   Closing date for 31 July 2009 draw is 30 June 2009. Closing date for 31 January 2010 draw is 31 December 2009.

2   Restricted to entries with UK and Eire addresses only. BPP employees, their families and business associates are excluded.

3   No purchase necessary. Entry forms are available upon request from BPP Learning Media Ltd. No more than one entry per title, per person. Draw restricted to persons aged 16 and over.

4   Winners will be notified by post and receive their cheques not later than 6 weeks after the relevant draw date.

5   The decision of the promoter in all matters is final and binding. No correspondence will be entered into.